Detox!

Detox!

The Spiritual Path of Jesus
for 21st Century Men

Craig S. Pesti-Strobel

RESOURCE *Publications* • Eugene, Oregon

DETOX!
The Spiritual Path of Jesus for 21st Century Men

Copyright © 2021 Craig S. Pesti-Strobel. All rights reserved. Except for brief quotations in critical publications or reviews, no part of this book may be reproduced in any manner without prior written permission from the publisher. Write: Permissions, Wipf and Stock Publishers, 199 W. 8th Ave., Suite 3, Eugene, OR 97401.

Resource Publications
An Imprint of Wipf and Stock Publishers
199 W. 8th Ave., Suite 3
Eugene, OR 97401

www.wipfandstock.com

PAPERBACK ISBN: 978-1-7252-8024-3
HARDCOVER ISBN: 978-1-7252-8023-6
EBOOK ISBN: 978-1-7252-8025-0

02/22/21

Scripture quotations marked (RSV) are from the Revised Standard Version of the Bible, copyright © 1946, 1952, and 1971 National Council of the Churches of Christ in the United States of America. Used by permission. All rights reserved worldwide.

Scripture quotations marked (NRSV) are from the New Revised Standard Version Bible, copyright © 1989, 1993 National Council of the Churches of Christ in the United States of America. Used by permission. All rights reserved worldwide. http://nrsvbibles.org.

Scripture quotations marked (NIV) are taken from the Holy Bible, New International Version®, NIV®. Copyright © 1973, 1978, 1984, 2011 by Biblica, Inc.® Used by permission of Zondervan. All rights reserved worldwide. www.zondervan.com The "NIV" and "New International Version" are trademarks registered in the United States Patent and Trademark Office by Biblica, Inc.®

I dedicate this book, first, to the memory of my father, Vincent S. Strobel (1930–2011) who provided the model of a man of integrity, love, and faithfulness. In addition, I dedicate this book to my brothers, Jeff Strobel, Todd Strobel, Brett Strobel, Nick Strobel, Kurt Strobel, Burke Strobel, and Nathan Strobel, all of whom have sought in various ways not only to emulate our father, but also to seek ways to walk the Path that Jesus taught in ways that reflect their own personalities and personal commitments. Through each of them, the world has been blessed.

Contents

List of Diagrams | ix
Acknowledgements | xi
Introduction: Curing a Sickness | xiii

1. The Way of Love | 1
2. Next Mindify Yourself! | 12
3. Becoming Men | 21
4. Mapping the Terrain | 31
5. What is Spirituality? | 46
6. Life Disciplined | 56
7. Reading the Bible | 78
8. Jesus and His Male Disciples | 88
9. Turning the Tables | 95
10. Son of Magnificat | 106
11. Sorting Things Out: Tempting Jesus | 116
12. "The Spirit Is Upon Me": Jesus' Inaugural Sermon | 126
13. Changing Our Minds | 136
14. Counting the Cost | 144
15. Family | 156
16. Women | 166
17. Friends | 184
18. Foes | 190
19. Mending the Strands: Forgiveness | 204
20. Conclusion: Walking in Our Integrity | 218

Bibliography | 231

List of Diagrams

Figure 1—Map of the Territories (Dynamic Interaction Model of Human Relational Development—Basic Model) | 33

Figure 2—Expanded map of the Territories (Dynamic Interaction Model of Human Relational Development—Full Model) | 36

Figure 3—Personal Mapping | 44

Figure 4—Example Map | 45

Figure 5—Power Survey | 124

Acknowledgements

THIS BOOK HAS GONE through five revisions to reach its present edition. It was started in 2004 and completed in 2020. Various chapters have been shared with several reading groups and writing retreat participants. Unfortunately, I have not kept a list of everyone who has commented or offered feedback. My apologies, but I do wish to express my appreciation for everyone's thoughts and comments over the years about material that was included, or material that you convinced me to exclude.

Teri Watanabe (awordsworthwriting.com) did the first job of copy-editing the fourth revision, and I appreciate her comments that helped strengthen my style and worked to make it more consistent. I also want to thank the editorial and typesetting staff at Wipf and Stock Publishers in Eugene, Oregon for their attention and assistance during the publishing process.

Introduction

Curing a Sickness

THIS BOOK IS WRITTEN to cure a sickness.

It is a sickness that has reached epidemic proportions in the United States of America. It is a sickness that festers in the hearts and minds of nearly half of the population, and has resulted in the deaths of thousands of innocent people, the gender-based terrorizing of women and children, the brutalization of persons of color and forceful deportation of persons born on the soil of other nations, among other presenting symptoms. Consider the following:

1. As of November 14, 2017, there had been 317 mass shootings (with four or more persons wounded or killed) in the United States in 2017. The previous year ended with a total of 483 mass shootings.[1] The overwhelming preponderance of shooters were men.

2. An upsurge in white supremacist groups began with the election of Barack Obama in 2008, and culminated in a rise in hate crimes since the election of Donald Trump in 2016. The FBI reported a high of 6,121 identifiable hate crimes in 2016, up from 5,818 such crimes in 2015.[2] This supremacist activity culminated in the "Unite the Right" rally in Charlottesville, Virginia, in which torch-wielding white men shouted racist, anti-Semitic and Nazi-era slogans, while gun-wielding militia members—all of them white, mostly young

---

1. These statistics are compiled by the Gun Violence Archive, www.gunviolencearchive.org.

2. These statistics were reported by the Southern Poverty Law Center, https://www.splcenter.org/hatewatch/2017/11/13/fbi-hate-crimes-reach-5-year-high-2016-jumped-trump-rolled-toward-presidency-0, accessed November 22, 2017.

men—wandered the streets in threatening fashion. Many of the slogans proclaimed the United States to be a "Christian nation."

3. In the 2016 and 2020 elections, Evangelical Christians overwhelmingly voted for Donald Trump, who admitted to groping women and sexual pandering. In 2017, Judge Roy Moore was accused by several women of sexual abuse while they were teenagers, and he cited the relationship between Joseph and Mary (who presumably was in her late teens at the time of their engagement) as justification for his actions. Christian pastors flocked to uphold him. This prompted the *#MeToo* outpouring on social media in which millions of women across the country shared their own stories of being sexually harassed, touched, groped, and violated at home, at school, in the office, on the street, and even in churches. It is safe to say that there is not one woman who has not experienced some form of sexual harassment in her lifetime from her male colleagues, bosses, relatives, and strangers.

4. Gun rights activists and members of paramilitary militias are overwhelmingly male, and aggressively parade their lethal weapons in public rallies in order to intimidate and frighten legislators and ordinary citizens, many of whom have suffered from gun violence. For example, on January 31, 2020, fully armed guns-rights activists—all men—freely walked into the Kentucky State Capitol building and were waved around metal detectors, freely walking around the capitol carrying semi-automatic rifles, while people carrying umbrellas were not allowed to bring those umbrellas in "because they could be used as weapons."[3] Similar rallies were held in Virginia when the legislature considered controlling access to the type of semi-automatic rifles used in recent mass-killings in the United States.

These four symptoms are just a few examples of an epidemic that has infected the bodies, hearts, minds, and souls of North American men. This epidemic is a virulent form of masculinity that is destroying things—destroying the planet, destroying democracy, destroying families, destroying women, destroying men. Read the headlines—the *#MeToo* movement has pulled away the curtain revealing the lascivious

---

3. "Fully Armed Rally-Goers Enter Kentucky's Capitol Building with Zero Resistance," by Peter Wade, *RollingStone*, Feb. 1, 2020, accessed February 3, 2020, at https://www.rollingstone.com/politics/politics-news/fully-armed-rally-goers-enter-kentuckys-capitol-building-with-zero-resistance-946606/.

Introduction

culture of men in power. Politicians, presidents, CEOs, media magnates, entertainers, actors, untold numbers of bosses and managers, coaches, sports doctors—all satisfying their personal sexual lusts, fantasies, and appetites through the power they wield over the women in their sphere of control and influence.

Churches, synagogues, and temples are not exempt. Search the Internet, find the YouTube channels where religious leaders preach the supremacy of men over women, who refuse to allow women in positions of leadership, who proclaim control over women's bodies in the name of saving the unborn but who then leave women on their own to fend for themselves and raise the children who were once the precious unborn but are now problems—women's problems.

Look at the millionaires and billionaires who, in lusting after ever more wealth, scrape the earth bare, build pipelines across the sacred lands of indigenous peoples, only to have those pipelines burst and leak millions of gallons of toxic oil onto those lands. Millionaires and billionaires groping and fondling their ways into one another's boardrooms and bedrooms, plotting and planning which politicians to buy, setting the price on this democracy here or that government there, secretly arming this or that militia, provoking this or that white supremacist group.

It is the form of masculinity that kidnaps and traffics girls and young women into international sex slavery. It is the form of masculinity that terrorizes female partners, wives, girlfriends into submission, forbidding them to have friends or access to finances, and killing them when they try to escape. It is toxic. It destroys everything it touches. It sucks the joy and vitality out of life. It scorches the earth and eviscerates the soul. It is toxic.

It is time to Detox.

While it may be safe to say that not every man in the United States is a white supremacist, or has committed acts of violence, or has sexually harassed or assaulted women (or men), the fact that these behaviors are tolerated or even defended in some churches reveals a severe and willful ignorance of the life of integrity, nonviolence, respect for women, and active embrace of the outcast and marginalized that Jesus lived and taught his followers, especially his male followers.

It is time to turn this around. It is time to Detox.

There is a cure for this toxic form of masculinity that is life-giving, that seeks the welfare of others, that respects and cares for the earth and all its creatures. It is the way of thinking, acting, and being that was lived and taught by Jesus of Nazareth 2000 years ago. He taught it to his male disciples, and demonstrated it with his female disciples. Sadly, it has been largely ignored and even countermanded by the legions of male hierocrats who came to power as Christianity was absorbed and co-opted by the Roman Domination System of empire and male power and privilege. This is one of the great ironies of histories, because Jesus specifically *forbade* his (male) followers to "lord it over one another" in the way the rulers of the nations did.

It is time to redeem the redemptive Path of Jesus from its imprisonment in the dungeons of doctrinal authority and hierocratic obfuscation.

It is time that men who claim the name of Christ begin to live the life that Jesus Christ came to teach them to live.

It is time to take hold of the truly life-transforming power of Jesus Christ to heal the inner wounds that lead to violence and abuse.

It is time that men purge their minds and behaviors of the systems of thought that relegate other human beings to being expendable labor, or commodities to bargain or sell, or less than human because they are of another religion or skin color or national origin or gender identity.

It is time that men cleanse and purify themselves of the lust for power and domination that Jesus decried.

It is time for men to study, practice, and live the Way that Jesus brought and taught.

This book offers a systematic program to do just that. This book speaks to the men of today in the words that Jesus spoke to the men of his day, addressing the same situations that face men today: the prevalence of violence, harassment and exploitation of women and children; the virulent hatred of anyone deemed to be "foreign" or "alien;" the treatment of persons as commodities to be bought, sold, or worked to exhaustion in the name of making a profit; the loss of moral and ethical integrity to the extent that falsehoods are paraded as truth, and many other acts that can only be described as wicked, all of which derive from the core sin of the use and abuse of power.

The men of Jesus' day would be able to relate to this list. Jesus showed them a way out of the systems of power and domination, human abuse and exploitation that he called "the world." He offered a way for men to rescue and cleanse their souls and minds from the perversions of these systems, and gave them a new way of living that was grounded in the radical way of love. Not a sappy, sentimental, gushy mushy kind of love. His love was the kind that made a person willing to lay down their life for their friends. It's the kind of love that you cannot dismiss. It is the kind of love that makes us as human beings, and in its absence, breaks us.

In the pages that follow, we will seek out the words and lived example of Jesus as we look at the ways we have been socialized into the systems of power and violence, and explore the Spiritual Path that Jesus lived and taught. The basic themes that we will explore are:

- Reversing hierarchies of power
- Non-cooperation with systems of domination
- Alternatives to violence and oppression
- Repentance as the act of radically changing our ways of thinking and behaving
- Considering the cost of discipleship
- Men's relationships with their families
- Men's relationships with women
- Friendship and inter-mutuality
- What it means to love our enemies
- The power of forgiveness
- Walking in our integrity—ethical and moral living

Taking the Detox Path of Jesus is perhaps the most significant thing you can do with your life. I say this not because I have completely succeeded in this quest. No, I am simply one beggar telling another beggar where he has found bread. And this bread that I have found is the Bread of Life. It is a Way that is Truth and Life. It is all about a Love that will not let you go. And it is this Love that wants to change the world.

— 1 —

The Way of Love

Detox! JP21 is an integral part of a program of reclaiming the spiritual life teachings of Jesus for all the world to explore in the twenty-first century. This larger program is called *Reboot! JP21*,[1] which is grounded in the conviction and Biblical evidence that Jesus gathered followers in order to teach them a new way of living and thinking intended to raise the level of human consciousness, expanding the hearts and minds of all who sought to apply his teachings and life example to their own lives. Small communities of his followers set up new micro-societies that slowly started to exert influence on the larger communities around them—until the Christian movement turned into a hierarchical institution, and was subsequently co-opted and subverted by the Roman Empire after Constantine's nominal conversion to Christianity.

What Is the Reboot! JP21 Process All About?

Reboot! JP21 is based upon the conviction that Jesus did not come to establish a vast, powerful institution called the Church (in any of its denominational permutations). Rather, his life work was devoted to teaching and demonstrating the possibility we all have for lives transformed by an expanded and higher consciousness based in an immediate and intimate relationship with the Love in which the entire universe is centered, and which holds all things together. What he bequeathed to the world through his early followers was a Path, a Way. This is demonstrated by the fact that the earliest name for any gathering of his followers was the Way.

1. See the JP21 website: https://www.conspiritu.org/reboot-jp21.html.

What flows from this conviction is the simple conclusion that the Way of Jesus does not consist of doctrines, theologies, and speculations *about* Jesus, rather it consists of a *way of living* that expands our awareness of who we are, and how we are interconnected with the human and more-than-human world around us, that roots us deeper into those interconnections, with the result that we work to manifest that same expanded awareness and action in the cultural and social systems in which we live. It is a Way of Love, but not a sappy, sentimental sort of love. It is love that is action *on behalf of* and *in the best interests of* the other.

Detox! JP21 is specifically addressed to men and is a process of unlearning and disentangling from the dysfunctional and maladaptive systems into which we have been enculturated, and then immersing and embedding in a system that affirms life in its diversity and interconnectedness. It is a process that is lifelong, because the hooks and roots of our dysfunctional world have spent many years infiltrating our consciousness, and shaping our thoughts, behaviors, and value systems.

A twenty-first century analogy for the spiritual path that Jesus taught and demonstrated to his followers is the idea of a computer Operating System. Every computer has an Operating System, which is a complex, interconnected set of instructions that tells the computer how to run its basic operations, and how to utilize and run any additional software programs and applications designed to run on that computer.

Computer Operating Systems owe their existence to an interdisciplinary field of research and exploration that emerged in the mid-twentieth century: Cybernetics. The word *cybernetics* comes from Greek *kybernētikḗ*, meaning "governance." *Kybernḗtēs* is the governor or "helmsperson" of the ship. Contemporary cybernetics began as an interdisciplinary study connecting the fields of control systems, electrical network theory, mechanical engineering, logic modeling, evolutionary biology, neuroscience, anthropology, and psychology in the 1940s.

This new field of cybernetics was vital to the development of computers and the electronic systems at the heart of computers. Cybernetics looks at how systems operate, and how they give rise to certain results, or behaviors. Talking about systems is important for us to understand the elegance and beauty of the spiritual path that Jesus called the Kingdom of Heaven.

Systems of Thought and Behavior
That Govern and Control and Even Manipulate Us

What is a system? Systems Theory and the study of Cybernetics gives us this definition: "A set of detailed methods, procedures and routines created to carry out a specific activity, perform a duty, or solve a problem. An organized, purposeful structure that consists of interrelated and interdependent elements (components, entities, factors, members, parts etc.). These elements continually influence one another (directly or indirectly) to maintain their activity and the existence of the system, in order to achieve the goal of the system."[2]

Systems Theory has recognized that human beings live, move, and have their being in the midst of complex systems of social organizations, governments, religions, etc. Worldviews operate to regulate, define and maintain these systems.

A system operates by being an all-encompassing complex of factors, including values, educational processes, religious teaching, popular culture, political and military control, economics, and legal structures. As we work to dismantle and disentangle ourselves from these maladaptive and destructive systems, we begin by analyzing and understanding how these systems operate and how they infect our hearts and minds. This is the first step for moving into the Next, Bigger Mind that is a central component of what Jesus called the Kingdom of Heaven.

In order to understand how these systems function beneath our level of conscious awareness, think of what it is like to be a fish whose entire life is lived immersed in water. Everything about you as a fish is adapted to living in water. Gills have evolved in order to filter out oxygen dissolved in water. Your musculature and body shape are designed to move you through water. In fact, you are only aware of water as the normal medium in which you live, move, and have your being.

Systems are the "water" in which we as human beings live, move, and have our being. Systems have shaped our thought processes, our desires, our intentions, and our perceived needs. Systems determine our value, and devalue us if it suits the purposes of the system and the interests served in the perpetuation of the system. Telling the truth about how systems operate as well as understanding the nature of these systems is vital in order to begin disentanglement.

---

2. "System: definitions," *Business Dictionary*.

So, we have a general Operating System—a Life Operating System, if you will—that guides our thinking, provides us with a set of values and principles to live by, tells us what to like or not like, what is acceptable to do and how to do it, what to avoid, how to find meaning in what we do, and so on. It is bound up in our emotions and feelings, such that we feel pain or pleasure when we do certain things or certain things are done to us. Our joys, fears, pleasures, amusements, aversions are all powerful motivating factors, and are key elements of our Life Operating Systems.

Our personal Life Operating Systems are shaped and "programmed," if you will, by the greater social systems in which we swim like fish. These systems exert strong control over our lives, not always for our good.

Our Systems Need to Be Changed—
We Need to Reboot! with a New Life Operating System

So, why am I spending all this time talking about systems, cybernetics, and computers? The point is that Jesus addressed the social and religious systems of his day in a way that is systematic in itself. Jesus doesn't just spout cute little slogans that look good on your refrigerator or car bumper. He didn't just say, "Love your neighbor," he sent his disciples out into situations where they would have to touch lepers, heal the sick, hang out with Samaritans and Gentiles. They had to encounter the prejudices that had been instilled in them by their society and religion. They had to rearrange their ways of thinking. He demonstrated ways of overcoming these conditioned ways of acting and thinking as he walked along the highways and byways, touching the untouchable, speaking with those he wasn't supposed to speak with, arguing with the teachers and preachers of prejudice, purity, and privilege.

The thing about the Jesus Path is that it is a full-meal deal. It provides a way to disentangle our minds from the junk that our societies, religions, organizations, and networks of associations have dumped into our hearts and minds. Jesus understood how human beings are formed and shaped by the cultural environments in which they live. He also understood how those environments can be changed by the people who live in them, as those very people undergo a transformation of heart, mind, and life.

The Gospels all depict Jesus beginning his ministry saying "Repent! The kingdom of God is at hand!" If he had come today, he might say, "Reboot! You are about to commit a fatal error that will cause your life system to crash!" We start on the *Jesus Path* when we recognize that the path we are currently on is not working, or is perhaps even dangerous or perilous to our health and the health of the world. In computer talk: our life is giving us "error messages" and it is time to disconnect from a dysfunctional system, purge our operating system of the old, and download a new Operating System. Time to "reboot."

JP21 Is Based in Love

The practice and power of love is central to the message and life of Jesus Christ. In fact, one of Jesus's close friends, John, the son of Zebedee, who became known in later centuries as John the Evangelist, was so overwhelmed by the power and quality of Jesus' life as a revelation of love and a revelation of God, that he makes the radical claim that the path to knowing God is followed by loving one another: "Whoever does not love does not know God, because God is love" (1 John 4:8 NRSV).

St. Jerome, in his commentary on Chapter 6 of the Epistle to the Galatians[3] tells the well-loved story that this same John the Evangelist continued preaching in Ephesus even when he was in his 90s. The evangelist was so enfeebled with old age that the people had to carry him into the Church in Ephesus on a stretcher. And when he was no longer able to preach or deliver a long discourse, John would lift himself up from the stretcher on one elbow and simply say: "Little children, love one another." Then he would lie back down and his friends would carry him back out. Every week, he gave the same short sermon with exactly the same message: "Little children, love one another." One day, someone asked him about it: "John, why is it that every week you say exactly the same thing, 'Little children, love one another'?" And John replied: "Because it is enough."

The love that Jesus brought to the world was not meant to be a one-time event. Jesus clearly commanded every one of his followers to practice a radical, self-giving form of love that could turn former enemies into friends, turn empires upside down, and change the course of history. This kind of love never ends, and it continues to grip the lives of those who come into contact with it, melting lives, purifying out the dross and recasting lives in golden splendor.

I know this because it recast mine. Let me tell you what happened.

---

3. Jerome, *Comm. in ep. ad. Gal.*, 6, 10.

My Personal Spiritual Journey

I was raised in the church. My family started attending Whitney United Methodist Church in Boise, Idaho when I was about two years old, and we went every Sunday we could. I took church seriously, and listened closely to what the minister said every Sunday, read my children's Bible and looked at all the pictures, went to Sunday School faithfully for years and was a regular in the youth group. All eight of us boys did this and my two parents set the example. I took this following Jesus stuff seriously.

When I started High School, I started to rebel and chafe against some of my parents' restrictions, with particularly pronounced conflicts with my mom. One conflict was that I started getting involved in drugs at school. I was pretty stealthy about it all. I was never allowed to grow my hair long or wear bell-bottoms or cool pants with holes in them even if bandana patches covered those holes. I fooled people pretty well with my clean-cut exterior. I continued to go to church, listen to the sermons, and wonder about what this Jesus stuff was all about, and how it really made a difference in my life. (Do you hear that phrase again: "make a difference?") But all the while I had this other life at school.

By the end of my sophomore year, 1972, I reached a crossroads in my life. I had registered for a Senior High Camp at Sawtooth United Methodist Camp. In fact, I was on the camp council for a camp that was designed to restart the Senior High Camping program at Sawtooth, but this other part of my life was pushing at me. So, I made a bargain with God before heading up the dusty road that year: either God did something tremendous at that camp, or I was going to get heavier into drugs. That's just the kind of challenge God enjoys.

One night as the twelve youth and three adults at that camp sat around in a circle in the lodge talking about deep stuff, I suddenly sensed this voice speaking to me. It said, "Who do you think you're fooling, Craig Strobel?" I "heard" it several times. It was a voice so loving and so truthful that it cut clean through all the crap I was throwing up in my life, and speared my heart. I knew it could only be Jesus. Tears were streaming down my face and a friend helped me pray to Jesus for forgiveness and to turn my life over to him. I remember being flooded with such an overwhelming flood of joy that I leapt over tall sagebrush bushes in a single bound, as if I were Superman.

Rebooting Meant a New Start

The same power that raised Jesus from the dead touched my dead-end life and raised it into a new Easter beginning. I was limping along acting religious by doing all the churchy religious things, going to church, Sunday School, youth group, youth rallies, but the power of religion had previously escaped me. What needed to happen was that I needed to die to a whole way of life that was a clear path to death. This is what Paul means when he says, "Do you not know that all of us who have been baptized into Christ Jesus were baptized into his death? Therefore, we have been buried with him by baptism into death, so that, just as Christ was raised from the dead by the glory of the Father, so we too might walk in newness of life" (Romans 6:3,4). This newness of life was not an instantaneous event. Rather, it has involved a lifelong process of disentangling myself from the destructive and maladaptive systems of the world around me. It has involved "downloading" a new Life Operating System. The death Paul talks about is this process of disentangling and dismantling the old Life Operating System in order to make room for the new Life Operating System that Jesus called the Kingdom of Heaven.

This new life eventually led me into the ministry where I have served churches for the past thirty-eight years. But as I have worked as a religious leader I have noticed that much of my time has been spent being an administrator of the church rather than being a minister to the spiritual lives and longings of people. I have witnessed spiritually eager people come to church and get involved only to be turned off by the attitudes of some of the members. Others have left because some religious leaders in the media preach hateful things or urge people to do things that are deeply disrespectful of other religions or faith expressions. Some come to church looking for the love of God and leave because of the hatefulness of people bearing the name of Jesus Christ. I have always wanted to find these people and tell them that the Way of Jesus is nothing like what they have experienced, that the Way of Jesus *is* all about love, in spite of what they experience in some churches.

(Why should I have to use that phrase, "in spite of"? Isn't that the saddest thing in the world to say?)

This book also grows out of a very personal place of pain in my own life. I have been married and divorced twice. Each divorce pierced my heart like a barb, because it laid my life open before my eyes. In college, as I served in a leadership position in my college Christian fellowship, I committed myself to being a sensitive, caring and enlightened husband, a "new male." I paid close attention to what women were openly saying about their lives and what they needed in a relationship. I felt I could offer my marital partner just that: a partnership based upon mutuality, where we each brought our individual skills, desires, dreams and avowals together and offered them for the good of the relationship. I enjoyed cooking and was a good cook and did a lot of the cooking in both marriages. In both marriages, I worked next door, was home more, and regularly cleaned the house. In addition, I did the gardening and yard work. I tried to share household tasks as an equal partner in each marriage. But those commitments were not enough to cement these two relationships. Something more was needed, and the divorces underscored the fact that something was lacking. But what was it? That question implanted itself in my soul.

The second barb thrust in my heart by my divorce was perhaps the sharpest of all: I was a pastor. I had committed my life to Jesus Christ and my vocation to his service as a Christian minister. From this basic commitment flowed all my other commitments, including my marriage and my children. My devotion to my family was grounded in my devotion to my Lord and Savior, and to his teachings and life example. I knew that my parishioners looked to my life to see if "it could be done," if the Christian life as described in the New Testament could actually be lived, if it was actually possible. To that end, in part, I vowed not to become a pastoral workaholic. I was home when my children or wife came home, and I dedicated evenings to the family. I served small rural churches and we pared down the administrative oversight to two or three essential committees that met once a month, or even less frequently. I did my visitation during the day, leaving the evening for my family. I believed that it was a part of my ministry to model for my congregation a strong, cohesive, caring family wherein both parents were equal partners in raising their children. I wanted to show the men in my congregation that it was in them to be loving nurturers of their children and their wives. They had that capability, and, in my conversations with many of them, I also knew they had the desire to live out the love of Christ. They just needed guidance and examples and support. I committed myself to provide these for them.

These are all commitments I still have. But my divorces forced me to examine *my life* more closely. I needed to begin telling deeper truths about myself to myself, because only then would I be set free, as Jesus promised in John 8:32. I also needed to tell those truths about myself to God, especially as I experienced God in my relationship with Jesus Christ. I realized that I needed to continue to abide in God's word, I needed to make God's reality, God's teaching, God's presence my dwelling place, which were all ways to render in English what I read in the original Greek in my study of the Bible. I could do the Biblical study and research in my office. I now needed to do the application in my life. Ah, yes, now there was the rub.

This Search is Personal and Not Just Theoretical

This book grew out of that very personal search for a life more deeply planted in the word of Jesus Christ, for a life of devoted discipleship, a life where my heart's home is the dwelling of God. It is a search for a life of deeper truth-telling about myself to myself and to God. It is, at its core, *a search to live out the Path of Jesus in the midst of the challenges and opportunities of the twenty-first century.*

In order to be a twenty-first century man who desired to pattern and shape his life after the example of Jesus, I realized that I needed to return first and foremost to his life and teachings and see if there was something he said that directly addressed what it means to follow him *as a man*. I started to read the Gospels more carefully, paying attention to when it was apparent he was talking to his male disciples, and when he was addressing larger groups of disciples, some of whom were women as well as men. I paid attention to what Jesus said and did in regards to the social conventions of his day, but more particularly to how he dealt with those who had power over others, whether they were in positions of teaching authority, governmental authority, or social hierarchy, such as men over women or husbands over wives.[4]

What I discovered was not only a scathing indictment of the relationships between men and women in our homes and our society, but, more significantly, I uncovered what I believe to be a clear demonstration of a specifically male spirituality, based in the life and teaching of Jesus Christ. I further discerned that throughout the Gospels, Jesus strove to instill this spirituality within the lives and minds of his male followers.

---

4. I use the preposition "over" deliberately. The social relations of his day were hierarchically stratified, and based upon the domination of one group or class by another. That this was the accepted and expected order of things should make the proclamation of Christ's emptying himself of the power, domination and authority of divinity in Philippians 2:6–8 even more shocking. Just what is this Jesus all about?

Furthermore, I realized that this spirituality was not simply meant to be a set of lofty teachings, clever aphorisms or points to ponder, but rather, a way of life deeply rooted in the spirit and power of the One who had emptied himself of all divine prerogatives and power and became servant of all. To be a new creation in Christ as Paul talks about in 2 Corinthians 5:17 means to enter into the full way of being and acting that Jesus demonstrated, and which is a full expression of who he is, and thus is a revelation of God's very self. What this means in terms of being a man after Jesus' heart in the context of our society is very specific, and is not necessarily what it means to be a woman after Jesus' heart in the context of our society.

Detox! JP21 Is a Path for Men of the 21st Century

And so, this book is addressed to men. I have realized that it is presumptuous of me to attempt to define for women what a female spirituality might be, because it would be informed entirely by my own masculine point of view, colored by my place of power and privilege in society, as well as by the sexual charge that is inherent in relations between men and women. I can speak to men because I am a man, who has experienced the things men tend to experience growing up from childhood into adulthood. In addition, I grew up the oldest in a family of eight boys, so in spite of the very strong influence my mother exerted upon me, I was heavily shaped by a masculine frame of thinking and living.

The following chapters outline the evidence for such a male spirituality by first examining the Gospels. As a Christian believer and more importantly, as a committed and professing *disciple* of Jesus Christ, I look first and foremost to him as my guide, as my exemplar, and as my interpreter of all matters concerning life and spirituality. This includes the interpretation of Scripture. Thus, it is that when I read the Bible, I read it through the lens, if you will, of Jesus Christ, of his life and teaching, of his death and resurrection. Jesus is the defining point, the Alpha and Omega, the beginning and end of Christian male spirituality.

Therefore, I invite you to join me in a journey of deep exploration into what Jesus taught his male disciples about following him in his way. We begin this journey by considering what it means to be a man in today's society. We will look at the issues men face in term of socialization and development of a purpose and direction for our lives. We will explore how the search for a meaningful and purposeful life is central to the development of the male psyche, and how the social contexts for exploring such lives have become fragmented and subject to abusive and destructive behaviors. We will frame our journey using a model I developed for understanding personal development in its personal, interpersonal and social interactions.

The next section discusses the nature of spirituality and the role of spiritual disciplines in forming character and molding behavior according to the deepest values and beliefs that a person holds. That is, how do we "walk the talk?" How do we get our actions to align with what we say we believe about the world, or about how to treat one another? How do we avoid becoming hypocrites, preachers of religion but not practitioners?

Since the main sources for learning about Jesus that are authoritative in the Christian community are the Gospels contained in the New Testament of the Bible, it is important to delineate how we will use the Bible in our exploration of the spirituality of Jesus. The next section identifies passages in the Gospels that refer to men or men's issues specifically, and describes how to read and interpret the Bible in a way that leads to deeper personal and social understanding.

The final section investigates the various contours and themes of male spirituality. Significant sections of the Bible are explored for the light they shed upon how Jesus addressed and responded to the social inequities and roles played by men in his day.

Embracing the Path of Jesus as a twenty-first century man is perhaps the most significant thing you can do with your life. It may also be the most difficult thing you have ever done with your life. If you find that to be true, you are on the right path. Jesus called it a narrow path that few would tread upon. Welcome to the journey.

— 2 —

Next Mindify Yourself!

THIS BOOK REPRESENTS THE possibility of a new beginning in life. Whatever your reasons for reading this book, it is ultimately all about making a new beginning. The idea of making a new start in life is compelling. Think of the various roads in life that you've taken that just ended up nowhere. I have a friend who says that a dead end is just another place to turn around. You know, the Bible doesn't condemn dead-ends. It just says, "Turn around!"

The path of Jesus begins with turning around. In the Bible, the word for this is "repent." And speaking of beginnings, in all four Gospels, Jesus begins his ministry by hanging out with John the Baptist and adopting his message of repentance. Let's look at Matthew's and Mark's versions:

Matthew 3:1-17 (NRSV)

[1]In those days, John the Baptist appeared in the wilderness of Judea, proclaiming, [2]"Repent, for the kingdom of heaven has come near." [3]This is the one of whom the prophet Isaiah spoke when he said,
"The voice of one crying out in the wilderness:
'Prepare the way of the Lord,
make his paths straight.'"
[4]Now John wore clothing of camel's hair with a leather belt around his waist, and his food was locusts and wild honey. [5]Then the people of Jerusalem and all Judea were going out to him, and all the region along the Jordan, [6]and they were baptized by him in the river Jordan, confessing their sins.

⁷But when he saw many Pharisees and Sadducees coming for baptism, he said to them, "You brood of vipers! Who warned you to flee from the wrath to come? ⁸Bear fruit worthy of repentance. ⁹Do not presume to say to yourselves, 'We have Abraham as our ancestor'; for I tell you, God is able from these stones to raise up children to Abraham. ¹⁰Even now the ax is lying at the root of the trees; every tree therefore that does not bear good fruit is cut down and thrown into the fire.

¹¹"I baptize you in water for repentance, but one who is more powerful than I is coming after me; I am not worthy to carry his sandals. He will baptize you with the Holy Spirit and fire. ¹²His winnowing fork is in his hand, and he will clear his threshing floor and will gather his wheat into the granary; but the chaff he will burn with unquenchable fire."

¹³Then Jesus came from Galilee to John at the Jordan, to be baptized by him. ¹⁴John would have prevented him, saying, "I need to be baptized by you, and do you come to me?" ¹⁵But Jesus answered him, "Let it be so now; for it is proper for us in this way to fulfill all righteousness." Then he consented. ¹⁶And when Jesus had been baptized, just as he came up from the water, suddenly the heavens were opened to him and he saw the Spirit of God descending like a dove and alighting on him. ¹⁷And a voice from heaven said, "This is my Son, the Beloved, with whom I am well pleased."

Mark 1:1–11 (NRSV)

¹The beginning of the good news of Jesus Christ, the Son of God.

²As it is written in the prophet Isaiah,
"See, I am sending my messenger ahead of you,
who will prepare your way;
³the voice of one crying out in the wilderness:
'Prepare the way of the Lord,
make his paths straight,'"

⁴John the baptizer appeared in the wilderness, proclaiming a baptism of repentance for the forgiveness of sins. ⁵And people from the whole Judean countryside and all the people of Jerusalem were going out to him, and were baptized by him in the river Jordan, confessing their sins. ⁶Now John was clothed with camel's hair, with a leather belt around his waist, and he ate

locusts and wild honey. ⁷He proclaimed, "The one who is more powerful than I is coming after me; I am not worthy to stoop down and untie the thong of his sandals. 8I have baptized you with in water; but he will baptize you in the Holy Spirit."

⁹In those days Jesus came from Nazareth of Galilee and was baptized by John in the Jordan. ¹⁰And just as he was coming up out of the water, he saw the heavens torn apart and the Spirit descending like a dove on him. ¹¹And a voice came from heaven, "You are my Son, the Beloved; with you I am well pleased."

Let's look at what John the Baptizer had to say about starting over. In Matthew's version, John says, "I baptize you in water *for* repentance." It doesn't say, "John was baptizing *after* the people repented." In the Gospel of Mark, it says that John practiced a baptism *of* repentance. Let's pause a moment and look at that word, "baptism."

The original Greek word, *baptizma*, means to immerse. It has the same sense and uses of the English word, immerse. For instance, have you ever immersed yourself in a good book? You were baptizing yourself in that book. It doesn't mean "to dunk somebody in water." It simply means to immerse.

But, I do have to say, there is something powerfully dramatic about being immersed in water. I remember when I was young, my mom taking us to swimming lessons. But I could just never get the hang of things. I didn't like putting my head in the water, and the whole stroke, turn your head, take a breath, stroke thing just wasn't going to happen. Several summers went by like this. Then finally, one summer at Boy Scout camp, we were at Warm Lake in Idaho, and I was taking swimming lessons along the lakeshore. I finally plunged myself in the water and glided along the bottom for about three seconds. But it was amazing! I felt the power of the water all around me, I felt like a fish, and suddenly the whole swimming mystery was solved. Total immersion in the experience changed everything.

This is what John is talking about. New life doesn't happen by just wishing for it. You have to jump in, full-bodied.

John is talking about a life immersed in the power and presence of God. Water immersion symbolizes this. Jesus will come to immerse them in the power of the Spirit. John is all about preparing for this immersion in the Spirit. We have to prepare ourselves for this. How? By *telling the truth* about our lives—confessing our sins—and how off the mark we are, how off-path we have wandered, how lost and confused, how injured and hurt, how self-centered and hurtful we are. John preaches a baptism of repentance—an immersion in this self-examination, telling the truth, and starting over.

Now we need to pause once again and look at the next word, "repentance." The original Greek is *metanoia*, which literally means to change one's mind, to change the direction of one's mind, and thus one's life. In fact, *metanoia* also translates as "beyond the (normal) mind," and the force of the verb indicates going beyond our normal consciousness or way of thinking into a deeper, bigger mind, the "mind of Christ" as Paul calls it in Philippians. *Metanoia*, or repentance, then, means redirecting our lives from our small self-centered minds into the bigger mind of God. John preached about immersing oneself in repentance, or *metanoia*.

John says Jesus will come to immerse us in the power of the Holy Spirit. So, Jesus came down the River Jordan to meet John. If you are like me, you probably ask, "Why did Jesus have to repent?" But remember, *metanoia* means to move into a bigger mind in order to start over, and Jesus comes to symbolically demonstrate that he embraces this bigger mind of God. In essence, he is embracing his divine nature, and his divine mission to show us a path to God. And what happens next blows everything away, and people listening to this story in Mark's time would have been blown away.

Jesus goes down in the water to show the world that he is ready to embrace the bigger mind of God. He wades in the water with John. Now, at this point of his Gospel, Mark makes a very dramatic statement: ". . . just as he was coming up out of the water, he saw the heavens torn apart and the Spirit descending like a dove on him." *Torn apart*. There are two places in Mark where the Greek word is used that means torn apart (*schidzomenous*): here and in Mark 15:38. This is the story of the crucifixion of Jesus. He cries out, someone runs up to give him vinegar on a sponge, and, then verse 37 and 38: "Then Jesus gave a loud cry and breathed his last. And the curtain of the temple was torn in two, from top to bottom."

Now this curtain is highly significant. This was the outer curtain veiling the innermost part of the Holy of Holies, the place where God's presence resided. David Ulansey explains that, according to the Jewish historian Josephus,

> . . . this outer veil was a gigantic curtain 80 feet high. It was, he says, a 'Babylonian tapestry, with embroidery of blue and fine linen, of scarlet also and purple, wrought with marvelous skill.

Nor was this mixture of materials without its mystic meaning: it typified the universe . . .

Then Josephus tells us what was pictured on this curtain:

"Portrayed on this tapestry was *a panorama of the entire heavens* . . . [emphasis Ulansey's]."

In other words, the outer veil of the Jerusalem temple was actually one huge image of the starry sky! Thus, upon encountering Mark's statement that "the veil of the temple was torn in two from top to bottom," any of his readers who had ever seen the temple or heard it described would instantly have seen in their mind's eye an image of *the heavens being torn*, and would immediately have been reminded of Mark's earlier description of the heavens being torn at the baptism.[1]

This is what happened to Jesus and what he came to do: open heaven to us. Not after death, but now. The path of Jesus is nothing less than a path into a bigger mind, an expanded consciousness, the metanoia John preaches. Our minds literally have to be changed. But this is no easy task. Anyone trying to escape the clutches of addiction or trying to heal from an abusive upbringing, or recover from PTSD knows that "changing one's mind" is not like changing the sheets or changing one's clothes. It actually entails changing the very quality and content of one's mind, and changing the configuration of the neurons in the brain. It involves developing a new mode of thinking and perceiving the world. It involves quite literally an expansion of consciousness. Paul called it having the mind of Christ, Jesus called it the Kingdom or Realm of Heaven (or God) that is within us and in our midst. This is what Jesus came to help humanity realize and develop into. But there are a lot of things that have to be deconstructed, taken apart, disassembled, in order to be rebuilt and reconfigured in our mental landscape. This is the work of the Spirit within us. And that is what Jesus immerses us in—the power of the Holy Spirit. And this transforms us. It transforms our direction in life, it transforms our focus in life, it transforms the world around us by the things we do, and it transforms our very reality.

In the 65th chapter of Isaiah, God says, "For I am about to create new heavens and a new earth; the former things shall not be remembered or come to mind." Jesus saw those heavens torn open, and felt the holy power of those heavens poured out upon him. And he pours out the same

---

1. Ulansey, "The Heavenly Veil Torn," 123–25.

Holy Spirit power upon you. Every person who seeks this new way, this new path. We can all start over. No dead ends. Just new life.

Jesus allowed himself to be baptized by John because he was showing the world that he embraced the fullness of this new life, which is a path into a bigger mind, an expanded consciousness, what John was calling *metanoia*.

A Closer Look at Metanoeîte

So, let's take a closer look today at this metanoia stuff that both John and Jesus talk about. The verb used by John and Jesus is *metanoeîte*. It is an interesting word. It is made up of two parts: the first part is *metá-*, which, when used as a preposition, can mean "after," "next," "with," "behind," etc. The second part, *noeîte*, is the imperative of *noéō*, which means to direct one's mind towards something, to perceive, to notice. The noun form is *noûs*, which can mean "mind," "disposition," the total inner or moral attitude, "insight," "inventiveness," "reason," "consciousness," i.e., the mental side of human beings by which we show ourselves to be feeling, willing, thinking beings.

So, when you put these two words, *metá* + *noéō*, you get a word that can mean "change one's mind," "come to a later or new thought," or even "come to the next mind." In early Christian circles, it was often used in a way that meant to convert, such as conversion to Christianity from another system of belief. It also was used in ways to indicate an attitude of deep sorrowfulness or regret for what has done in life, which could lead to a change in behavior, belief, or way of life.

I have come to believe that John and Jesus used this word in a much stronger and more expansive sense. The fact that they use the imperative form of the verb indicates that there is a strong urgency to the type of change they are talking about. I believe that they were urging the people of their time—and every time and age since then—to actually "move into the next mind." I believe they meant something bigger and wider and deeper than simply "being sorry or regretful" about something.

Next Mind

For instance, John and Jesus both say to move into the bigger mind because "the kingdom of heaven is at hand/has come near." Something new is happening here, not a simple shift in morality, not simply choosing to be "good boys and girls," not simply "being nice" or trying to get along. To be in the kingdom, or, as I prefer, the *realm* of heaven, is a higher order of being than we are accustomed to in everyday life. It is a higher order of thinking, a higher order of compassion, it is a higher order of valuing other human beings, it is a higher order of understanding how the earth works as a natural system. It is a higher order because being in the realm of heaven means to begin to perceive things from the perspective of God. It means thinking from the perspective of, and from the *intention* of the Divine Source and Force from which all Reality springs forth. Therefore, I believe the best translation for metanoia, when referring to how John and Jesus use that word, is to talk about the "Next Mind."

In fact, if Jesus came today, he just might say "Next-mindify yourself!" Move into the Next Mind, which is actually a Bigger Mind. But let's pause for a moment to think this through.

How many times have you or anybody you know said, "I've changed my mind about this (or that)?" Usually we mean that we have changed our thinking or opinion or ideas about something. But we use this funny expression that seems to imply that our mind—the seat of consciousness, of awareness, of thinking, of creativity and imagination, of decision-making—has suddenly become, well, *different*.

What if our minds *could* become different? What if we were able to somehow upgrade our entire mental apparatus and process the same way we upgrade our computer software and operating systems?

Well, guess what? We *can* upgrade our minds. In fact, our minds are *designed to be upgraded*. Let me say that again: *our minds are designed to be upgraded.*

Think about it (pun intended): Do you think about things the same way you did five years ago? Ten years ago? When you were in High School? Elementary school? Kindergarten? Have you been altered by surviving a traumatic event? Have you traveled to a foreign country to visit or live for any length of time? How did that affect the way you think about the world?

The ability to adapt, modify, alter, and enlarge our pattern of thinking is the central characteristic of what is called *consciousness*. What do we mean by "consciousness?" Basically, consciousness is the inner state of awareness and responsiveness to one's environment, social context, and life situation, as experienced through sensations, emotions, volitions, and thoughts. The idea of awareness plus responsiveness underscores the fact that human consciousness is *self-aware*, meaning that we can think reflectively about our own inner psychological state and process of thinking and emoting. Because of this ability to reflect upon our own inner state of mind, humans over the centuries have developed ways of directly intervening and altering their own states of mind. Great religious and spiritual teachers across the world in various times and places have often been masters of consciousness, and have taught their followers techniques for expanding consciousness, along with affecting positive social change as a direct result of such expansion of consciousness.

This is what John and Jesus were teaching people: *the expansion of personal consciousness and social consciousness are interrelated and interdependent phenomena.* John told people that they couldn't presume upon their ethnic or genealogical status to prove how good or privileged they were. They had to change their entire lives and way of doing things. Things were going to have to be changed because the Realm of Heaven was at hand, and God's way of doing things is not the world's way of doing things. That is the first thing that has to be acknowledged. The first thing to do, then, is to confess, to tell the truth about the way things are—in our personal lives, but also in the world at large.

And so, *Metanoeîte*—next-mindifying ourselves—begins with *telling the truth*, but it doesn't end there. It's not enough to admit where we've gone wrong in life. It's not enough to acknowledge that the world is pretty messed up. John and Jesus are interested in striking at the heart or root of what is actually dysfunctional and destructive behavior—and that is our embeddedness in dysfunctional, destructive, and oppressive systems.

There is a winnowing out and an uprooting that needs to occur in our very process of thinking and behaving, and in the very basis for our attitudes and responses in life. Because we are by our very nature social creatures, our attitudes, language, beliefs, values, sentiments, prejudices, ideas, and everything else about us are formed by society. We actually have to disentangle ourselves from all the dysfunctional and destructive patterns of life that our dysfunctional and destructive world has implanted within us. As we disentangle ourselves, we also work to change the way our world works. Humans have made the world the way it is, humans can unmake the world the way it is.

This whole repentance/conversion thing is not as simple as it appears. Even if one goes with *metanoia* meaning a change of mind (which still can have levels to what that means), even changing one's mind so that one's behavior is significantly changed is no easy task. Our minds and brains have been literally shaped and formed by everything around us: our language, our every interaction growing up, what we watch constantly on TV or movies, or on our computers, the steady stream of stuff that comes to us on Facebook or Twitter or SnapChat or any of a dozen social media. All of this creates a form of mind that is self-focused, prone to consider violence as a solution to most problems, commodity and acquisitionally-oriented, and, in our culture, obsessed with sex. All of these things reflect the destructive dysfunctionality of our world. And so, we seek to allow ourselves to be transformed by the work of God within us, and we also seek to transform the world we live in according to the Realm of Heaven. In other words, *Metanoia* needs to produce results, bear fruit. Bearing fruit is not instantaneous, but is the result of a long process of growth and development.

That is just what was happening there alongside the Jordan River, 2000 years ago. People came to John. He told them, just as he tells us today, here in the twenty-first century, here in this place on Planet Earth, "Next—mindify yourselves! The Realm of Heaven is here, and you can live in it. But you can't just dip your toes into it. You have to jump in! Your whole body, your whole mind, your whole soul, your whole self—everything—has to get immersed in the New Life of God, the New Way of God. The Realm of Heaven is here, and God is ready to change things.

So, jump in!

Your Next Mind awaits!

Your Next Life awaits!

The Next World awaits!

Jump in!"

— 3 —

Becoming Men

"So, young man, what do you plan to be when you grow up?"

If I had a dollar for every time I was asked that while growing up, I would have no educational debts today. Aside from the absurdity of asking that of someone whose favorite activity was watching Rocky and Bullwinkle on TV, my personal observation, is that the question was seldom posed to girls my age. My recollection is that when it was, they would often answer, "I'm going to be a mommy," which would receive approving smiles. Having observed this upon a few occasions, I once decided to answer, "I'm going to be a daddy." This elicited a puzzled look and the reply, "Well, you can be a daddy, but what are you going to *do* with your life?"

This led me at a young age to conclude that being a mommy was both an occupation as well as a state of being, apparently, whereas being a daddy wasn't. Being a daddy was fine, even noble, but it wasn't sufficient. It was as if being a father was limited biologically to the donation of sperm to assist with the fertilization of an egg—a process that led to the development of a baby, the gestation and birth of which automatically conferred the identity of mother to the woman. But, from conception on, the presence of a father always seemed to be an historical rather than an existential event.

Luckily for me, my father remained on the scene and was very active in our lives. In fact, he has served as a very powerful example of what fatherly love is all about—which made the response to my comment about being a daddy all the more puzzling to me. It turns out that I was not alone in my puzzlement.

At root were deeper issues that were just being identified culturally. With the rise of the women's movement and feminism in the 1960's and 1970's, women began to closely examine their experiences of oppression, violence, inequality of opportunity and the undervaluing of motherhood. The default reply, "I'm going to be a mommy," was not an adequate expression of the longing in women's hearts, and not a large enough arena for the potential creativity and intellectual ability that over one half of the world possessed. The primary problem that feminism identified as needing to be addressed was patriarchy. Patriarchy literally meant the rule of the fathers, and originally referred to the authority men had over their families, but that authority was seen to expand to include the rule of men over society as well as male control of the economic, power and decision-making structures of society.

For generations, men were assumed to be the model of the generic human person, as well as its quintessential exemplification. When writing about the human species, the preferred term was (and continues to be in many quarters) "mankind." The Declaration of Independence declared that "all men are created equal," and the laws of the land quickly revealed the lie of the presumed universality of "men" and "Mankind." Those who were "equal" were male, white, and (for a brief period) landowners.

Catherine MacKinnon describes how maleness has been presumed to be the standard for humanness:

> ... [V]irtually every quality that distinguishes men from women is already affirmatively compensated in this society. Men's physiology defines most sports, their needs define auto and health insurance coverage, their socially defined biographies define workplace expectations and successful career patterns, their perspectives and concerns define quality in scholarship, their experiences and obsessions define merit, their objectification of art defines art, their military service defines citizenship, their presence defines family, their inability to get along with each other—their wars and relationships—define history, their image defines god, and their genitals define sex. For each of their differences from women, what amounts to an affirmative action plan is in effect, otherwise known as the structures and values of American society.[1]

---

1. MacKinnon, *Feminism Unmodified*, quoted in Mason, *Crossing into Manhood*, 51.

Many of these presumptions have been challenged by the women's movement and feminists. These challenges have forced men to look at their lives and the world around them more closely, carefully and critically. What men have begun to discover and confess is that things aren't so great at the "top of the heap" either. Men die at younger ages than women, engage in more risky and self-destructive behaviors than women, and the virulent social virus of violence is associated with men more than women in several ways. For example, "89 percent of all violent crimes are committed by men; each year 1.8 million women are physically assaulted by their husbands or boyfriends; wars are initiated, conducted, and consummated primarily by men; and three times as many men as women are murdered."[2]

From those statistics an interesting and sobering observation emerges: not only are men more frequently the perpetrators of violence, men are more often the victims of violence.

As a pastor, I have seen the many ways violence mars men's lives and the lives of those around them. I have had men begin talking with me about some experience they had during war, and then break down and have to leave the room because the memories and emotions are too overwhelming. More than once has this occurred during a church board meeting. Often their wives will sit there with a sad look on their face and say, "Every once in a while, when the war comes up in conversation, this will happen. I can't comfort him or talk with him about it."

So deeply has the violence of war affected men for generations that the psychological establishment was forced to acknowledge the lingering effects of the battlefield with a diagnosis: Post Traumatic Stress Disorder. Studies of this disorder have provided the groundwork for understanding how traumas of various sorts affect people emotionally and psychologically. These psychological effects then play themselves out in family relationships and occasionally on the public stage.

When I was in college, a neighbor of mine returned from Vietnam and stayed at his parents' house while he figured out what to do with his life. One morning his brother awoke to find him in his bed, dead from a heroin overdose. Like many soldiers of the Vietnam era, my neighbor had been introduced to drugs in Vietnam as a way to cope with the stresses, fears and horrors of that war. Heroin was widely available and, for those who did use it, addiction and death became the all-too-frequent

---

2. Boyd, *The Men We Long to Be*, 25. Boyd is citing statistics compiled by Myriam Miedzian in her book, *Boys Will Be Boys*, 7.

end. Not only had my neighbor died, but his whole family was left with the memory of finding him dead and knowing the cause. The violence of war keeps on giving, long after its occasion has passed.

Violence is a man's issue, and it is an issue that injures and oppresses men as much as women. It is also tied to issues of power and domination, since the threat or use of violence is always used by one group to maintain its domination of another group. And time after time, group after group has sought to overthrow their dominators through violent means. Jesus lived and taught what Biblical scholar Walter Wink has described as a "Nonviolent Third Way" of responding to domination and violence. It is a way that does not seek to perpetuate the violence, but rather to transform the situation nonviolently while also confronting and engaging the powers of domination.[3]

This Nonviolent Third Way arises out of the sort of compassion for the world that Jesus exemplified and acted out of whenever he encountered human suffering, oppression and injustice. He looked out upon the masses of humanity and was moved inwardly with compassion (Matthew 9:36; 14:14; 15:32; 20:34; Mark 6:34; 8:2). But he did not respond to their plight by taking up arms or advocating violence. Instead, he said, "Love your enemies and pray for those who persecute you" (Matthew 5:44 NRSV). Instead of revenge, he taught forgiveness (Matthew 6:15; 18:21,35; Mark 11:25; Luke 6:37; 17:3,4; John 20:23). Instead of rigid adherence to rules and regulations, he lived and taught a way of living that responded to true human need (Luke 13:14–16; 14:1–6).

Even though violence, power and domination are key issues for men, they need not be the main determinants in our lives. Jesus taught and modeled for his male disciples a way of life that does not rely on domination or violence, but which encourages the ripening of all the latent goodness and majesty within men. My experience with men bears out this positive side of what I am calling "men's issues."

In my many varied contacts with my fellow men, I have sensed that men long to lead lives that are productive and creative, which enrich the family and community. Men long for deep friendships and family relationships that are fulfilling. Men yearn to give themselves to something significant and meaningful and to find purpose and meaning in their lives through that giving of themselves. In other words, men sense that

---

3. See, for example, Wink, *Engaging the Powers,* and *The Powers That Be.*

there is a better way of being in the world than what society has force-fed them, and they are beginning to seek it out.

The men's movement in our own time has developed in partial reaction to the women's movement, but also in response to these deeper longings—longings that men have started to explore as a result of women exploring what gives their lives significance and meaning. In this way, the women's movement has unleashed the possibility for women and men both to identify those social and personal forces that dehumanize them and to actively rearrange the world in ways that bring fulfillment, joy and meaning for all persons.

This longing for deeper fulfillment in life arises out of men's search for a place and purpose in the world. This is related to the question posed to me years ago by all those inquisitive adults, "What do you plan to be when you grow up?" What they meant was, "What are you going to *do* when you grow up?" but in the world of manhood, *being* is often confused with *doing*. This is a result of a particular psychological bridge that boys are forced to cross on the way to manhood that girls do not have to cross on their way to womanhood.

Valerie Saiving described this bridge in concise detail in 1960:

> The close relationship between mother and infant plays the first and perhaps the most important role in the formation of masculine and feminine character, for it means that the person with whom the child originally identifies himself (sic) is a woman. Both male and female children must learn to overcome this initial identification by differentiating themselves from the mother. But the kind and degree of differentiation required of the boy are strikingly different from what is required of the girl . . . The boy's process of differentiation from his mother is much more complex and difficult. He learns not only that he must grow up but that he must grow up to be a man; that men are different from women, since they do not have babies; and that he must therefore become quite a different creature from his mother. Instead of imitating her, he must relinquish completely his original identification with her. He also finds that, while he is not and never will be a woman, neither is he yet a man. It will be many years before he can perform sexually as a man, and therefore he does not need to be guarded, like his sister, against sexual activity before he is ready for it. He is thus permitted far greater freedom than the girl. But this freedom has its drawbacks for him, since along with it goes a certain set of standards which he must meet before he is judged to have achieved manhood.

He must learn this or that skill, acquire this or that trait or ability, and pass this or that test of endurance, courage, strength, or accomplishment. He must *prove* himself to be a man . . . Growing up is not merely a natural process of bodily maturation; it is, instead, a challenge which he must meet, a proof he must furnish by means of performance, achievement, and activity directed toward the external world. And even so his reward for achieving manhood is not easily grasped in imagination. It is quite obvious to a child what motherhood is; it is not nearly so obvious what it means to be a father.[4]

Nor what it means to be a man. In many traditional cultures, young boys and girls are raised together in the women's compound, so that the boys are first socialized according to the women's culture. At a later point, often around the age of thirteen, the boys are then taken from the women's compound and the men then initiate them into the men's culture, which sometimes includes even a separate variation of the language they had learned growing up! Early anthropologists such as Margaret Mead, Arnold Van Gennep, Victor Turner and others described surprisingly similar patterns of separating boys and girls around the age of puberty, and then engaging in an intense period of instruction in the meaning and role of men and women in their culture. Manu Ampin describes the general African pattern of initiation into adulthood as "tak[ing] the young initiates out of the community, and away from the concerns of everyday life, to teach them all the ways of adulthood: including the rules and taboos of the society; moral instruction and social responsibility; and further clarification of his/her mission or calling in life."[5] This pattern of initiating boys into manhood, and thus into a deep sense of purpose and place in the world, has been repeated in various ways around the world in traditional cultures.

This pattern of initiating boys into manhood is lacking in most industrialized countries. One major reason for this has been the cultural shift involved with industrialization and the mass movements of people away from rural areas and agrarian lifestyles into urban communities. Whereas in the rural situation boys would see their fathers at work, and would be involved in helping them from a very early age, this was not so in the cities. Men would work very long hours—often 16–18 hours a

---

4. Saiving, "The Human Situation," in Christ and Plaskow, *Womanspirit Rising*, 30–31.

5. Manu Ampim, "The Five Major African Initiation Rites."

day—away from the family, and return home exhausted, with no time or energy to meaningfully or lovingly interact with their families, let alone pass on any tips about manhood to their boys. Often what boys saw happen to their fathers was not anything they wanted to repeat or emulate in themselves anyway. Wendell Berry expresses it this way:

> It is clear to me from my experience as a teacher, for example, that children need an ordinary daily association with *both* parents. They need to see their parents at work; they need, at first, to play at the work they see their parents doing, and then they need to work with their parents. It does not matter so much that this working together should be what is called "quality time," but it matters a great deal that the work done should have the dignity of economic value.
>
> ... [D]espite their he-man pretensions and their captivation by masculine heroes of sports, war, and the Old West, most men are now entirely accustomed to obeying and currying the favor of their bosses. Because of this, of course, they hate their jobs—they mutter, "Thank God it's Friday" and "Pretty good for Monday"—but they do as they are told. They are more compliant than most housewives have been. Their characters combine feudal submissiveness with modern helplessness. They have accepted almost without protest, and often with consumptive relief, their dispossession of any usable property and, with that, their loss of economic independence and their consequent subordination to bosses. They have submitted to the destruction of the household economy and thus of the household, to the loss of home employment and self-employment, to the disintegration of their families and communities, to the desecration and pillage of their country, and they have continued abjectly to believe, obey, and vote for the people who have most eagerly abetted this ruin and who have most profited from it. These men, moreover, are helpless to do anything for themselves or anyone else without money, and so for money they do whatever they are told. They know that their ability to be useful is precisely defined by their willingness to be somebody else's tool. Is it any wonder that they talk tough and worship athletes and cowboys? Is it any wonder that some of them are violent?[6]

In North America, this situation was exacerbated as a result of being a largely immigrant society. As long as immigrants settled in communities with others of their original ethnicity, it was possible to pass on traditions

---

6. Wendell Berry, *The Art of the Commonplace*, 68, 70.

and for initiatory rites to occur. But as the great salad bowl of society became tossed and mixed, with people claiming multiethnic ancestry and increasing mobility, there were no community and social structures to initiate boys into manhood. In a very real sense, then, modern urban culture and the extreme mobility of society have displaced men—from their families, from their heritage, and from their traditions—thus displacing them from the sources of their identity and wisdom about what it means to be a man, a father, and a mate.

This displacement represents a crisis in manhood precisely because the central existential concern for men has always been to find or make their place in the world. Whereas girls have a place in society biologically defined for them, as Saiving describes, boys have to find or create their place. In other words, men have had to artificially construct a means to identify and claim their place and thus their legitimacy in the world. Hence the inquiry, "What do you want to be when you grow up?" is not merely idle chit chat, but rather a warning that the very serious business of discovering one's reason for being looms just over the horizon, so it is time to begin preparing oneself to face its demands.

This search for place in the world can have very creative results. It is the driving force behind the development of the public sphere of societies, in distinction from the development of the private or domestic sphere, which traditionally across the world is the province of women. Men's search for place fuels the urge for exploration and discovery, for acquisition of knowledge and territory, for invention and work and labor of all kinds.

Unfortunately, this can easily lead to very negative results, such as when men create social systems based upon the domination of peoples and the creation of class-stratified societies that concentrate wealth in the hands of a very few and leave the majority at minimal subsistence level. Or when these societies become empires and take over other societies and their natural resources by means of violence and war. The inventive urge has resulted in the rise of industrialism, which separates humans from the natural world and subsequently reduces both to commodities consumable by the industrial society.

The search for place and identity is the primal experience of male development. Of course, to speak of the search for "place" is to use a spatial metaphor for what is essentially an inner process that is expressed externally in the world in such things as behaviors, actions and construction of things as diverse as buildings, governments, and philosophical and religious systems. For millennia this external world was primarily the province of men, of the patriarchy. Women were often usually excluded from this sphere or prevented from participating in its construction, even though the domestic sphere was foundational to and constitutive of the larger patriarchal society. Part and parcel of the construction of this patriarchal society was the development of models of manhood that were based upon a need to exert power over others, and preserve positions of privilege and authority.

All of these situations arise out of men trying to bear an edifice called "manhood" that has been created by social systems based upon power and domination, and the enforcement of rigid roles designed to preserve this system. Jesus taught his male followers that he had overcome this system, or world (the Greek word *kosmos* means the same, John 16:33) and they, too, were not to act as overlords or dominators, but were to act as servants, contributing to the welfare of others, and, thus, to society at large (Matthew 20:24–26; Mark 10: 42–44; Luke 22:24–26).

This oppressive edifice of manhood is the artifice of a larger social system constructed (mainly) by men as the means for finding their identity and place in the world. And all of this is because of the primal experience of needing to establish an identity separate from that of the mother and the feminine domestic sphere. So it may be that one of the core male issues is the separation of the boy from his mother, but toward what? As James Dittes frames it, ". . . to rescue and mold his identity as male, a boy has to put distance between himself and the one who gave him life, his mother. A man has had to choose between maleness and intimacy with life."[7] The task for boys to become men is not only differentiation from but also identification into something new. But is it actually necessary, as Dittes suggests, to choose between maleness and intimacy with life? Is it not possible to seek out a way of being in the world that participates fully, intimately and deeply in life itself, albeit in a specifically male mode?

It is in specifically this context that Jesus' teachings make sense. Each Gospel writer takes a slightly different view of who Jesus was and what he did and taught, but the general pattern emerges of Jesus as someone who was in touch deeply and intimately with the source of Life itself in a cosmic sense and identified himself with that source, or *as that source*, such as when he says in John, "I am the truth and the way and the life," and, "I am the resurrection and the life." These words indicate a vision of

---

7. Dittes, *Driven by Hope*, 11.

manhood that is not divorced from life, but immersed deeply in it to the point of identifying oneself *with* life. From this identification with life itself, there follows the dedication of a man to live according to a Way of life that is governed and constructed around that cosmic Life. To follow Jesus is to find one's place in the world *within oneself,* and to find that there in that inner core is one's true home, there in one's heart. It is in that home that one offers hospitality to God. And it is out of that home-of-the-heart that one extends hospitality to the rest of creation—the natural world, humanity, one's friends and family.

Because men spend so much time in the external world constructing and finding their place, the internal world is often less explored and somewhat unfamiliar. The unseen world of feelings and hidden influences are very real, and my experience tells me that men have very deep and significant feelings. But they often remain in an unexplored territory. But every unexplored territory is a landscape begging for discovery, a task to which we now turn.

— 4 —

Mapping the Terrain

ON THE LAST DAY of his life, Jesus has a meal together with the men and women who have been his closest friends, followers, supporters and confidants for the preceding three years. In the midst of the meal he starts talking about going to his father's house to prepare a place for his disciples. Thomas, the one who was always bold enough to ask the questions everyone else was thinking, asks him, "Lord, we don't know where you are going. How can we know the way?"

Jesus looks at him with that look that had always cut through the crap and says simply, "*I am the way, and the truth, and the life*" (John 14:1–6 NRSV).

From this story, the earliest disciples of Jesus were called followers of "the Way" (see Acts 9:2). The word for "way" in Greek is *hodos*, and is also found in the name of the second book of the Bible, Exodus, which literally means "way out" or exit. But the word more specifically refers to a path or road, usually one that was well-traveled and thus dependable as the way to use in order to get to where you want to go.

Interestingly, the same notion of the well-worn and, thus, dependable path appears in Islam where *sunnah* refers to this well-worn, proven and true path. The way of life that the prophet Muhammad taught his followers was called the *sunnah*. Those who are said to follow this path of the Prophet are thus called *sunnis*.

In Chinese, the word for a path or road, or way, is *dao*, and Daoism is that particular religious philosophy that one follows to achieve a life of balance, harmony and long-life (or even immortality).

It is common to speak of the religious and spiritual life as being a journey or pilgrimage. The thing about a journey, though, is that it starts one place and ends somewhere else. That's what the spiritual life is like. We start one place and eventually find ourselves someplace else. We start one person, and are someone else at journey's end. Something about the trip changes us.

In the Gospel story, Thomas protests, "We don't know where you are going. How can we know the path?" Which road are we to take? How do we find our way? What will guide us? As we begin the pilgrimage that this book represents, we might well ask the same question Thomas asks. If we undertake this journey of the soul to commit to the Path of Jesus for the twenty-first century, where will it take us and how will we know the way?

And so to that end, we begin with a little orienteering.

When I was in grade school and junior high, I was active in my local Boy Scout troop. My favorite thing to do was go camping. As I advanced in rank and experience, I became more adept at reading a map and using a compass to find my way around. The importance of this skill was impressed upon us when our scoutmaster would take us out as Tenderfeet into a forest for a hike away from camp, and then broke us up into small groups and set us loose to find our way back on our own. Always with us was one more-experienced boy who knew the way back, but who lagged behind to see how we did. Occasionally we would find our way back through luck or recognizing some physical feature, but more often than not, the groups would wander uphill and downcreek, occasionally crossing streams that were never crossed on the journey out and struggling up ridges where the path out had been level. Finally, at some point, the small band would confess to being totally lost, and the older boy would lead them home, using a map and compass. From that experience the newer boys learned to appreciate the skill of reading a map, and using a compass properly.

What I want to share with you in this chapter is a map of where we will travel in this book, and why this particular route will get us to where we want to be. Like all journeys into strange and new territory, there will be a lot to see and a lot to get used to. At times you may find yourself saying, "When will we get there? Are we almost there?" But of course, as any true explorer knows, there is no "there" there. The journey becomes our home.

So why a map? So as not to get lost. And so as to undertake the journey with purpose and direction. And to get a sense of the lay of the land.

If you travel to London or to New York or the San Francisco Bay Area, one of the best ways to get around is on the mass transit system, especially the subway systems (the "tube" as it is called in London). Each system has a map of the lines and stops laid out in a highly stylized, representative fashion. Its sole purpose is to show the relationships between the various stops, but bears only the vaguest resemblance to the actual layout of the city or region it serves. For that, you need a more detailed street map, or even a topographical map. But for getting around on the tube, the schematic map does just fine.

I have put together a sort of schematic map to guide our journey into the spirituality of Jesus for men. Figure 1 below sketches this journey as it traverses between three contiguous territories, named "Personal," "Inter-Personal," and "Social/Cultural." Moving between each territory is a two-way information highway of sorts. As we visit each territory, we discover that there is a constant exchange along these highways.

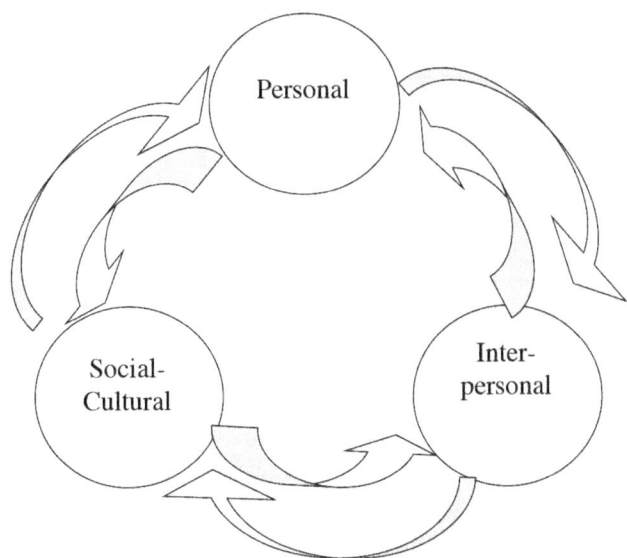

Figure 1 – A map of the Territories
(Dynamic Interaction Model of Human Relational Development —
Basic Model).

For example, the Personal territory receives from the Inter-Personal territory such things as words, ideas, values, affirmations, scolding, love, anger, laughter, jokes, yelling, screaming, beatings, tender caresses, teachings and so on.

From the Social/Cultural territory, the Personal territory receives things such as worldviews, philosophy of life, values, language, education about history and mathematics and science, religion, political loyalties and struggle, large-scale prejudice, occupational identities, ideas and practices concerned with power, ethnic and national identity and loyalty, and so on.

But the Personal territory can also be seen to be contributing to these other territories as well. The Personal realm expresses itself in various ways through interaction with the Inter-Personal: returning love, acting out love or anger or sadness or joy, hitting back or running for protection, drawing up defensive bulwarks or reaching out in vulnerable intimacy. To the Social/Cultural territory, the Personal contributes assent and support or dissent from its programs, contribution of ideas and new knowledge, artistic expressions and creativity, bodies for armies or protest lines.

Of course, each territory represents some aspect of how we as individuals relate and interact with the people in the world around us. We exist as self-contained persons, with our own set of internal thoughts, ideas, experiences. But we are highly permeable in that we have received most of these things from our interactions with our family, friends and culture.

Think, for instance, of a newborn baby. Being the oldest of eight boys, I had plenty of experience helping to raise my younger brothers. I would bend over them and make funny noises at them, hoping to elicit some response from them. I would offer them toys, and play "pick up the dropped toy" with them as they experimented with the force of gravity. They soon learned Baby Newton's first law of gravity: a dropped object will always be replaced on a highchair tray when an older family member is nearby. As they got older, they picked up language and an occasional phrase from the older brothers that didn't always thrill my parents, but there it was. We played together and argued with each other. Sometimes something of mine would turn up missing and I would know where to find it, with much complaining to my mother and scolding of my brother.

So, we each grew through this interaction as individuals within a family system. If I were to map this out I would depict a flow of words and actions going from my parents in the Inter-Personal realm to me in the Personal realm. Then many of these words and actions would return back out to my parents or to my brothers or even my friends. The saying is true that we live what we see every day.

All that I have just described is thoroughly documented and explored by psychologists, developmental specialists and sociologists. All of it relates to spirituality. This is because spirituality has to do with how we exist in our internal life, and how that internal life is expressed through our attitudes, words and deeds in our families, with our friends and in society at large. It's all about relationship.

In other words, we are built for and by relationality. To be a person means to be in relation. Personality is the potential to be in relation as well as the particular qualities of relating that an individual manifests. Martin Buber describes this when he says, "Individuality makes its appearance by being differentiated from other individualities. A person makes his appearance by entering into relation with other persons."[1]

In fact, if you gather together all of Jesus' teachings, and lay them all out, you will find that the vast majority have to do with how to live together and get along. Next to that are the teachings that have to do with the character of God, and the nature of God's relationship with humankind. This is to say, more of Jesus' teachings are ethical than theological.

Expanding the Map

When we begin to talk about God, we realize that the map we have in hand is inadequate as a guide through the spirituality of Jesus. There are two more territories that need to be added: the Divine Realm, or realm of God, and the realm of the Environment, or Nature, or Earth. Poetically, humankind has been depicted as being a marriage between heaven and earth, or the divine and the earthly. In Genesis, God walks along a riverbank, bends down and scoops up a fistful of clay. God fashions the lump into a torso, rolls two tubes of clay for legs, two more for arms, adds a head. But it is still inanimate clay. So, God bends down and breathes into the clay and it comes alive. Mud becomes flesh, moisture becomes blood and cells. Skin and bones form. Nerves pulse and eyes open.

This story reminds us that we are not self-existent: we owe our life to a Source of life beyond us, and we are shaped by that source from the very common stuff around us. Thus, we maintain relationships with the earth and with God, or the Divine. The second map, below, depicts the

---

1. Buber, *I and Thou*, 62.

interworkings and interconnections between our human realms and the realms of the divine and the earth or natural world. This map attempts to depict in two dimensions what is really multi-dimensional.

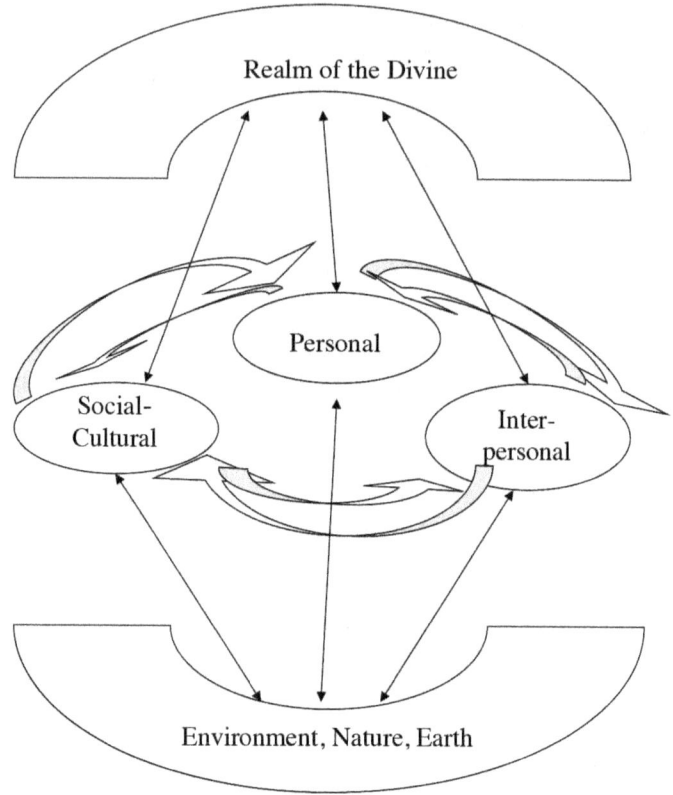

Figure 2 – Expanded map of the Territories
(Dynamic Interaction Model of Human Relational Development —
Full Model).

Sandra Schneiders, a professor of Biblical Studies and Christian Spirituality at the Jesuit School of Theology in Berkeley, California defines spirituality as "the experience of conscious involvement in the project of life-integration through self-transcendence toward the horizon of ultimate value one perceives."[2] (Her definition is meant to be applicable to all forms of spirituality, and thus is non-sectarian in its wording.) Her definition offers a commentary on our map. "Conscious involvement in

---

2. Schneiders, "Approaches to the Study of Christian Spirituality," 16.

the project of life-integration" describes work that begins in the personal arena and extends out in deliberate connection and interaction with others in the world and the closer arena of friends, family and intimate communities. It is a project of integrating all the internal stuff into a way of life, behavior and relating to others that is not random or haphazard but is lived with meaning and purpose and significance. This is what she means by "self-transcendence toward the horizon of ultimate value (that) one perceives." What brings meaning, significance and coherence to our lives is how all our individual stories resonate with and participate in a larger story of more cosmic proportions. We are part of something quite a bit larger than our little bounded experience, and integrating our lives into that larger something, that greater story is the work of spirituality. We shall explore this is greater depth in the next chapter.

Mud and Bones

The creation story from Genesis reminds us of the importance of our earthiness. We are material, physical creatures. We have flesh-and-blood bodies that hunger and thirst, grow strong and vital and then become enfeebled and die. We eat, drink, excrete, laugh and run, sing and sob. We have brains and nervous systems that mediate sensations, thoughts, ideas, feelings, emotions and creativity between our inner world and the world beyond us. Because of this, spirituality focuses a lot upon practices done in and with the body. Things such as prayer, meditation, fasting, yoga, and contemplation all feature some sort of discipline of the body and mind. Scientists have even done research on people while engaged in these various practices and have charted the inner workings of the brain. Some researchers even speak of the "God part" of the brain, which they claim is responsible for such things as transcendence, out-of-body experiences, feelings of unity with all of life, euphoria, and ecstatic states. Some use this research to reduce spirituality and religion to being merely neurological processes, regulated and determined by biochemistry and nothing more.

My response is that these neurological, biochemical processes are the *media* and *means* whereby the meaning, purpose and significance of our lives is communicated inwardly to us and outwardly from us. We *are* mud and bone, as it were, but we are also more than simply that. So it is that every religion develops various physically-based practices that serve to discipline the body and mind so as to alter behavior according to certain norms, to sharpen inner awareness of the volatility and ephemerality of emotional states, to gain clarity and knowledge of the sources of undesirable behaviors and attitudes, and to reduce the individual's dependence upon the outside world for gratification and a sense of self-worth. Some practices involve not so much discipline and deprivation as an alteration of circumstances. New living arrangements or social groupings may be called for, or actions on behalf of society at large. This involves placing the body in new locations, and perhaps taking risks with and within the body.

In other words, the territories of the Personal, the Inter-Personal and the Social/Cultural are the playing fields of spirituality. Each territory has a set of issues that need to be addressed, and, as a consequence, a set of tasks that address those issues. It is the purpose of this book to look at those issues, and to sketch out the way that Jesus' spirituality helps us as men to navigate the territory of our lives without getting lost, but with integrity, meaning and grace. To that end, with map in hand, we will use the life and teachings of Jesus as our compass and guide along the way.

Mapping the Social/Cultural Arena

The Social/Cultural arena is the world of everyday life, of the evening news, of school, church and work. It is the arena that provides us with our worldview—that particular set of ideas and behaviors that tells us what is real and not, what is worthwhile or not, what questions to ask and how to answer them, where to go in life (and on vacation) and how to get there. It is the arena that provides us with language itself, and knowledge in its wake. Education, entertainment, government, community and religion all are created in and regulated by the Social/Cultural arena.

It is also the world of wars, global warming, slavery, prejudice, pogroms, terrorism, militaries, reservations, ghettos, and prison camps. All that is good in humanity finds its expression there, as well as all that is depraved and destructive. The Social/Cultural is the great stage upon which all the little dramas and comedies, tragedies and farces of collective humanity are played out. But the Social/Cultural arena is also like the air we all breathe in, the song that remains within every mind, the dance step we are all taught, the joke we all share. It is impressed upon our very neurons and hidden in our bones and flesh. It is, as Morpheus says to Neo in *The Matrix*, "the world that has been pulled over our eyes." It is everywhere and we are always in it, even in our moments of remotest solitude.

Mapping the Inter-Personal

The Inter-Personal arena is just as its name suggests—it is that territory of relationships that exists between persons as they relate to each other, one-on-one. It is the realm of parent and child, brother and sister, friend to friend, teacher and pupil, supervisor and worker, doctor and patient and so on. It characterizes the great bulk of our everyday interactions.

The Inter-Personal in many ways serves as the conduit whereby the values, worldview, customs and language of the Social arena are communicated to us and implanted in the Personal arena. But the Inter-Personal arena has its own internal dynamics and characteristics, as well as issues to be addressed and tasks to do the addressing. There are ways of interacting and communicating that are conducive and helpful for communication, and there are ways that block communication or make it very difficult. Some relationships are so severely strained that any work towards healing has to be addressed to the relationship itself as well as to the individuals involved in that relationship. The work of forgiveness and reconciliation works in this arena.

But this is also the arena of friendship, of marriages, family life. It is an arena that can be filled with joy, laughter, great enthusiasm and incredible creativity. It is the realm of singing in choirs or playing in a band. It is the arena of performing plays or playing sports. It is the arena of sleepovers and birthday parties, of sharing secrets with a special friend, and of consoling one another in our deepest grief.

It is no accident that Jesus did not engage in his ministry as a solo performer, a one-man band. He gathered men and women around him not only to be his disciples and carry on the work after him, but also to share his burdens, lighten his way with laughter, sharpen his message with their questions, and buoy him up in the stormy passages with their trust and confidence in him. The community of believers is thus a central ingredient in the spirituality that Jesus taught.

Mapping the Personal

If we were to take a magnifying glass to our map of the Personal, we might find it contains such issues as how we think about ourselves, internal conversations about ourselves and about our families and friends, ideas about what is important in life, our opinions, values we hold, things we enjoy, and so on. We might also find such things as memories of being hurt or abused, of violence done to us, experiences of terror, of heart-wrenching sorrow, of betrayal, disappointment and despair. These experiences don't just sit there. Instead, they move in, set up shop and develop a whole cottage industry of territory acquisition and hostile takeover of the inner landscape of the personal. Often these remembered and internalized experiences are at war with the values and ideals we hold. This internal conflict simmers and sometimes rages, and spills out onto the highway to the Interpersonal, and our families or friends receive the brunt of our internal struggle. Sometimes it spills out on the highway to the Social/Cultural and we engage in destructive or violent behavior. Sometimes our attitudes or beliefs assume the form of institutions with an acceptable face, but nonetheless are characterized by violence against or oppression of others.

On the other hand, our experiences of personal violations may be contained in safe locations, cordoned off by what we can only call reverberations of grace or mercy, and our experiences of harmony, enjoyment of difference, appreciation of beauty and wonder at creation, enjoyment of family and friends dominate our inner landscape. These might find expression as our predominant mode of being in the world.

Each of us have been formed and shaped by all of our experiences growing up and long afterwards. Developmental psychologists help us to understand the effects of these experiences in our early years, and have identified how personalities, behaviors and psychological states arise as a result of and response to these experiences and events. For those of us whose psychic landscapes have been marred and ravaged by violence, trauma, abuse or extreme deprivation, we may have developed particular protective and adaptive behaviors that become hardened and "cast in concrete," or so we think. At the least, these behaviors may become automatic and even comfortable, regardless of their effect upon the world around us.

This, and much more, is the landscape of the Personal. The spiritual tasks at the Personal realm tend to focus on developing self-awareness of this inner landscape, consciousness of how this inner landscape gets expressed in our language and physicality, stocktaking of our attitudes and values, and scrutiny of our behavior and treatment of those around us and of those halfway across the globe.

Anna's Story

To get a handle on how this terrain mapping works, I would like to relate a story about several generations of a family. The family does not actually exist, but is a blend of several families I have known over the years. The story begins with the mother, Anna, who was born in the heat and blood of the Second World War in Eastern Europe. As the Nazi army and SS staff ground their way through Poland and Hungary, one SS officer spied a young Jewish woman that met his fancy. In spite of the Aryan ideal of blond hair and blue eyes, he was captivated by her dark flashing brown eyes and raven-like hair. But since she was an inferior race, she was free for the taking and so he took her, possessed her for an evening and then discarded her as he moved on to the next town, the next conquest.

Anna was born nine months later, and as the Nazis were rounding up Jews for the camps, her mother frantically sought shelter for this child that, although a product of her violation and shame, was nonetheless flesh of her flesh. In desperation Anna's mother took her to the local Catholic Church and pleaded with the priest to take and hide the child from the Nazis. As the priest looked at the child's dark hair but yellow-hazel eyes, he discerned the deeper story and took the child in. And so Anna was passed from family to family westward across Europe. Over the course of several years she was housed with families that cared for her as one of their own, but she also lived in homes where her life was little more than as a housemaid, where the "real" family would go off to the theatre and leave her behind to wash the clothes and fix the dinner. At one house, the grandmother called her "the bastard child," and never used her real name. At another house she was sexually molested. Finally she made her way to the family of a Dutch physician, who was preparing to emigrate to the United States. The war by now was over, but Europe was in a shambles. Anna was in her early teens, becoming a woman, and afraid of leaving the continent that had been home. But she would take a piece of it with her. All the uncertainties about where she was going to live next, all mistreatment at the hands of women and men, the abuse, as well as happy moments, times of laughter.

In America she had to start over. A new language, new customs, a bedroom that was hers alone. Her new family actually adopted her, and were the first loving, stable parents she had known for a long time. But the past had buried itself deep inside her skull, her behavior was erratic. She was prone to emotional outbursts, and she felt the eyes of everyone at school looking at her, probing her secrets, knowing things about her that she didn't even know. She became very controlling of her environment. Everything had to be just so. Everything had to be in just the right place. She became obsessive about it. She wouldn't allow anyone else to clean the house. She was meticulous, and the house sparkled with cleanliness under her care, but woe be unto the person who moved a chair or left a coat on the floor.

After High School she met a man who was interested in her, and they started dating. They married and six months later their eldest, a boy, was born. Over the years two other children were born. Anna became a terror at home. She flew into rages and beat her children. Afraid of what might happen to her children if they wandered away from her hawk-like watch, she would lock them in their rooms when they came home from school. No slumber parties, no neighbor children over for snacks and games. As her children grew up, they chafed against her rules. Their father spent more time at the office, and then at the bars before coming home. He tried at first to intervene when Anna threw dishwater on their oldest son and then made him scrub the floors with his pants, but she withheld sex from him for 6 months, and refused to feed the family until they all apologized to her. When the oldest son graduated from high school he immediately joined the army to get away from home. He joined a unit that was sent to the Middle East and was put in charge of political detainees. He and a woman enlistee became sexually involved, and they engaged in sexual exploits in front of the prisoners, and then sexually humiliated the prisoners. He was court-martialled for that activity and imprisoned in a military jail.

Anna's middle child, a daughter, tried to keep the family together. She attended her brother's court-martial and corresponded with him while he was in jail. She studied hard in school, not only to please her parents, but also as a way of escaping or rising above the chaos of her family life. She went on to college and graduate school, becoming a mental health counselor. She also tried to keep her younger sister away from the crowd that she had started to hang out with surreptitiously, but this youngest child soon got hooked on methamphetamines, and took to stealing her mother's jewelry to pay for her habit. When her mother confronted her, she pulled out a knife and slashed her mother across the face and fled. This began several years of living on the streets or on the couch of anyone who was interested in her for a few weeks.

This story, which is a composite of several true stories, doesn't have an ending. It is ongoing. I tell it to illustrate how the Personal, Inter-Personal and Social arenas all work to make us who we are, but how we also act upon those arenas as well. In Anna's story we see how the events of the world around her (the Social arena) first made its indelible marks upon her. Because of social attitudes, prejudices and the domination of one group (the Nazis), Anna was conceived and then given away by her mother. These social forces labeled her: "bastard," "foster child," "housemaid," "problem," "immigrant," "foreigner." These social labels were communicated and impressed upon her in the Inter-Personal arena by the families with whom she lived and the people she interacted with on a daily basis. Everything imprinted itself upon her and lodged its way deep into her memory and psyche—all deep in the Personal arena. And it was in the Personal arena that she devised ways to cope with the pain and hatred and hurt. Her mind found places to go when she was being abused physically or emotionally. Her awareness was heightened about everyone else's emotional state and she found ways to protect herself. These protective mechanisms were manifested in behaviors that would be given various names over the years: hysteria, paranoia, obsessive-compulsive, psychosis, and Post Traumatic Stress Disorder. The Inter-Personal arena of her family life was thus also affected and shaped by how the inner turmoil of her Personal arena expressed itself outwardly with her children and husband. Her children, in turn, internalized what they received from their parents' behaviors, and each developed their own coping behaviors and personal decisions about how to live in and react to the world around them. The children externalized these behaviors by acting out upon that world (the social arena) in various ways. The traumas of one generation were then passed along onto the next generation.

I tell this story as a way to dramatize in a rather raw fashion the principle behind mapping the terrain as I have done in this chapter. I developed the diagram of the Personal/Inter-Personal/Social arenas for workshops I have conducted in Nonviolence and Peacemaking as a way to show how integrative the work must be, because the issues of domestic violence, personal attitudes, language, emotional health, religious beliefs, political action, social attitudes, war, trauma, fear and foreign policy are all interwoven in the lives and psyches of persons in power and on the ground, at the front lines on both sides, and back at the home front.

There is a powerful word of hope and promise in all of this, however, which is the core of this book. The spirituality that Jesus taught is directed at healing and transforming all three of the arenas of our inner and outer life. Jesus brought healing for inner wounds and taught ways of acting and thinking that replaced the traces and tracks of injury and hurtfulness with practices of compassion, mercy, kindness and love. He modeled these traits and insisted upon their centrality in human experience. He taught about forgiveness and accountability, about justice and kindness, mercy and integrity. Jesus believed in the possibility latent within each person to transcend the dictates of their circumstances, and to become agents of transformation of the world around them. Jesus knew that human decisions had made the world the way it was, and that transformed humans could remake the world according to a better way of being. This way of being was the Kingdom of Heaven—that realm of existence that was rooted in and empowered by the Spirit and vision of God. The spirituality that Jesus taught and lived was a vision of something greater, an action plan for achieving it, and a program to equip and outfit people for life according to its contours.

It is that hope-filled spirituality that we are exploring in this book. And hopefully, the journey and exploration will transform us as well.

Reflections and Personal Exercise

The following exercise is designed to help you map the terrain of your own life experience. For this exercise you will need a very large sheet of paper, and some colored pens. If you don't have colored pens, a single pen or pencil will do. The purpose of using several colors is to trace the different events in the three arenas described in this chapter.

Lay the paper out horizontally, and divide it into three sections horizontally as such:

Social
Inter-Personal
Personal

Figure 3 — Personal Mapping

In the top section, develop a rough timeline of significant social events across your lifetime. You may want to further divide the horizontal lines into time periods, either generally or by years. The choice is yours, because the point of this exercise is for you to have something useful for you.

Early years	Grade School	Jr./Sr. High	Young Adult	Middle Years	Older Years
Social					
Inter-Personal					
Personal					

Figure 4 — Example Map

In each of the other arenas, list significant events or occurrences. It is important to list as much as possible, the good with the bad, the painful and hurtful as well as the happy and pleasant. Draw arrows from events in the Social and Inter-Personal arenas to the Personal arena indicating what you received from those events. What phrases or statements became embedded in your consciousness? What feelings? What physical experiences? Label these.

Draw arrows from the Personal Arena into the other arenas indicating what your response was, or what pattern of behavior you developed. Was there anything you did that was shared in the social arena such as performing, doing artwork, playing sports, writing stories or opinion pieces, inventing things, developing software, putting on fund-raisers, serving as a volunteer firefighter? The list is endless. The important thing to do is to get a picture of how your life has unfolded as a result of the interaction of these three arenas, and how this interaction has shaped you as a person.

This project should be ongoing. It is a personal project, so you do not need to share it with anyone unless you truly want to divulge your life story. Rather, keep it rolled up as you read through this book, or as you gather with other people in a support group based upon this book. As you diagram your life in this way, look for those things that are painful and perhaps in need of healing. Look for attitudes and behaviors that in the context of this book and in the context of your spiritual journey do not square with following after Jesus' heart or way. Identifying these things explicitly will help you to know what areas of your life will need your attention, and the healing salve of the unconditional love of God.

— 5 —

What is Spirituality?

IN THE MOVIE *SECONDHAND Lions*, the character Hub, played by Robert Duvall, gives his speech about "what every boy needs to know about being a man" to young Walter, played by Haley Joel Osment. He says,

> Sometimes the things that may or may not be true are the things a man needs to believe in the most. That people are basically good. That honor, courage and virtue mean everything; that power and money . . . money and power mean nothing. That good always triumphs over evil. And I want you to remember this . . . that love . . . true love never dies! Remember that boy . . . remember that. Doesn't matter if it is true or not, a man should believe in those things, because those are the things worth believing in . . . . . . got that?

Spirituality is all about how we live according to the things that are most important to us. These things are spiritual in that they form us at the deepest places in our lives, and they provide for us a way of life steeped in meaning and significance. Spirituality is about "the things worth believing in," and then seeing how those beliefs play out in our lives.

Before we even begin to discuss what Jesus taught and lived as his example of a male spirituality, it is important to explore for a bit what spirituality is all about. For some people, the term spirituality is foreign and exotic sounding. To others, it refers to something in contrast to religion, something more personal and private. In fact, spirituality and religion are tightly wound together, and have the same goal: the transformation of human persons—individually and collectively.

What is Spirituality?

Let me return to something we looked at in the previous chapter regarding the Personal Arena. You might recall Sandra Schneiders' definition of spirituality as "the experience of conscious involvement in the project of life-integration through self-transcendence toward the horizon of ultimate value one perceives."[1] Her definition offers a more precise way to understand what Hub is trying to convey to Walter in *Secondhand Lions*. "Conscious involvement in the project of life-integration" describes work that begins in the personal arena and extends out in deliberate connection and interaction with others in the world and the closer arena of friends, family and intimate communities. It is a project of intentionally and consciously integrating all that lies within us internally into a way of life, behavior and relating to others that is not random or haphazard but is lived with meaning and purpose and significance. Schneider's "ultimate value" is what Hub refers to when he speaks about believing in "things that really matter."

Spirituality is not something added on to our human experience. Rather it is part and parcel of who we are and how we are as humans. As Schneiders points out, spirituality is actually a characteristic of being human.

> It is the capacity of persons to transcend themselves through knowledge and love, that is, to reach beyond themselves in relationship to others and thus become more than self-enclosed material monads. In this sense, even the newborn child is spiritual while the most ancient rock is not. But we usually reserve the term spirituality for a relatively developed relationality to self, others, world, and the Transcendent, whether the last is called God or designated by some other term.[2]

It has become commonplace and even fashionable to separate out spirituality from religion, as if they were foreign substances to each other like oil and vinegar, that had over time accidentally found their way to each other and had gotten shook up together. Essentially a salad dressing for the soul, but now times and tastes have changed and a defatted dressing is the way to go, so let's just pour on the vinegar: spirituality without the superfluities and inconveniences of religion.

But the better analogy is to think of religion and spirituality as the sodium and chloride that are closely bound to each other as salt. In

---

1. Schneiders, "Approaches," 16.
2. Schneiders, "Religion vs. Spirituality: A Contemporary Conundrum," 165.

practice and principle, they can be separated, but not easily, and in fact, salt is not a simple combining of the atoms of sodium and chlorine. Each undergoes a change in order to become bonded to the other, and the new product of their joining—table salt—does not bear any resemblance to the individual elements that make it up.

Another way to think about the relationship between religion and spirituality is to consider religion to be the container or carrier of spirituality, like a chalice holding wine. The chalice carries and contains the wine, and without the chalice, the wine would spill out on the floor. The wine needs the chalice in order to be available for drinking. The purpose of the chalice is to contain the wine. Each are dependent upon the other. Religion is an essential part of spirituality as its carrier.

So let's be clear about this—religion and spirituality have grown up together, and like all siblings, have at times fought with each other, played with each other, confided in each other and tattled on each other. But forever related they remain.

Let's look closer at what we're talking about here.

As a child growing up, I was fascinated with how things worked. I would take apart old clocks and radios and small motors to see how they worked. I soon became able to fix things because I knew how the various parts were supposed to work together. One time I even delighted my father who asked me to look at a malfunctioning vacuum cleaner. I determined that what was needed was the small brushes in the electrical motor in the floor nozzle. We went down to the store and paid $1.50 for the replacement parts, went home and installed them and the unit worked fine after that. The dealer wanted to sell him a whole new motor, or even a new floor nozzle. Taking things apart had its advantages.

So let's do a bit of "taking things apart" in regard to religion and spirituality in order to understand what we're talking about, and especially to understand how what Jesus taught and lived actually works. That is the key point for Jesus' spirituality for men—it is designed to work.

Let's begin with the word that some people want to get rid of or at least ignore, "religion." It is actually an interesting word with a long history, but its Latin roots will suffice. It is made up of two smaller words, *re-*, which means to restore or go back to an earlier condition, and *ligio*, from *ligare*, which means to bind. *Ligare* is related to words such as *ligament*, which binds muscles to bones, and *lignin*, the substance in plants that binds cells together. Thus, religion has to do with binding back together what has come unraveled. As the fabric of our world becomes more and more frayed, surely something is needed to repair its tears and mend its breaches (or breeches if you will.) That is the proper place for religion.

"Spirit" comes from the Latin *spiritus*, which is the noun form of the verb *spirare*, "to breathe." *Spiritus* originally meant "breath," but came to refer to that force that animated or gave life to living things. Thus, it was more than simply taking in air—it referred to the unseen forces that made life possible—forces that were under the control of the gods or God. In Christian teaching, the Holy Spirit was that aspect of the Divine that had direct contact with human beings, and which animated the physical body, taught the mind and conversed with individuals as person-to-person.

In Genesis, the Spirit is with God at creation, and hovers over the primordial waters. The psalmist says, "When you hide your face (all creatures) are dismayed; when you take away their breath they die and return to their dust. When you send forth your spirit, they are created; and you renew the face of the ground" (Psalm 104:29–30 NRSV). Jesus tells his disciples that he will send the Comforter and Advocate, the Holy Spirit to be with them and to lead them in all truth (John 14:16–17, 26; 15:26; 16:13–15). Paul speaks of the Spirit bearing witness to our spirits (Romans 8:16) and interceding for us when we don't know how to pray (Romans 8:26–27).

Spirituality, then, has to do with how we live our lives in relation to that which is both beyond us and within us, which empowers us to life, and which teaches us about that life and how to live it.

Jesus worked with his male followers to develop their character as persons according to the deeper spiritual meaning and constitution of life. When I say the spiritual constitution of life, I am referring to how the world and universe is put together according to the design of God, and how the relationships between the various parts of life express the intent of the Designer. The spiritual constitution of life relates to how things are meant to be, and how our meaning and purpose in life is found by living in accordance with the design of the universe.

When Jesus refers to himself as the Way, the Truth and the Life (John 14:6), he is speaking directly about how he embodied this deeper purpose-filled and significance-drenched aspect of life. Simply put, a Christian (male) spirituality is to enter into the heart of Jesus, to explore his Way, his Life and his Truth, and to live it out in daily life. It is more than thinking correctly about doctrine or agreeing with religious ideas or statements. It is all about *how* one lives his life in the world, how he treats the members of his family, his co-workers, with what sort of integrity he goes about living out his values and beliefs. Putting it another way, the integrity of our lives is reflected in how congruent our everyday actions are with what we believe.

Integrity and Congruence

Eugene Peterson describes this eloquently in his essay, "Transparent Lives," where he talks about the congruence between what one believes and how one lives out that belief:

> If there's a single word that identifies the contemplative life, it is congruence—congruence between ends and means, congruence between what we do and the way we do it. So we admire an athlete whose body is accurately and gracefully responsive and totally submissive to the conditions of the event. When Michael Jordan played basketball, he was one with the court, the game, the basketball and his fellow players. Or take a musical performance in which Mozart, a Stradivarius and Yitzak Perlman all fuse indistinguishably in the music.
>
> The words of Jesus that keep this in focus are "I am the way, the truth and the life"(John 14:6). Only when we do the Jesus truth in the Jesus way do we get the Jesus life. But this isn't easy. It is easier to talk about what Christians believe, the truth of the gospel formulated in creeds and doctrines. We have accumulated a magnificent roster of eloquent and learned theologians who have taught us to think carefully and well about the revelation of God in Christ through the Holy Spirit. It is easier to talk about what Christians do, life as performance, the behavior appropriate to followers of Jesus codified in moral commandments and formulated in vision statements and mission strategies. We never lack for teachers and preachers and parents who instruct us in the mores and manners of the kingdom of God. None of us here are likely to pretend perfection in these matters, but most of us are pretty well agreed on what's involved.
>
> But what counts on my agenda right now is the Christian life as lived, lived in this sense of congruence between who Christ is and who I am—being in Chicago right now at this busy heavily trafficked intersection of the kingdom of God, Christ playing in my limbs and my eyes.[3]

---

3. Peterson, "Transparent Lives."

Spirituality has to do with how congruent one's life is with one's professed beliefs—how one's behavior, thoughts, actions, speech, and even politics align with what one professes to be ultimately true and significant about life as a human creature in this universe. Spirituality is not so concerned with the content of one's faith—*what* one believes—as much as it is concerned with *how* those beliefs form and shape the character and life-expression of the believer.

Here I have just introduced a bit of a neologism: "life-expression." By "life-expression" I am referring to everything that makes up a person's lifestyle—what one watches and does for entertainment, what one does with money, how that money is obtained, and so on—as well as a person's values, their treatment of family, friend and stranger, how they vote on election day, what they tolerate in their community and what they don't, as well as what they allow themselves to say and how they say it. Life-expression is an all-encompassing way to talk about how an individual moves through the world based upon the quality of their inner life. The keyword here is *expression*, which literally means to "press out." Life-expression is how one's inner life is brought out from within and manifested in everyday life. Life-expression is the arena of spirituality. And as Peterson so eloquently describes it, it is concerned with integrity and congruence.[4]

This is the spirituality with which Jesus is concerned—a life of congruence and integrity. But it is also concerned with the nature and quality of one's relationships in family and in the world. In the teaching and example of Jesus, faith is not a set of propositions or doctrines to which one gives assent. He states this clearly in Matthew 15:7–9 (NRSV):

> You hypocrites! Isaiah prophesied rightly about you when he said, "This people honors me with their lips, but their hearts are far from me; in vain do they worship me, teaching human precepts as doctrines."

The spirituality of Jesus is concerned with aligning one's heart with God's heart, and with living the life that arises out of that alignment. Jesus taught that if one had seen him, they had also seen the Father. So in order to understand the heart of God one must study and follow closely how Jesus lived *his* life, and to look to its congruity and integrity. This,

---

4. This helps to explain Jesus' continuous disgust with hypocrisy and duplicity, and with his sympathetic approval of those who confess to a lack of faith—the latter are being honest and forthright whereas the former are not.

of course, is precisely what it means to be a disciple—to be a student of another. And so in this book we will not only sit at Jesus' feet to listen to his teaching, we will also observe his actions and pay special attention to his behavior and treatment of those with whom he came in contact. The points of congruence and places of integration within his life and teaching will serve as our model for how we can lead lives of congruence and integrity.

However, it does not take much life experience to realize that people do not lead totally congruous lives. Far too often, people espouse one set of values but live by another set. Or people have suffered traumas or abuse that leaves psychological scars that affect how they relate to others, or how they move through the world. A quick scan of the headlines of the newspaper or evening news reveals a world that is not in congruity with its deepest values or highest principles. The best way to describe it is a world that is broken and badly in need of fixing.

Part of what is unraveled in life is our own integrity as humans. Not only moral integrity, but also our wholeness as persons. We need to be rewoven ourselves. We need to be made whole again. The religion of Jesus is designed to restore us to wholeness. One way it does this is by being holistic.

"Holistic" refers to the wholeness of a thing, or a thing in its completeness. Holistic religion addresses the human person in their wholeness. Holistic religion and spirituality addresses the human thirst for knowledge and understanding, as well as deeply felt commitments and sense of connectedness to ultimate concerns and purposes in the world. It also provides embodied practices that work at the physical level of the body and brain. Contemporary research in neurophysiology demonstrates that neurological circuits in the brain can be altered by changes in behavior. Spiritual disciplines work precisely because they alter the brain's neurological connections.

A holistic religion also addresses our embeddedness in social networks and communities. Humans are formed by virtue of their interaction with other humans, and spiritual transformation best occurs in the context of spiritually-engaged religious communities. As we look closely at the things Jesus did and taught, we will discover how holistic it is.

Roadblocks

The greatest roadblock to leading a life of integrity is the tendency within men to compartmentalize their lives, their thinking, and their behavior. This sort of compartmental way of being separates things out into neat categories, like "duty," "morality," "job," "family," "faith," "pleasure," "wealth," and so on. Each category becomes a waffle compartment that is separate and discrete from every other compartment.

We are all aware of the travesties of men in places of influence and trust who have betrayed that trust through sexual abuse of children and youth. These offenses have occurred most notoriously in the Catholic Church, but abuses can be found in every denomination of Christianity as well as other religions and faith groups. In my own experience, there were several well-respected ministers in my own conference who were discovered to have abused children and youth.

What we can clearly see in each of these men is that their lives were unresolved and disintegrated. Each of these men's lives were lived not only in separate compartments, they were almost like separate lives. However, these men were not suffering from split personalities, because each had full awareness of the various pieces of their lives, and moved between them smoothly and seamlessly. But somehow, the pieces were egregiously disconnected in certain very significant ways. There were major incongruities in their lives that were never resolved.

One of the spiritual tasks that faces us as men is to cut holes between these compartments so that they become more permeable, so that what we proclaim in our "Faith" compartment flows into our "How We Treat Our Spouse" compartment flows into our "How We Treat Our Fellow Workers" compartment flows into and shapes what we do in our "How We Vote" compartment.

Spirituality as Integration with Life and Its Source

The spirituality that Jesus lived and taught was a process of life-integration that brought together all the scattered fragments of a person's inner world (the personal arena discussed in the previous chapter) into a coherent whole and aligned them with a pattern of life rooted in the very order and organization of the universe itself. Since persons develop as *persons* through their relationships and connection with other persons, this alignment with the order of the universe is also personal in nature.

The power and principle of order and coherence in the universe provides the context, potentiality and possibility for all things to be, and is Being itself.

Let's unpack this for a moment. The idea that there is a primal and foundational reality that underlies the ordinary reality we experience with our natural senses is found at the core of religious traditions around the world. This was referred to as the "Perennial Philosophy" by the philosopher Leibnitz, and popularized by Aldous Huxley in his book by that title. Tony D'Souza summarizes the basic outlines of this concept as follows:

1. There is infinite, changeless reality beneath the world of change.
2. This same reality is at the core of every human personality.
3. The purpose of life is to discover this reality experientially; that is, to realize God while here on earth.[5]

In the Gospel of John, Jesus provides what we might call the mission statement for his ministry: "I have come that they may have life, and have it to the full." (John 10:10). The opening of the Gospel of John makes clear that Jesus provides this pathway to fullness of life precisely because he was himself the ordering force that had brought all things into being:

> In the beginning was the Word, and the Word was with God, and the Word was God. He was with God in the beginning.
>
> Through him all things were made; without him nothing was made that has been made. In him was life, and that life was the light of men. The light shines in the darkness, but the darkness has not understood it.
>
> The true light that gives light to every man was coming into the world.
>
> He was in the world, and though the world was made through him, the world did not recognize him. He came to that which was his own, but his own did not receive him. Yet to all who received him, to those who believed in his name, he gave the right to become children of God—children born not of natural descent, nor of human decision or a husband's will, but born of God.
>
> The Word became flesh and made his dwelling among us. We have seen his glory, the glory of the One and Only, who came from the Father, full of grace and truth.

---

5. D'Souza, *The Way of Jesus*: xvii.

> No one has ever seen God, but God the One and Only, who is at the Father's side, has made him known. (John 1: 1–5, 9–14, 18 NIV)

John here declares that Jesus is God revealed to humankind in the flesh of Jesus. Jesus came to reveal the nature of God (i.e., the "infinite, changeless reality beneath the world of change") to humankind. That nature is pre-eminently known and experienced as love. It is this love, mediated directly by the Holy Spirit that transforms persons and brings life to its fulfillment (i.e., "to realize God while here on earth.") These are things worth believing in, and worth living by, as Hub says in *Secondhand Lions*.

What this all boils down to is this: *Christian Spirituality involves the transformation of human persons through the experiential presence of the love of God as taught and lived by Jesus and mediated by the Holy Spirit.* This will be our definition and description of Christian Spirituality to guide us as we consider what it means to walk on the Path of Jesus in the twenty-first century.

— 6 —

Life Disciplined

One of the most heavily-watched athletic events is the Olympics. Whether it is the precision and grace of figure-skating, the power and physical mastery of gymnastics or the endurance and strength of the marathon, every event highlights the hard work and dedication necessary for humans to achieve their full potentials. Each athlete may begin with certain innate abilities but these remain merely a latent possibility until that athlete submits himself or herself to a systematic and rigorous training program. This training program is more than simply strength and endurance training. Integral to the discipline of the body is discipline of the mind.

This fact was brought home to me in an essay that a student once wrote in an English composition class I taught. She was a state-ranked cross-country runner, and her essay described the thought processes that went on in a typical run. Constantly she had to gauge not only her own energy reserves, but also she had to monitor the movements of the other runners. Instead of focusing upon the pain and weariness of her legs and the rest of her body, she trained herself to focus on what she could do and to feel beyond the present moment. Her essay impressed me with its careful detailing of the complex psychology of running. More importantly, it reinforced the idea that athletic achievement requires integrated mental and physical discipline.

In the same way that most human beings are born with the capacity to walk but require specialized training and development in order to become dancers or professional athletes, so also the spiritual capacities latent in every person need to be developed and disciplined. They need to be *practiced*. Just as baseball or football players in their spring training engage in a series of drills, agility exercises and weight training, so those who want to follow in the way of Jesus must engage in those spiritual drills and agility training of the heart that are necessary to become proficient as a player on Jesus' "team."

Using the analogy of sports, religion can be thought of as belonging to the realm of the team and sport in general, while spirituality relates more to the realm of the individual athlete, and his or her training and development as a player on any given team. In the previous chapter, I spoke about the derivation of the word "religion" from its Latin origins meaning to "rebind." With this basic meaning of religion in mind, it is most helpful to understand religion as being that human social force that seeks to repair what is broken, to reweave what is frayed, to reconnect what is disconnected, to reintegrate what is disintegrated. Spirituality serves as the personal and individual application of this social tendency towards collective cooperation, order and harmony. A popular political slogan expresses this notion succinctly: "Think globally, act locally." Spirituality acts at the local level of the individual person. Its methods, ideas, and perspective on the world arise out of the global perspective of religion.

It may seem strange to speak of spirituality as having a "perspective," but it does. Spirituality works to align the thoughts, words and actions of persons with that which is of ultimate value, significance and meaning to them. Religion is the container and bearer of meaning and value. Because of their more global perspective, religions articulate particular worldviews about what is of value in the world, and how to live according to those values. Religions also articulate how those values can be attained, and how they govern the actions of individuals and societies. Spirituality serves as the way to cultivate those values in the conduct and behavior of individuals, especially as they relate to other individuals. You can see from this description how religion and spirituality weave their way throughout the personal, inter-personal and social arenas we explored in Chapter 3.

Spiritual but Not Religious: Objections to Religion by Its Principled Despisers[1]

In spite of this intimate association between spirituality and religion, a growing number of people in North American and European societies today identify themselves as being "spiritual but not religious." What might cause people to abandon religion while embracing spirituality?

Although the factors are undoubtedly numerous and complex, one powerful factor has to do with a human failing as old as humanity itself: hypocrisy. When churches and church leaders act in ways contrary to the core teachings of Jesus, people wonder about the integrity of the religion itself. When pastors condemn the sexual practices of some persons but engage in sexual immorality themselves, people wonder about the integrity of the leaders of religion. When churches enter the political arena and push for the election of certain politicians or support particular political parties, people become suspicious, especially when the politicians elected go on to lie, divert funds to benefit large multinational corporations, foment wars, ignore civil rights or international treaties. People perceive a deep moral and ethical disconnect between what churches proclaim and what they practice in everyday life.

This is a problem not only in Christianity, but in other religions as well. At the time of the writing of this book, the United States has been engaged in a war with Iraq, although it is not clear with whom in Iraq the U.S. troops are engaged. Over the years of that conflict, reports came in daily of small guerrilla actions by certain Iraqi factions against other Iraqi factions or against U.S. troops. Often these actions were incited by Muslim clerics, who were as often as not carrying out campaigns against rival clerics, or against clerics who call for moderation and conciliation. There is strong evidence that young Iraqis have become disenchanted with the clerics' war rhetoric, and who perceive that the idea of jihad as articulated by these clerics is in keeping with neither the Qur'an nor the sunnah (the teachings and example) of Muhammad.[2]

In Sri Lanka, there have been fierce and bloody conflicts between Buddhists and the immigrant Tamil population, who are predominantly Hindu. The sight of Buddhist monks rioting and committing acts of

---

1. This section heading is a deliberate reference to a book written in 1799 by the German Protestant theologian Friedrich Schleiermacher that was entitled: *On Religion: Speeches to Its Cultured Despisers*."

2. Tavernise, "Violence Leaves Young Iraqis Doubting Clerics."

violence shocks those who understand Buddhism to be a religion of peace and enlightenment, and a path to overcome those rapacious cravings that lead to acts of violence.

Clearly, it is entirely possible for the practitioners of religions to live and behave in ways that negate and deny the very foundations upon which those religions are built. This is because religions are made up of human beings, and human beings are far from perfect or even consistent in their dealings in the world. In fact, people have a tendency to do things as a group that they would never consider doing on their own. Reinhold Niebuhr examined this phenomenon in his 1932 book, *Moral Man and Immoral Society*.[3] In that book and later books, Niebuhr argued that "human nature would always complicate even our highest ideals and our greatest accomplishments. This insight necessitates a humility in every human endeavor, especially faith and politics."[4]

Those who look askance at those proclaimers of religion who fail to "practice what they preach" would find good company with Jesus. Jesus frequently took the religious leaders of his time to task for failing to live up to the religious demands they placed upon other people. In fact, he referred to them as "hypocrites," a term adopted from the theatre of the Greeks of his time. The Greek word *hupokritês* was actually the word referring to actors in the theatre. The actors of that time would wear large masks to represent the character they were portraying. By employing this word Jesus was saying that the religious leaders to which he was referring were nothing more than play-actors, putting on the mask of religion without actually allowing it to affect or change who they were beneath its façade. The following passage from Matthew illustrates his attitude graphically:

> Then Jesus said to the crowds and to his disciples: "The teachers of the law and the Pharisees sit in Moses' seat. So you must obey them and do everything they tell you. But do not do what they do, for they do not practice what they preach. They tie up heavy loads and put them on men's shoulders, but they themselves are not willing to lift a finger to move them.
>
> «Everything they do is done for men to see: They make their phylacteries wide and the tassels on their garments long; they love the place of honor at banquets and the most important

---

3. Niebuhr, *Moral Man and Immoral Society: A Study of Ethics and Politics*.

4. Krista Tippett, "Moral Man and Immoral Society: The Public Theology of Reinhold Niebuhr."

seats in the synagogues; they love to be greeted in the marketplaces and to have men call them ‹Rabbi.›

"Woe to you, teachers of the law and Pharisees, you hypocrites! You shut the kingdom of heaven in men's faces. You yourselves do not enter, nor will you let those enter who are trying to.

«Woe to you, teachers of the law and Pharisees, you hypocrites! You travel over land and sea to win a single convert, and when he becomes one, you make him twice as much a son of hell as you are. (Matthew 23:1–7, 13–15, NIV.)

It must be kept in mind, of course, that this tendency to play-act at the thing we profess is not exclusive to the practitioners of religion. There are politicians who fail to abide by the Constitution they are sworn to protect, doctors who care more for money than the health of their patients, lawyers who find ways to break the law without being caught or punished, scholars who plagiarize the research and writing of others (including their students) and claim it to be their original work, bankers and investors who engage in financial schemes that are illegal and unethical but make them very wealthy, and CEOs of large businesses who decry government regulation of their business while engaging in business schemes that result in the government having to bail out the industry to prevent catastrophic financial collapse.

In the previous chapter I spoke about spirituality as being about the congruence between the values we proclaim and the lives we lead. Clearly, the search for a congruent and coherent life is directed expressly at the issue of hypocrisy. An incongruent and hypocritical life is a broken and unraveled life, and it is the work of religion and spirituality to mend and reweave just such a life, not only individually but also corporately. My plea here then is simple: let us not abandon the valuable vocation of religion in our embrace of the calling of spirituality. Both are necessary. The pursuit of one without the other is incomplete and will have only partial results.

Jesus provides for us the model of a life that is both religious and spiritual. He was born and died a First-Century Palestinian Jew. He was embedded completely in the religious practices of First Century Judaism. He was circumcised shortly after birth, brought to the temple for dedication, attended Passover celebrations with his family and followers in Jerusalem, attended other pilgrimage festivals, and even allowed himself to be baptized by John in the Jordan river as part of a Jewish renewal movement. He quoted the Hebrew Scriptures extensively, disputed points of the law with religious authorities and teachers, and the Gospel writers quote exclusively from the Hebrew Scriptures when speaking about Jesus and his fulfillment of the scriptures. His final meal with his followers was a Passover Seder, adapted slightly to impress upon his followers his own work in leading them to spiritual freedom in a way analogous to how Moses had led the Israelites to freedom out of Egypt hundreds of years earlier. Several times when Jesus healed persons, he immediately commanded them to go show themselves to the priests at the temple for confirmation of their healing and to offer the proper sacrifices of purification and thanksgiving. Clearly, he was both spiritual *and* religious. What Jesus taught his followers was how to go to the heart of religious practice and drink of its life-giving waters. At the same time, religion did not exist for its own sake, but served as the vehicle for the work of the Spirit of God in the formation of persons according to the way of God.

Formed by the Spirit

Recall that in the last chapter I defined Christian spirituality as involving the transformation of human persons through the experiential presence of the love of God as taught and lived by Jesus and mediated by the Holy Spirit. The notion of "transformation" implies the change or adaptation of something from one form or state to another. Sometimes transformation can involve a simple change of status, such as when a student graduates from one grade to another or at the completion of a course of study. Another kind of transformation has to do with a change in appearance, such as when a house is redecorated and repainted, or when a person has a "makeover" of their hairstyle and personal appearance. The work of transformation of persons by the work of the Holy Spirit refers to an inner change of attitude, belief and commitment that results in an outer change of behavior and habit.

This work of spiritual transformation can be both sudden and gradual. In fact, it is usually a combination of both. In the example of a person graduating from a course of study, the moment of commencement represents a sharp change in status—one moment a student, the next a graduate, an alumna or alumnus. But much work and study has gone on in order to achieve that moment. Knowledge has been gained bit by bit, and skills have been acquired gradually. Yet the work of education is not over. Skills and knowledge must be applied and assimilated into the practical demands of jobs and employment. The transformation from student to graduate is, in a sense, instantaneous, whereas the transformation of the person from their life before being a student to their life as an employed person is long, progressive and ongoing.

The same is true in the spiritual life. A person may have a sudden, life-changing experience that forever alters their direction and priorities. But in order for this change to have lasting effects, the person must find ways of acting that are in accord with this new direction. They must also redirect their thoughts and attitudes along lines in concert with this new direction. What they need to do is to adopt a set of *practices* that serve to reinforce their new life and to help establish the change as permanent.

To speak of practices returns us to a very interesting positive flipside of our discussion about hypocrisy. Recall that the word "hypocrite" in its original Greek context referred to actors in theatre. In order for any actor to be prepared for an actual performance, they must run through their lines and movements on stage over and over again in order to memorize their part. This is called "practicing." Similarly, athletes on a team practice together as a team over and over so that they develop their skills and learn how to work as a team. They have certain "plays" that they need to know as a team in order to compete in a game. In order to compete well and effectively, these plays must be so well-rehearsed and practiced that they are second nature to each player and to the team as a whole. In essence, through repeated practice and rehearsal, actors and athletes each internalize their lines, parts, routines and plays to the extent that the actor fully embodies their character such that they seem to actually be that character, and the athlete executes their plays so well that they seem to have been born to the game, or such that they *are* football or baseball itself.

This is the work of *formation*. Human beings have as part of their normal developmental process the natural capacity to learn, grow, change, and adapt. Human beings are malleable and formable. This is true physically as well as intellectually, emotionally, psychologically and spiritually. Human behaviors are shaped by a wide variety of factors as we saw in the chapter about Mapping the Terrain. This is because humans are fundamentally *shapeable*.

Because of this malleability, the primary way humans are formed spiritually is through the process of engaging in a set of practices that serve to reinforce and fashion their behaviors and attitudes according to a particular set of values and beliefs about the world. These practices are called *spiritual disciplines*.

Virtually every religious system in the world has developed a set of attendant disciplines, and most of these disciplines are remarkably similar across the world. Practices such as meditation, prayer, almsgiving or acts of charity, corporate worship or devotional practice, and ritualized activities are among the disciplines most common around the world. There is evidence of these disciplines having been practiced for millennia—a testimony to what humans have found to be efficacious in all places and at all times.

Jesus was a practicing Jew in first-century Palestine. The Jewish spiritual disciplines for which we have evidence that he practiced include prayer, study of the Scriptures of his time, acts of charity, and the observance of religious rituals and festivals. In addition, Jesus spent time alone in the natural world, engaged in fasting, urged repentance, performed works of mercy and justice as well as works of love and compassion. He engaged in acts of forgiveness and reconciliation, and worked to establish a new form of community among his disciples and followers. Let's look at these in greater depth.

Prayer

One of the most common of human spiritual practices is prayer. Prayer is found across the world in a variety of forms, and employs a wide variety of techniques and methods of articulation.

At its heart, prayer is the formal or deliberate stating of an intention for oneself or for another person or groups of persons, or even for a situation. That is, a person desires that a certain thing will happen, or a particular state of being or set of circumstances be achieved, and they formulate that intention into words. This is the essence of prayer. In traditions such as Christianity, Islam, Judaism, the prayers are directed to God, who serves as the one who listens to and receives such stated intentions or prayers. But prayer is also found in Buddhism, Hinduism, Paganism and Wicca, and indigenous and traditional societies across the globe. It is a well-nigh universal human practice. What is unique in Christian prayer is how this practice is grounded in the life and teaching of Jesus Christ, and how it is often directed to him in a conversational manner, as if face-to-face.

Richard Foster in his book *Prayer*[5], identifies at least 21 kinds of prayer in the Christian tradition alone. Foster groups these types of prayer into three basic directions: inward, upward and outward. Prayer engages the person praying in a process of personal transformation, which occurs within. But there is also the human need for intimacy, and especially intimacy with God. In the Christian tradition, God is a God of deep personal relationship, who goes in search of fellowship with human beings, even becoming like them in order to have an up-close-and-personal relationship. Thus there is an upward movement to prayer. But prayer also moves the person praying out into the world. Even though prayer is usually private (Jesus urged his followers to pray in secret), the fact that prayer involves the naming of our intentions for one another and for the world demonstrates that it has a strong social dimension to it as well.

The power of prayer arises from the fact that it is first and foremost an activity of the will of God. In his instructions on prayer to his disciples, Jesus gives them an example of how to pray. He said

> "This, then, is how you should pray: 'Our Father in heaven, hallowed be your name, your kingdom come, your will be done on earth as it is in heaven. Give us today our daily bread. Forgive us our debts, as we also have forgiven our debtors. And lead us not into temptation, but deliver us from the evil one" (Matthew 6:9–13 NIV).

Significantly, Jesus begins the prayer by grounding it in the nature of God and God's will. Prayer is a holy act, because God is holy. And because God is holy, prayer needs to be grounded in God's will for the world. That is, our intentions, as voiced in our prayer, must be rooted firmly in God's intentions. Christian teaching over the centuries has emphasized that Jesus came to reveal the will of God to humankind. Keeping that in mind, we can understand that by teaching his followers how to pray, Jesus was also teaching them that it is the will of God *that* we pray. The very act of praying manifests the will of God in a very concrete and specific way. The following is my definition of prayer, which expresses this notion: "*Prayer is that part of the will of God that needs the vehicle of human expression in order to be manifested in the material world.*"

Prayer is a way of attuning our wills to the greater Will that pervades the universe. The God that called all things into being and that upholds and sustains all things desires to be known by us, and prayer is

---

5. Foster, *Prayer*.

that mechanism of knowing and being made known. Prayer is the cornerstone of the spiritual life. As in all avenues of human knowing of other persons, it is based in communication, conversation and dialog. It is also based in an honest opening of one's heart and inner life to the other, in this case, to God. The Psalmist expresses it eloquently:

> O LORD, you have searched me
> and you know me.
> You know when I sit and when I rise;
> you perceive my thoughts from afar.
> You discern my going out and my lying down;
> you are familiar with all my ways.
> Before a word is on my tongue
> you know it completely, O LORD.
> You hem me in—behind and before;
> you have laid your hand upon me.
> Such knowledge is too wonderful for me,
> too lofty for me to attain.
> Where can I go from your Spirit?
> Where can I flee from your presence?
> If I go up to the heavens, you are there;
> if I make my bed in the depths, you are there.
> If I rise on the wings of the dawn,
> if I settle on the far side of the sea,
> even there your hand will guide me,
> your right hand will hold me fast.
> If I say, "Surely the darkness will hide me
> and the light become night around me,"
> even the darkness will not be dark to you;
> the night will shine like the day,
> For you created my inmost being;
> you knit me together in my mother's womb. (Psalm 139:1-13 NIV)

Prayer is, in essence, an act of radical intimacy with God. God is radically intimate with us in that we are entrusted with the task of acting as conduits for God's work of blessing the world in acts of compassion, mercy, justice and love. We are radically intimate with God by opening ourselves to God's guidance and to the shaping of our lives and characters by the Holy Spirit. There is no other way to be spiritually formed by God.

Study of Scripture

Jesus studied the scriptures of his time, and knew them deeply. On several occasions in the Bible he quotes them outright, or makes comments upon them. For instance, in the chapters in Mathew referred to as the Sermon on the Mount (chapters 5–7), Jesus quotes from the books of Deuteronomy, Exodus and Leviticus—three of the books of the Torah. At another point, he disputes with other religious leaders and scholars of his time, the Pharisees, Sadducees and scribes, about their interpretations and application of various points of religious law, which was contained both in the written scriptures of his time as well as the oral interpretations of that law.

It is in the nature of Scripture that it bonds a group of people in a shared experience and understanding of God, and what it means to be the people of God, however that may defined by that group. The Scriptures become that common touchstone that helps to mediate differences, which provides a common language for morality and disciplined living, and describes the means by which we may gain access to mystery. Jesus studied the Scriptures of his time because they were the spiritual teachings and proclamations of his people, and they gave witness to the One he called *Abba*, "Father."

In a later chapter I will discuss in greater detail the importance of the study of the Bible in spiritual formation, and I will suggest various ways to read the Bible with the intention of allowing *Abba* God to speak to us through its stories, poetry, teachings and rules of life.

Alms-Giving or Acts of Charity

Every human society has come into existence as a result of the cooperation of humans with one another. This has meant that people contribute their talents, abilities and even material substance towards the security and sustenance of the group or society as a whole. But every society has also had to reckon with the fact that not everybody is able to contribute equally, and that some members of its group are more vulnerable than others, whether because of their age, or because of disability, injury or disease. The giving of alms arose in societies around the world as a means for those on the margins of society to survive. There is evidence that the group of disciples who traveled with Jesus not only received monetary support from others, but also maintained their own fund for giving to the poor.

But there were other forms of charity as well. "Charity" is from the Latin, *caritas*, which means "love for all people." Jesus' ministry was characterized by his compassion for all the people with whom he came in contact. He helped people in whatever way he could to find greater purpose or hope, to be physically made well, and to be restored to their family and friends. He engaged in a ministry of healing, teaching and casting out demons that drew throngs of people everywhere he went.

This work of charity, or love for all people, was rooted in compassion. "As he landed, he saw a great throng, and he had compassion on them, because they were like sheep without a shepherd" (Mark 6:34 RSV). The Greek word we translate as "having compassion" is vivid: it literally means to be moved deeply within one's gut. Compassion was not an intellectual concept to Jesus, it was a direct, visceral experience that was the result of meeting people face-to-face and being open to their needs and struggles in life. He literally felt their pain and desperation, and responded out of the resources he possessed, either materially or emotionally and spiritually. Matthew summarizes his activities this way: "... many who were demon-possessed were brought to him, and he drove out the spirits with a word and healed all the sick. This was to fulfill what was spoken through the prophet Isaiah: 'He took up our infirmities and carried our diseases'" (Matthew 8:17 NIV).

Works of charity that are based in compassion are the manifestation of God's presence in the world. This is because, as the writer of 1 John proclaims, "God is love" (1 John 4:8). The writer of the Gospel of John declares that it was because of God's great love for the world that Jesus was sent into the world, to manifest and actualize that love in specific, concrete ways. All acts of charity that arise out of human compassion for others are rooted, therefore, in the nature of God, and are ways that the "Love of God" moves from being a concept to being a living reality.

Devotional Practice and Worship

I have already described how Jesus observed the various Jewish festivals and religious rituals. There are numerous references in the New Testament to his participation in synagogue services. In addition, he spent much time alone in prayer and communion with God. All of these are acts of devotion and worship.

"Worship" derives from the Old English word *weorth*, which meant what its modern form, "worth" denotes: that which renders something valuable and desirable. The worship of God recognizes that God is the source of all that is valuable and desirable, and that communion and fellowship with God is to be desired above all other things. This is expressed eloquently in a hymn of praise in the Book of Revelation: "You are worthy, our Lord and God, to receive glory and honor and power, for you created all things, and by your will they were created and have their being" (Revelation 4:11 NIV). This pithy little hymn describes the basis for worship of God (creating and granting being to all things), as well as the content of worship (offering to God honor and glory and power).

Humans naturally tend to find value and worth in things, and to seek after that which they value. It is a basic driving force of human behavior. Acts of devotion and worship help to direct this natural tendency toward God and toward ultimate concerns. One way we demonstrate that something is of value to us is by the time that we devote to it, especially time that is our own to give, not time required to make a living or put food on the table. For instance, how much time do you spend each week watching or playing sports? How much time hiking in the woods or fishing? How much time working on projects? The time that you spend, that is your "free time" to use as you wish, is a direct indicator of the value you place on the thing you are doing.

Devoting time in the worship of God is a formal declaration of the high value we place in the life that has been made possible for us by the grace, mercy and love of God. Worship is the acknowledgement of our complete and utter dependence upon God for everything. It is not always easy to admit our dependence upon others for our well-being, but it is the most well-established fact of life: we are fully dependent upon forces outside of ourselves for our well-being, in fact for our being at all.

One of the hugest myths of our time is the fantasy of the "self-made man." There is no such thing. A professor in the seminary I attended, Dr. Doug Adams, used to remind us of this fact graphically. He would say, "Do you know how you can tell a self-made man? He has no belly button!" There right in front of us, as an ever-present reminder of our dependence upon others for our well-being, sits our belly button. Any time we feel too certain of our self-sufficiency and individual cleverness, we need only to pat our belly to remind ourselves that we are a product of forces and laws and creatures and people far beyond our reckoning and even our recognizing. Worship is the vehicle whereby we acknowledge our dependence upon these forces and creatures and people by acknowledging the One responsible for their being in the first place.

Worship helps bolster the spiritual life by reminding us and reinforcing within us the knowledge that we are part of something vastly grander and more profound than our own bounded and limited perspective. When I was in seminary, I lived in an apartment that was set on a hill overlooking the San Francisco Bay. I would often go up on the roof and look out over the city and across the bay to the Golden Gate Bridge. I could see cars driving on the bridges and boats making their way across the water. Whatever problem I had that seemed so overwhelming and pressing faded in intensity and diminished in size as I gazed out upon the larger world around me. The problems didn't disappear, but the very exercise of gazing out onto a larger landscape helped me to realize that I was indeed part of something beyond my narrow point of view, and this helped me to understand that no problem was insurmountable, nor was it interminable.

Worship is just this sort of gazing out upon a larger landscape—a landscape that is universal in scale and unlimited in its timeframe. Nothing in human experience lasts forever, and this realization is a powerful antidote to despair and anxiety. Worship expands our horizons, lifts our spirits, and elevates our values.

The one thing in life we have absolute control over is how we act in the world—how we relate and react to others. The choices we make day to day about how we respond to those around us—what we say, how we treat people, how we spend our time, where we go, what we do—these are in our power of choice. It has been aptly said, "What we are is God's gift to us, what we do with ourselves is our gift to God."

This act of acknowledging in worship our dependency places us firmly in the midst of the complex network of relationships that make life possible. The remaining spiritual practices that follow are the means whereby we contribute to the well-being of others, and thereby become the channels and instruments of God's grace in the world.

Time Alone in The Natural World

Quite often in my ministry I have spoken with men who would rather spend time out in the woods hunting, or out on a lake or by a river fishing, or hiking up a mountain than come to church. They would often confess to me that they felt closer to God out in nature. In researching the ministry of Jesus, I have come to believe they got it half-right. Jesus did spend significant amounts of time in the natural world as a means to restore his soul and refresh his mind. After his baptism by John in the Jordan River, Jesus spent time in the wilderness in a time of fasting and prayer. The Gospels record that he was known to depart from the buzz of his disciples and the pressing crowds that followed him to "lonely places"—places that were apart from human habitation.

Spending time alone in the natural world was a way that Jesus used to reinvigorate himself after expending so much personal time and energy in service to others. However, this was always balanced by spending time in fellowship with his disciples, worshipping with them, and engaging in the sort of education and learning that can only occur in human society. The key word here is balance. Jesus balanced the intensity of daily human interactions with the solitude of communion with the natural world.

Humans are as much a part of the natural world as are other animals and plants, trees, rivers, mountains, sun and stars. We have developed over centuries and millennia in direct contact with the natural world, and human psychological health is dependent upon continuous engagement with the rest of creation. However, human civilizations have increasingly become separated and even alienated from the natural world. By losing contact with nature, humans can forget the fact that they are also creatures. They have a Creator. The human hubris of thinking that we are the authors of our own existence and the final arbiters of our actions arise out of this creaturely amnesia.

Spending time in natural places, and especially wild places can restore us to our place in creation. It works in concert with devotional practices by expanding our vision and exercising our sense of awe and wonder. The beauty we encounter feeds our souls in ways that we are unable to accomplish out of our own volition. The natural world comes to us as a tremendous gift—a blessing we have not earned and cannot claim to deserve. And so it serves as a tangible experience of God's grace.

Anyone who has taken time apart to go hiking or camping or even just sitting in a park or garden with no pressing agenda can understand the psychological and emotional benefits that that time apart can provide.

As I write this chapter, I am sitting in a cabin at a writer's retreat along the Imnaha River in northeastern Oregon. Steep canyon walls lift the horizon high above the river. Trees surround the cabin and embrace the river shores on either side. The unrelenting, unresting, as well as unhasting pace of the water as it tumbles and trips over the rocks outside my window calls me to a different pace of life. Along this river there is space to think and ponder, permission granted to wonder and consider, room simply to be and not prove myself. I can drop my pretenses, set aside my feigned self-importance and hang up for a time the demands placed upon me. The trees and rocks and river don't care if I am the CEO of a multinational company or a garbage collector. Here in this spot in nature I can simply be.

The times Jesus spent in the lonely places of the natural world were just such retreats from *doing* into the depths of *being*. Such time apart serves to settle us back and center us down into the blessed giftedness of life, a gift given to us beyond any consideration of whether we have earned it or deserve it in any way. Time apart in the natural world can return us to the mysteries of grace and providence.

Fasting

As Jesus began his ministry, he retreated to a place in the wilderness for a time of prayer and fasting. Fasting is a practice that has been linked with the pursuit of spiritual insight in cultures all around the world. It was practiced in concert with deep meditation by Siddhartha Gautama in his search for enlightenment; it formed a regular part of the practices of *sannyasins* in India for centuries; and in the Bible it was used not only in conjunction with acts of repentance and confession of sins, but also as a means to purify oneself and prepare for a deeper encounter with God.

The constant need for food occupies much of our time and energy as humans. In fact, it is the primary concern of all living beings. By temporarily stepping away from the all-consuming need to consume, our mental energy and attention can be directed to practices such as prayer, meditation and contemplation. As the body no longer needs to direct its energy resources to the acquisition, preparation, eating and digesting of food, it has more energy available for the work of the brain as it engages in these exercises of the mind.

Jesus enjoined the practice of prayer and fasting upon his disciples. At one point, he admonishes his disciples for their apparent failure to heal or cast out demons as being due to their lack of prayer and fasting (see Matthew 17:21). Of course, it was not a hard and fast rule. At other points in the Gospels, Jesus is asked why the disciples of John pray and fast while the disciples of Jesus don't (Matthew 9:14, Luke 5:33). What Jesus seemed to practice was a balance of spiritual disciplines, which is good instruction for us as well.

Repentance

When Jesus begins his ministry, he joins forces for a brief period with John the Baptist. The message both of them preach is "Repent! The Kingdom of God is at hand." The *Koiné* Greek word we translate as "repentance" is *metanoia*, which literally means to change or redirect one's mind. To alter the direction of one's mind means not only to redirect the direction one is headed, but also to change the manner in which one is traversing that path. Repentance is all about engaging in a clear and careful examination of the direction your life is taking, and seeking a better way. Someone has said, "a dead-end is simply another place to turn around." Repentance takes a dead-end and makes it into a cul-de-sac wherein we can seek a new direction in life.

Significantly, Jesus begins his ministry in two of the Gospels by calling people to a change of mind and a new direction in life: "From that time on Jesus began to preach, 'Repent, for the kingdom of heaven is near'" (Matthew 4:17 NIV), and "after John was put in prison, Jesus went into Galilee, proclaiming the good news of God. 'The time has come,' he said. 'The kingdom of God is near. Repent and believe the good news!'" (Mark 1:14–15 NIV).

Following Jesus is much more than adding his ideas to our overcrowded collection of good thoughts and helpful aphorisms for living. It requires a reordering of our priorities and challenges our most basic assumptions about what is important in life. Throughout his ministry, Jesus challenged and called into question the prevailing assumptions and practices of power and domination, value of persons, relationships between rich and poor, men and women, clean and unclean. His call to repentance was not just a one-time event. It was a lifelong practice.

The most basic form of repentance involves the daily examination of the things we have thought, said and done that day. Placing them up against the life, teaching and conversations of Jesus provides a good measure of what path we are on, and where we are on that path. The act of repentance, especially when done daily, serves as a continuous course correction for the path our life takes.

To seek out the spiritual life usually requires that we redirect our lives in some way. Whether it is due to a personal crisis, or the need to completely reorder our priorities, or the need to disentangle ourselves from social systems that are degrading, violent or dehumanizing, a spiritual life is at core a redirected life. Jesus speaks of repentance 25 times in the first three Gospels. So it is that it is usually the first spiritual practice any person must engage in when they start out on the spiritual path.

Works of Mercy and Justice

The Mediterranean world of Jesus' time was built upon layers and layers of social and economic relationships, with each layer exerting some form of dominance over the layers below it. From emperor to slave, power was exerted over and upon those farther down the ladder. One of the most striking things about Jesus is how he did things that went against this system of power and domination.

Everywhere Jesus went, his preaching and the things he did were received and experienced as "good news." He healed the sick, brought sight to the blind, cast out demons, caused the lame and crippled to walk, cured leprosy, and taught the common people ways to live under an oppressive political and economic system that restored their dignity without resorting to violence. He respected their dignity as persons and worked to re-instill that sense of dignity in those whom the rest of the world had counted as expendable and worthless.

Jesus didn't simply "put a band-aid" on people's problems, but he also addressed the social conditions that prevented people from being whole or healthy, or that favored one group at the expense of another. He also addressed ways of thinking and belief systems that did not have the well-being of persons as their ultimate goal or guiding principle. Several times he was criticized for healing on the Sabbath, and he replied with the comment "The Sabbath was made for man, not man for the Sabbath." If it was lawful to pull an ox out of a well on the Sabbath, was it not lawful to heal a person who had been in bondage to disease for several years?

We will look at this in closer detail in a later chapter. But it is important at this juncture to point out that his reaching out to social outcasts, the unclean, beggars, women and foreigners was not a series of quirks of behavior or accidents in life. They were conscious, deliberate acts that reflected the set of his mind. They were acts so significant that the early Christian community made sure to remember them and later to preserve them in the words of Scripture.

The basic principle Jesus operated from was the well-being and wholeness of every person. The spiritual practice that arises from this has to do with engaging in whatever set of actions that maximizes the well-being of persons in their wholeness as persons. This may involve addressing social inequities, overturning laws that discriminate or favor only a select few. It may involve advocating on behalf of marginalized or disempowered persons. It may involve being a supportive companion for a person whose self-esteem has been dashed, and helping them piece it together again. There is no shortage of places in the world in which acts of justice, mercy, love and compassion are needed.

The extension of mercy to those in troubled places and the work for justice for those experiencing oppression and injustice in whatever form it presents itself is a profound spiritual discipline that reflects the mind of Christ at work in us.

Works of Love and Compassion

Similarly, much of Jesus' ministry was involved in works of healing and restoration of persons to wholeness of mind, body and spirit. Over and over, the compassion of Jesus is highlighted in the Gospels, and serves as the wellspring from which his actions and behavior originated. In the way of life that Jesus lived and taught, love was not a warm, mushy feeling but rather a bold way of acting. If a person was broken in body, then he worked a physical healing. If a person was broken is spirit, then he worked to raise their self-appraisal and let them know their value in the sight of God. No one was outside the sphere of Jesus' kindness and help. What Jesus could do to help, he did. The only time he was unable to help someone was when they did not receive him or believe in what he offered to them.

Forgiveness and Reconciliation

In the course of any human relationship, someone is bound to hurt someone else. It is just the way of things. Sometimes that hurt is inflicted deliberately, other times it may be inadvertent or even done unawares. The practices of forgiveness and reconciliation seek to rebind the relationships that have become strained or unwound through injury or hurt. Forgiveness, as another mode of healing, was also at the center of the spirituality that Jesus exemplified. Jesus speaks about forgiveness 37 times in the New Testament. It is a central component in the Lord's Prayer, and it is one of the last things he says on the cross: "Father forgive them for they do not know what they are doing." He told Peter that he must forgive someone 70 times 7 rather than simply a few times.

Several times Jesus speaks about how to go about seeking forgiveness and restoring relationships that have been strained or broken. This included the relationship between humans and God, as well as person to person. So powerful was this practice and message of forgiveness and reconciliation, that, later on, Paul realized that it fueled his missionary effort in the Gentile communities.

Because the early Christian communities were based upon loving fellowship, it was necessary for there to be ways to repair that bond of love when trust had been betrayed or offense had been taken, as can easily happen in the course of human relationships. The spiritual practice of seeking and granting forgiveness, and the work of reconciliation is the work of mending the tears and rips in the social fabric that binds people together in community. Jesus said, "Blessed are the peacemakers, for they shall be called children of God." The work of reconciliation and of forgiveness is the work of bringing peace to human hearts and communities, and is a profoundly spiritual process.

Forgiveness and reconciliation are forms of healing and restoration to wholeness that work at the psychological and emotional level of human relationships. As social creatures, humans are formed by the interrelationships in their families and communities. Acts of forgiveness and the work of reconciliation help to maintain the strength of those bonds of relationship, and assure that those bonds are helpful and not hurtful to the people involved.

But most importantly, as indicated above, the work of forgiveness springs from the very character and nature of God. By pronouncing forgiveness upon those who crucified him, and calling upon God's forgiveness of them, he demonstrated to us that the work of forgiveness is dear to the heart of God.

A New Form of Community

The spiritual life cannot be lived in isolation. Jesus gathered what can only be described as a motley crew of people around himself. It was an unlikely cohort of individuals that included a (despised?) tax collector, a political zealot, four fishermen, religious idealists, unknowns, women of means, friends and someone who would eventually betray him to his political enemies. He demonstrated to them a new way of living and relating to others. He taught them deep and effective ways of praying and taking hold of the power of the Spirit of God. He modeled the way of justice and mercy. And he insisted that those who followed him should live the same way and treat each other and those outside the circle of believers as he had treated them.

It is one thing to preach a certain way of life, and another thing to live it out effectively. The work of repentance and personal transformation that Jesus modeled, taught and lived is hard. Nothing about it is easy, although it is all based upon what is most naturally placed within our hearts and minds. Everything we need to know about how to live we can learn from children, Jesus observed. But society, empire, family, and even religion can beat and contort our lives so much that we need to completely relearn a way of thinking and acting that is life-giving and that has at its center the promotion of the well-being of others.

Because it involves the reordering of our lives, as well as the reprogramming of our ways of thinking, it is not something that we can undertake on our own. The change of life that the spiritual path entails is so radically different from the way human societies operate that alternate social systems or groups are needed in order to provide support, guidance and wisdom to those who seek that path. Jesus gathered people around himself and strove to establish the sort of supportive community that would enable his teachings not only to be remembered and passed along to subsequent generations, but more importantly, to be cultivated, practiced and lived out by those who followed in his path.

Jesus did not simply provide a critique about the failings of the social systems he found around himself—he showed people an alternative way to live and be. At its best, the Christian community is just such a community of love, justice, mercy and compassion in the world. It has not always been able to achieve this, but it is certainly motivated by these concerns when it follows most closely the life example and teachings of the Savior it proclaims. In order to adopt this new way of being and acting in the world, we need to have the support of like-minded people who will assist us in our journey. Because we are formed as persons through our interactions with other persons, it is vital to be in a community that not only supports but also actively works to reinforce the development of the highest ideals and standards of behavior and treatment of others. Being in the new community of Jesus Christ we not only learn the content of faith, but we practice the ways of living it out in our daily lives. This is what Jesus meant when he talked about the *ekklesia*, or church. The *ekklesia* is that community of people who were *called out* (the root meaning of the Greek word) from the social and cultural systems of their time and who were shown a new way, the Way of Love.

This is still true today. What the church provides is the laboratory wherein the gold of the Gospel of Jesus Christ is refined in the crucible of human hearts. The content of faith is shared and the life it espouses is experimented with and finally embraced. In this process, we are formed by the Spirit of God and our minds and lives are transformed according to the heart of Jesus.

These disciplines and practices are all ways in which the Holy Spirit trains us and transforms us. But we are not trained and transformed for our personal benefit alone. Rather, we are transformed in order also to go out and transform the world according to the vision Jesus taught and lived every day. It is a way of living in direct communion with God, in vivifying and vital fellowship with other humans and in radical nurturance within the natural world. It is a way of being and acting that cultivates and protects life in its myriad expressions around the world. It is demanding work, and not everyone accepts its rigors. But it is the way to the heart of Jesus, and to the heart of God.

— 7 —

Reading the Bible

THIS BOOK IS ABOUT seeking to live according to the Path of Jesus as men of the twenty-first century. In order to do this, we will need to spend time as his disciples did—at his feet, by his side, and in circles of fellowship asking questions and sharing our own impressions of his teachings and life. Although we lack the possibility of doing this in the up close and personal manner of his first followers, we do have in our possession what the early church gleaned as being authoritative accounts of his life and teachings, such as could be used to instruct new converts to the faith. These accounts are what are found in the Gospels of the New Testament. But in addition to these written accounts, Jesus also promised that he would send One who would teach and instruct those who wished to follow in his Way. That One was the Holy Spirit, the Comforter and Advocate.

> If you love me, you will obey what I command. And I will ask the Father, and he will give you another Counselor to be with you forever—the Spirit of truth. The world cannot accept him, because it neither sees him nor knows him. But you know him, for he lives with you and will be in you . . . the Counselor, the Holy Spirit, whom the Father will send in my name, will teach you all things and will remind you of everything I have said to you. (John 14:15–17, 26 NIV).

In order to learn from Jesus and about Jesus, we will need to consult three main sources. The first is the Bible itself, as the primary source text. The second is the Holy Spirit. We access the Holy Spirit through prayer and contemplation upon the word of Scripture. Later in this chapter I will describe in greater detail this process. The third main source is the witness and experience of the community of his followers—across the millennia as well as in recent times. This third source includes study and consultation of the writings of those who were close in time and proximity to Jesus and his early disciples. It also includes the writings of mystics, saints, theologians and everyday people that the church has collected and preserved over the centuries. But it also includes the wisdom and struggles of the people in the pews or coffeehouse next to us.

What I will do in this chapter is describe briefly how the Bible was brought together in its present form, and how that process served to define the Christian community as a particular community. I will then look at certain issues around any attempt to reconstruct what the "historical" Jesus did and said. Then I will describe a way to read the Bible as if in a conversation with it dialogically, which will lead into a discussion of engaging the Holy Spirit in a spiritual practice of reading the Bible transformatively.

How the Bible Came to Be

The Bible came into its present form over the course of many centuries. The Old Testament, or Hebrew Scriptures, contains the oldest sections of the Bible, and predate Jesus and the origins of the Christian community by at least a century. The scriptures among the Jewish people of Jesus' time consisted primarily of the Law (*Torah*: the first 5 books of the Bible), and the Prophets (*Neviim*: which included Joshua, Judges, I&II Samuel, I&II Kings, Isaiah, Jeremiah, Ezekiel, Hosea, Joel, Amos, Obadiah, Jonah, Micah, Nahum, Habakkuk, Zephaniah, Haggai, Zechariah and Malachi). Jesus specifically refers to these collections of writings when he says, "Do not think that I have come to abolish the Law or the Prophets; I have not come to abolish them but to fulfill them. I tell you the truth, until heaven and earth disappear, not the smallest letter, not the least stroke of a pen, will by any means disappear from the Law until everything is accomplished" (Matthew 5:17–18 NIV).

In addition to these two collections, numerous other books were recognized as scripture, such as the Psalms, Proverbs, I&II Chronicles, and Job. These came to be called The Writings (*Kethuvim*). At the time of Jesus, this latter collection was in flux, and was not finalized as a collection until the first or second century after the time of Jesus. But Jesus was certainly aware of it, because he also quotes from the Psalms at various points.

It is customary to refer to this collection of books as the *canon* of scriptures. The word "canon" is derived from a Semitic word for a "reed" that was used as a measuring rod in ancient times. It passed into Greek and Latin and came to refer to anything that served as a standard against which other things were measured. A canon of writings, then, or scriptures, is that collection of literature that defines the standards of belief, behavior and acceptable activities of a particular group of people. In fact, it serves to define that group as a group, and delineates the boundaries of inclusion in the group.

What we call the Bible came into its present form as a canon during the course of several centuries. The Hebrew Scriptures (*Torah, Neviim and Kethuvim*) may have taken as long as a thousand years to reach its present form. The Christian Scriptures, or the New Testament, only took about 200 years to be written, circulated and collected in its present form. But this process of canonization was crucial for establishing the identity of both the Jewish and Christian communities. Of course, the earliest Christian communities were, in fact, part of the larger Jewish community, which at that time was undergoing a process of development and defining of its identity. The destruction of the temple in 70 C.E. forced a change in the religious identity of the larger Jewish communities, one that was no longer centered on the offering of sacrifices in Jerusalem. The surviving Jewish communities scattered around the Mediterranean re-centered their focus upon their canon of scriptures as interpreted and expounded by the rabbis, while the Jewish communities that became Christian centered their identity and religious life around the proclamation and worship of Jesus as the Son of God and the spreading of his teachings throughout the accessible world. The two communities took very different, and often antagonistic trajectories. But because of this common origin, they share to this day many scriptures in common.

I find it most helpful to view the New Testament, in its canonical form, as the resultant product of the early Christian communities' struggle towards self-identity. Recent discoveries of writings such as the Dead Sea Scrolls, and the Nag Hammadi collection of writings have demonstrated that there were a number of writings that purported to have some connection with the teachings of Jesus. But they were not accepted into the canon by the growing consensus of the churches. Instead, the selection of the four Gospels as we now have them, plus the inclusion of several letters of Paul as well as letters attributed to him, and to Peter,

James and others were selected as expressing the heart of the teachings of Jesus and the early Christian communities' witness to him.

This is no minor point I am making here. To follow Jesus Christ is to identify with him and his teaching and the life he demonstrated. The community of Christ should be molded and formed by his life and his teachings. What the New Testament becomes, in this analysis, then, is a manual of spiritual formation. In addition, the New Testament is a manual of the Church's identity. It contains the church's story—where it came from, how and why it exists, where it is going, and where its place in the cosmos is. But pre-eminently it contains a "program" of spirituality that forms people according to the vision of human potentiality and community that Jesus described and demonstrated.

The Gospels are the primary place to seek out this spirituality. They represent the distillation of this spirituality from four similar yet distinctive vantage points. Interestingly, most scholars believe that they were written after the letters of Paul, with Mark perhaps being written first. It is thought that they emerged in response to the need for the church as an enduring entity to preserve the testimony and teaching of the first-hand witnesses to Jesus. As the early apostles and other disciples of Jesus began to die, the early community sought a way to preserve the witness they made. One way to preserve this was in the writing of what came to be called "Gospels" or "Good News."

The thing about Gospels is that they were centered on a person and they were narrative in form—they told the story of the person. They are not a theological treatise or a statement of doctrine. Rather, there was something about this person that needed to be told, because his life had made a difference of some kind or was instructive as a guide by which others might live their lives. Telling the story about this person was "good news" precisely because life had been made better because of him, and if I as a reader learned about his life and applied what he taught and how he lived to my own life, it would be made better as well.

Thus it is that the Good News about Jesus Christ tells his story—it contains his teachings as well as examples of how he lived, how he interacted with the poor and needy, his followers and his opponents. Everything is worthy of reflection, and of application to our own lives. That is the purpose of a Gospel, to show how our lives can become Good News as well.

At this point, however, it must be pointed out that we cannot fully reconstruct what Jesus authentically said or did, as if we had a video camera following him around, recording everything he said or did, twenty-four hours a day, seven days a week for three years. The Gospels represent what the early church discerned to be the significant core of his life and teachings. This brief witness, contained in relatively few pages, if properly studied, digested and personally applied could transform a person from the inside out. What we have in the Gospels is the testimony of the early church as to how Jesus had transformed human history, and as a consequence, how he could transform the lives of human beings who lived, moved and had their being within the contours of that history.

At various points in time across the past century and a half, various groups of scholars have attempted to get behind the Church's doctrines and teachings about Jesus to try and discern the person of Jesus and reconstruct his life. This has been called the Quest for the Historical Jesus, after the title of a book by that name by Albert Schweitzer. Schweitzer's book described the first such quest in the late 1800s and early 1900s. A second quest re-emerged in the late 1960s through early 1980s, and a third quest emerged with the work pioneered by the Jesus Seminar, sponsored by the Westar Foundation in the late 1990s and early twenty-first century.

It is not the purpose of this chapter, let alone this book, to champion their cause or to critique it. Much very helpful and illuminating research has arisen out of these research projects. Archaeological and textual discoveries have added greatly to our understanding of the time period of Jesus and the early church, and I will draw freely and deeply upon these insights. At the same time, it is impossible to recreate a true, full and satisfactory picture of the person that Jesus was, nor describe just how he lived and all that he taught and did in such a way that his contemporaries and companions would recognize the Jesus they knew in the portrait we compose. Ultimately all such endeavors reveal more about us and our questions and concerns than they do about Jesus. Which, interestingly, is also true of the Gospels.

The Gospels are not slavish biographies or memoirs about Jesus. They are, rather, the proclamation of the early church of just what was potentially life-changing and world-changing about his person and his life. That is why I call the Gospels a manual of spiritual formation.

If I want to repair my car the way it needs to be repaired, in the way that the manufacturer has designed it, I go to a professional maintenance manual, such as a Chilton's. If I want to operate my computer program correctly and efficiently, I read the manual that is designed to

Reading the Bible

go along with that program. If I want my life to be transformed through my encounter with Jesus Christ, I must go to the manual of transformation that the early community of followers and witnesses to Jesus Christ produced—the Gospels.

At the same time, however, it is important to also realize that as we read the Bible, we always read it through the filters and lenses of our own lives, our social situation and the era in which we live. This is not a bad thing. Every age has done this. It is unavoidable as human beings. It is simply human nature to interpret what we read and hear and see through our experience, education and cultural worldview. If you ever have the opportunity to read the various commentaries and expositions of scripture that have been passed on down the centuries, you will be amazed at how different eras of human history have produced such different ways of interpreting the Bible. And yet, it is still the same Bible that speaks to the profound places in the lives of human beings across the centuries all across the globe, in every language and every cultural setting imaginable.

It is this universal communicability that makes it "scripture." The Bible functions as "scripture" when it incorporates into its great cosmic story all our myriad smaller stories. It does this not by adding our stories into its narrative, but by its ability to embrace our stories as being in the same family as its story. The Bible as Scripture is that family of the Holy Spirit into which we are adopted. And we are adopted into that family when we take on the story of that family as our own.

Let me illustrate what I mean by this. I have been married three times. In each marriage, I endeavored to learn the stories, histories and genealogies of those families into which I had married. Family stories had always been important to me growing up, and as part of my embrace of this new family I wanted to learn their stories as well. This had some urgency to me because I had children through two of the marriages, and I want my offspring to know their family history. Our family histories have shaped us in ways that we only dimly recognize, but their influence can be profound. Embracing these stories in all their majesty, mystery, madness and mundaneness helps us to understand our own inner soulscape and the cast of characters that inhabit it. But equally important, by embracing the stories of the family we marry into, we open our hearts to the members of that family and we become part of it.

So it is with the stories of God. By embracing those stories, we become part of God's family, and those stories become part of our inner soulscape. And the thing about the stories of God is that they also have the power to challenge us and to change us. Thus it is that as we embrace the Bible and its story, the Bible's story embraces our story. And since the Bible's story has a particular trajectory to it—the salvation of humans and the redemption of the world—then our lives share in that trajectory.

Dialoguing with the Bible

The approach to reading the Bible I would like to suggest is one that treats the Bible as if it were a person speaking with us. Previously I suggested a metaphor for understanding how the Bible changes lives: by adopting us into its family story. As we become part of this family, we need to enter into a relationship with it through conversation and dialogue—just as we would with any family. So it is, then, that I want to advocate a dialogical approach to reading the Bible as the best way to be formed spiritually by it.

Earlier I spoke of the Gospels as being a training manual of sorts for spiritual formation. I wish to shift the metaphor here a bit. In the earliest tradition of the church, such spiritual formation was done in a personal manner. New believers were taught about the Christian faith, lifestyle and ethics by those who were well-established in the Christian faith. This involved a long period of instruction, and was always person-to person. The scriptures were thus taught personally, and persons were formed spiritually through face-to-face interactions with other Christian believers. So, while I have spoken about the Gospels as being a manual of spiritual formation, it was always used in the context of the believing community.

In addition, the Holy Spirit, as promised by Jesus, was the Unseen Teacher involved in the work of spiritual formation. It was the work of the Holy Spirit to guide the process of formation within the individual, whereas the community of believers guided from without. The individual then essentially engaged in a dialogue with the Bible, with the community of believers and with God as expressed in the Holy Spirit.

When reading the Bible dialogically, we assume that the text of the Bible comes to us as a person, and speaks to us. We approach the Scriptures as we would a person with whom we enter into dialogue. But in order to have any sort of dialogue, we must respect the integrity of the person we encounter and not attempt to mold them according to our own designs and schemes. The same is true of reading the Bible.

There is an untamable wild aspect to Scripture that resists our attempts to sanitize it according to our predetermined expectations.

Scripture cannot be corralled as if it were a mustang needing to be broken according to our needs and desires. Rather, it is like the bohemian cousin who went to Harvard and then joined the Foreign Legion, fought alongside communist insurgents, danced ballet in Paris, developed computer technology with Saudi Arabia and Israel, and has now settled down to raise organic vegetables, breed miniature horses and trade stock on the Internet. It defies all our attempts to categorize and pigeon-hole it.

Three Steps for Reading

There are three basic steps to reading the Bible that can facilitate this dialogical approach, and which will serve as the basis for our exploration of the spirituality that Jesus taught his male disciples. These can be expressed two ways. The first is *Information, Transformation* and *Formation*. The other description is *Explication, Implication, Application*.

The first step (*Information* or *Explication*) is informative and explanatory in character. In this step, we approach the text as a book, containing certain information and knowledge that we seek. We get to know the Bible as a library of books, and we get to know how it is laid out. At this stage the critical and scholarly study of the Bible helps us to understand the background and cultural settings of the Bible, as well as the nuances of language and poetry in the original language as well as in its translations. Commentaries, Bible dictionaries, scholarly journals and books, lexicons, and other reference books are very helpful at this stage.

The second stage is transformative in character (*Transformation* or *Implication*). This is the stage in which we consider the implications of what we have read for our lives personally. This stage is much more prayerful, reflective and introspective. This is the stage in which we examine ourselves in the light of what we encounter in the Bible. We engage in dialogue with the text, asking it questions and allowing it to ask us questions. We can facilitate this process by posing questions to ourselves as if we were the text speaking to us. Or, putting it another way, as if Jesus were speaking to us through the text. It is helpful to creatively engage the imagination in this process. There is a form of reading the scriptures that was developed by St. Ignatius of Loyola that actively engages the imagination and the senses in reading. In effect, we place ourselves into the story by asking a series of questions such as "What do I see and hear? What do I smell, taste, or touch? Who are the characters and what's going on with them? If I were in this story what role would I play? If I were Jesus in this story, what would I be thinking, feeling, saying?" For instance, if we read the story about Jesus calming the storm, we can place ourselves in the story as the disciples fearfully crouching in the boat, or as Jesus being awakened, or even as a person on the shore who has just bid the disciples good-bye and is watching the storm come up. It is even possible to imagine that we are the boat carrying this fearful crew and observe the whole scene as a bystander. When the disciples cry out to Jesus, "Lord do you not care that we are perishing?" we can allow their voices to become our voices. As we move imaginatively into the text and become involved personally in its story, we can better allow the questions and teachings of Jesus to speak directly to us. In this way the story can begin to transform us, by confronting us and engaging us at the deepest part of our hearts and minds.

To become men after Jesus' heart means to sit as if in his circle, as his disciples, to hear his words and see his life, to watch his actions and to ask questions. It means to consider the implications of the answers we receive and then take these answers into our own hearts and lives. Ultimately, then, we will be sent out like his early disciples into the world as servants of its transformation.

The third stage in reading the Bible (*Formation* or *Application*), then, is formational as we commit to apply what we have learned to our lives. What practical changes are necessary in order to live according to the insights and instruction we have received in our transformational reading of the Bible? What changes in thinking are called for, and what changes in priorities and use of our time? What new attitudes or moral and ethical standards need to be implemented? What new associations and activities?

Structure of Subsequent Chapters

This threefold pattern of Explication, Implication and Application will serve as the basic structure for the following chapters as we examine the Gospel text for clues to the spirituality that Jesus taught the men who followed and dedicated their lives to him. In the first part of each chapter we will look closely at a specific part of the Gospel text, and consult scholarly research concerning that text. Then we will consider the implications of the text for our lives as men living in the context of our families, our work situations and our communities. Finally we will look at possible ways to apply these teachings and examples directly to our lives, especially in terms of the personal, interpersonal and social arenas in which our lives operate.

Bravery

This is not work for the faint-hearted or timid of character. It is difficult work to confront ourselves directly and deeply. It requires great moral and personal courage to look at our patterns of behavior and to assess honestly how they are wanting. It takes even greater courage to step out and go against the cultural flow in order to follow Jesus. His movement was counter-cultural then and it still is today. However, it leads ultimately to the greatest satisfaction of the human potential, and provides for the greatest fulfillment of the deepest desires of the human heart. To become a man committed to walking the Path of Jesus in the twenty-first century is the ultimate achievement for any man.

— 8 —

Jesus and His Male Disciples

THE CENTRAL IDEA OF this book is that Jesus taught and modeled for his male disciples a particular type of spirituality that addressed the specific exigencies of being men. Being men is not something that is a strict given, but is rather something built or constructed, like a house or a car or a well-tended garden. Only a small part of being men is actually biological, although there is evidence that the hormonal cocktail that imbues men with their maleness may cause men's thinking and behavioral patterns to develop in certain ways that are different from women's. Nonetheless, the quintessential feature of being human is our malleability, and any biologically-based gender differences are manifested as being different ways of being formed and shaped by culture and society.

In order to talk about the way Jesus endeavored to form his male disciples spiritually as *men*, it is first necessary to discuss how to tease out from the text of the Gospels any teaching that might be aimed specifically at men. To be sure, we do not have record of Jesus turning to his followers and saying anything like, "And now I will teach you men a spirituality designed specifically for you." Indeed, the large collections of his sayings and teachings such as the Sermon on the Mount in Matthew and the Sermon of the Plain in Luke are addressed to the large crowds of people who thronged about him, which included both men and women. So how does one discern any teachings directed specifically to men?

The first place to look is the context in which a particular teaching is found in the Gospel text. We will look for contexts in which something has happened to which Jesus makes a specific response. We will ask a basic set of questions: Do the actions of the disciples in this particular story make more sense for us to attribute them to men or to women? Do the teachings or response of Jesus make more sense if they were addressed to women or to men given their particular social setting and situations of the time? Do any teachings appear to address issues and concerns that are more easily or logically associated with men or with women?

In order to explore these questions, it will be necessary to identify the social contexts and the nature of the relationships between various classes and sets of persons within each section of the story. There is a technical term for these small sections of the story that I need to introduce here that will facilitate our study. The word is *pericope* (pronounced *per-i-ko-pee*), and it refers to any small section of a story or chapter that conveys a basic idea, thought or theme. For instance, a small group of sayings that are related could be considered a pericope. A parable told by Jesus could be considered a pericope. Or the parable plus the incident that gave occasion for the parable to be told can be one pericope. A specific incident, such as the feeding of the five thousand or the healing of someone can be a pericope. Obviously, the Bible is not formally broken up into pericopes. This is more an academic matter that assists those who study the Bible to speak about specific sections of the Bible. Since it will benefit our study of the Gospels, we will refer to these sections of Biblical material as pericopes.

One of the chief things we will look for when examining various pericopes for their potential articulation of a male spirituality will be whether issues of power and domination are addressed or involved. Just as in the world today, the Mediterranean world of Jesus' time was characterized by various hierarchies of privilege, status and power. These will be examined in greater detail in upcoming chapters, but it is sufficient here to identify these hierarchies as giving us a clue as to whether Jesus might be addressing his male disciples specifically or not. Of course, it will be necessary to place his disciples within their own particular hierarchies of the time.

Hierarchies of power are of significance to men because men tend to think in terms of rank, level of authority and power, and station in life. One only need to think of the military, or of political positions ranging from precinct committee chairs to president of the country, or of climbing the corporate ladder to see how this issue defines men's social interactions. Many scholars have pointed out that whereas men *tend* to think and relate in a hierarchical fashion in which power and final authority resides at the top and then flows down the pyramid, so to speak, women *tend* to think and relate in a more conciliar fashion in which relationships flow more horizontally, as if in a circle of participants. Naturally, this is a broad generalization to which individual exceptions can certainly be found, but the general pattern and tendency just described has been found to be a true depiction.

The social settings in which people are raised exert great influence in shaping the attitudes and behaviors of those people. When those social settings and their constitutive systems are set up so that entire groups of people are degraded or devalued and are considered expendable or commodities to be bought and sold, there are serious repercussions within the personal and interpersonal arenas we discussed in Chapter Three. The teachings and vision of the Bible from Moses through the prophets to Jesus and John the Baptist stand in stark contrast to societies structured around hierarchies of personal worth and expendability. These become men's issues when we examine the social systems to determine the place of men within these systems. This sort of social analysis will help us in discerning the specifically male issues Jesus addresses in his teachings and actions set in the context of the social order of his time.

This order was a basically a hierarchy of power, expressed politically, religiously and domestically. Politically, the emperor or king was at the pinnacle, with power flowing down to high elected officials and aristocracy (the so-called "plutocrats"), through the military as agents of enforcement of the government, tax collectors and other "civil servants," through landowners and merchants to the poor, the laborers and finally to slaves and children at the bottom. The place of women varied in this hierarchy, depending upon where they were socially and financially. Many women in the Greco-Roman culture of the time were skilled business people, and ran extensive trading operations, managed households, and so on. They did not have a place in the governmental hierarchy, but would have to influence policies indirectly, through conversations with men who were in positions of decision-making authority, such as their husbands or business contacts. A woman of rank, for example, could order a male slave or employee around, for example, but was still in a place of political dependence and deference to the men of her social rank. There were differences in social stratification according to whether one was a Roman citizen, of if one was a member of a subjugated people, such as the Jews, or Persians, or Egyptians or Phrygians, and so on.[1]

---

1. For an interesting glimpse into the wide variety of people who were under Roman rule, look at the list of groups named in the story of Pentecost in Acts 2:8–11.

Religiously, this stratification was expressed in varying ways, depending upon to which religious group one belonged. Many of the various Mediterranean religions had women in positions of authority, particularly serving as high priestesses in local temples. This was not true of Judaism, in the earliest forms of which, associated with Moses and the period of the wilderness wanderings, all official religious functions were performed by men. This is evident in the specific provisions in Exodus and Leviticus to the high priest and priests who serve in the temple being male, and from the tribe of Levi. Women were not allowed to offer sacrifices, nor to be within the part of the tabernacle or later temple in which the sacrifices were offered. It is instructive to note at this point that the word "hierarchy" actually means "rule of or by the priests."

At the time of Jesus, in the early first century, the exclusion of women from official religious functioning was even more pronounced. The temple at the time of Jesus even had a specific section just for women, the "Court of Women." The official scholars and interpreters of Jewish religious law, the scribes, were men, as were the rabbis and members of the Pharisees and Sadducees. The Jewish religion, in its public face, seems to have been the rather exclusive domain of men, at least in terms of authority and control of ritual as well as scriptural interpretation. This, of course, is the sphere in which the Gospels portray Jesus as having his ministry, or more to the point, this is the sphere with which Jesus' ministry came into conflict.

The final expression of hierarchy was in the domestic sphere, although this seems to have varied from culture to culture, and our dependence upon just a few references here and there hampers our ability to produce a fully accurate picture of domestic life in first century Palestine. For example, the Greek philosopher Demosthenes described the situation in Greek culture in the fourth century BCE as follows: "We have courtesans (*hetairai*) for our pleasure, prostitutes (that is, young female slaves) for daily physical use, wives to bring up legitimate children and to be faithful stewards in household matters."[2] Whether or not this described widespread practice within Greek society is not certain, and how long it persisted into the time of Jesus and his followers is likewise uncertain. In Roman society, which came into political prominence following the conquests of Julius Caesar in the middle of the first century BCE, women seemed to have had more rights, including the right to divorce

---

2. Demosthenes, *Neaream* 122: 655, quoted in Trull, "Is the Head of the House at Home?," para. 11.

and hold property. At the same time, in highly urbanized areas, such as Rome and other important cities such as Corinth and Ephesus, domestic roles tended to follow the models of the public power structures, so we can assume that even if women managed the household affairs, they were still subject to the authority of the men in the household, including their sons when they reached an age of decision-making authority.

Jewish practice seemed to have varied depending upon how influenced the household was by Greco-Roman culture, how urban or rural it was, and how connected it was to the religious authorities in Jerusalem and other communities. We know of some cultural practices, such as the prohibition of men speaking with women in public, of women's testimony counting as less than a man's, the right to write a certificate of divorce belonging to men only, and formal education being the privilege of boys and men, although this did not preclude informal and household-related education of girls and women from occurring. The fact that Mary sat at Jesus' feet and received his instruction, much to the frustration of Martha (who quite possibly might have wanted also to be sitting where Mary was!), indicates that the home could be the setting for women to receive education (Luke 10:38–41).

All of this is to indicate the various forms in which these hierarchies of power and domination were expressed. Jesus challenged these hierarchies of power by teaching and living a spirituality that turned the tables (literally at one point) on the various ways power was expressed and wielded by one group against another. Of particular interest to us is how he worked with his male disciples to change their view of who they were in relation to other men, and in relation to women.

At the base of all this lies a basic conviction I am working with throughout this book. Running through the Bible like a golden thread, and found pre-eminently in the life and teaching of Jesus, we can detect a recurring critique of societies based on stratified power and domination. This critique is sometimes explicit and at other times is implicit. In order to counter these systems of power and domination in their external social manifestations requires that persons confront the set of values, behaviors and ways of thinking that they have internalized as a result of living in their society. This becomes the spiritual quest, in which internal attitudes and ways of thinking and acting are taken on as tasks. These tasks are undertaken in order to overcome or transform the attitudes and ways of thinking and acting. Always paired with the internal work is a corresponding external task of reconfiguring social relationships at the local level, as well as at the larger level of the community, and eventually society. One thinks of the long process of banning slavery in North America and Europe to see how individual attitudes needed to be changed in order for there to be social support for broad sweeping political as well as economic and social changes to occur. And the fact that racial relations in the United States are still an explosive issue demonstrates how deep and pervasive are the attitudes and ways of relating and behaving that still need to be addressed.

A caveat is in order at this point. Jesus did not live and move as a social or political revolutionary. His ideas and behavior certainly overturned and shook up the mindset of his followers and disciples, and the social movement that arose in his wake changed the face of the Mediterranean world, and propelled significant changes in world history in the ensuing two millennia. But we will not find Jesus spelling out a well-articulated social or political theory, nor will we find specific guidelines about how to achieve social harmony and equity in human relationships. Indeed, even the idea of equity is a more modern concept, which arose after 1700 years of struggle and reflection in European culture upon basic ideas that Jesus taught and were preserved by the early Christian communities in the Bible. The centrality of the Bible and these teachings in European social thought provided the seedbed out of which arose ideas of democracy and equality that were ultimately rooted in notions of the equal worth of every individual. These notions were derived in turn from the Biblical convictions that all persons are children of one God, and that Jesus Christ was sent to the world out of God's great love for the whole of that world, not just certain classes within that world.

Jesus did not set out any sort of systematic teaching, nor did he elaborate formal doctrines or theological positions. What Jesus did was to teach situationally. He taught his disciples by how he interacted with people, which provided the situation for deeper teachings about God, and what it meant to live a God-infused life—a life after the Abba's heart, in other words. So it is, then, that as we read the Gospels in the Bible, we will read to determine the social settings in which Jesus speaks and acts. We will look to discern whether the context explicitly or implicitly relates to the social situation of men at that time. We will then reflect upon the implications these teachings have for our own time and social situations. And then we will consider various ways we can apply these teachings and life examples in our own daily lives. In the following chapters, we will look at several situations that provided these "teachable moments" for his disciples. But first, let's look at several occasions that demonstrate how Jesus turned the tables on these hierarchies of power, and how Jesus provided practical avenues for a new set of relationships to be experienced and lived by his followers. It is to these teachings that we turn at last.

— 9 —

Turning the Tables

IN 1978, I WENT to England for a semester of study abroad during my college years. While there, several of us took a tour to Stratford upon Avon where we toured various houses or points of interest concerned with Shakespeare or his time. At one house, set up to look like a house of Shakespeare's era, the tour guide explained to us the origins of various common expressions in English. One set of expressions had to do with the table at which the family ate and presumably did other things as well. For most people who had very little money, the table consisted simply of a board set up on some sort of supports. Chairs were a rarity, so usually the family stood around the board. If there was a chair, usually the father sat at it, as in a place of authority, and after a while the person seated in a place of authority came to be referred to as the "chairman of the board." Perhaps you have sung that grace, "Evening has come/the board is spread./Thanks be to God / who gives us bread"? The board being spread alludes to this earlier reference to a board. After several months of usage, the board would become quite dirty and full of crumbs, so the board would be turned over and the bottom side of the board would then become the top side, and was the preferred side until it, too, was dirty or cut-up. This gave rise to the expression of "the tables being turned," which came to refer to any reversal of fortune or circumstances.

The spirituality that Jesus demonstrates to his male disciples was a table-turning spirituality. It seems as though he was continually challenging the presumptions of the men who were his disciples concerning the order of things they took for granted, which might be construed as God's plan for things. The stories of the earliest contact between Jesus and his male disciples depict this propensity of Jesus to turn the tables and establish a new way of living, relating and thinking. In this chapter, we will look at two such "calling out" stories in which Jesus calls his disciples out of their accustomed vocations into a new and unknown way of being. In addition, we will look at another story in which Jesus "calls out" his disciples from an old hierarchical way of relating into a new way of thinking and relating that overturns and even reverses cultural hierarchies.

Explication

Leaving

The first thing that Jesus did with his male disciples, which is instructive for male spirituality, is that he got them to leave behind their familiar pattern of life. All four Gospels depict Jesus rounding up his male disciples by calling them *out* of their vocations and positions in life. Let's look at several of these stories.

> As Jesus was walking beside the Sea of Galilee, he saw two brothers, Simon called Peter and his brother Andrew. They were casting a net into the lake, for they were fishermen. "Come, follow me," Jesus said, "and I will make you fishers of men." At once they left their nets and followed him. Going on from there, he saw two other brothers, James son of Zebedee and his brother John. They were in a boat with their father Zebedee, preparing their nets. Jesus called them, and immediately they left the boat and their father and followed him (Matthew 4:18–22, NIV).

> As Jesus walked beside the Sea of Galilee, he saw Simon and his brother Andrew casting a net into the lake, for they were fishermen. "Come, follow me," Jesus said, "and I will make you fishers of men." At once they left their nets and followed him. When he had gone a little farther, he saw James son of Zebedee and his brother John in a boat, preparing their nets. Without delay he called them, and they left their father Zebedee in the boat with the hired men and followed him (Mark 1:16–20 NIV).

> One day as Jesus was standing by the Lake of Gennesaret, with the people crowding around him and listening to the word of God, he saw at the water's edge two boats, left there by the fishermen, who were washing their nets. He got into one of the boats, the one belonging to Simon, and asked him to put out a little from shore. Then he sat down and taught the people from the

boat. When he had finished speaking, he said to Simon, "Put out into deep water, and let down the nets for a catch." Simon answered, "Master, we've worked hard all night and haven't caught anything. But because you say so, I will let down the nets." When they had done so, they caught such a large number of fish that their nets began to break. So they signaled their partners in the other boat to come and help them, and they came and filled both boats so full that they began to sink. When Simon Peter saw this, he fell at Jesus' knees and said, "Go away from me, Lord; I am a sinful man!" For he and all his companions were astonished at the catch of fish they had taken, and so were James and John, the sons of Zebedee, Simon's partners. Then Jesus said to Simon, "Don't be afraid; from now on you will catch men." So they pulled their boats up on shore, left everything and followed him (Luke 5:1–11 NIV).

These three stories represent various tellings of the same basic event: the call of Peter, Andrew, James and John. All four were fishermen, up in the Sea of Galilee, which was also known as Gennesaret. In order to understand the significance of what Jesus was asking of these four men, it is helpful to understand something of what was happening with the fishing economy of Galilee.

The fishing economy around the entire Mediterranean during the time of Jesus was literally booming. Methods had been developed for preserving fish, which made it possible to transport fish across the Roman Empire. Fish was particularly prized among the rich in Rome, and fish from as far away as Galilee could be found on the tables of Roman citizens, particularly those rich enough to pay for it.

A complex economy arose along the shores of the Sea of Galilee as a result. The fishing economy was strictly controlled, with entire families receiving fishing rights from the Roman authorities, paying taxes and tolls on fish that were caught and sold, and strictly watched to be sure that only those authorized by the Roman authorities were allowed to fish.[1] Scholars have pointed out that the entire economic structure of the Greco-Roman world was designed to enrich the aristocratic elite, especially through the imposition of various taxes and polls. People did not simply choose an occupation in the manner in which we are able to today. Rather, one had to secure permission and licensing from the Roman authorities, pay fees, and be subject to inspections by those authorities.

---

1. For a thorough discussion of the Galilean fishing economy, see K. C. Hanson, "The Galilean Fishing Economy and the Jesus Tradition," 99–111.

Those same authorities also regulated who could engage in purchasing and trading items produced or harvested by others.

To step outside of this complex system of economic and political relationships was to place oneself in a highly risky and tenuous position. Not only did a person surrender their livelihood, but they also set aside their status and place within the society. A person's identity was determined to a great extent by their place in the social economy of their time and location. What Jesus asks of Peter, Andrew, James and John is not simply to change jobs as we might view it today. He was in fact telling them to undergo a radical revision of who they were as men. Their identity and self-understanding would change. And since that identity was embedded in the network of relationships of which they were a part, to be removed from that network placed them in what sociologists refer to as a "liminal state."

A liminal state is a state of being in which one is neither here nor there, as it were, but somewhere in between. "Limen" is the Latin word for threshold, so a liminal state is one in which one is on the threshold between an old way of being and a new way of being. In religious traditions around the world, liminal states are highly significant times of spiritual transformation and religious experience. They also signify a change in one's status within a community, a change of identity, and a consequent change in the way in which one related to others in that community. This is precisely what Jesus was enacting in the lives of his male disciples. By calling them out of their fishing boats, he was inviting them to cross a threshold from their accustomed way of life, their familiar set of relationships and attitudes, even their previous understandings of God, and enter into a new land, a new territory, a new realm of being. This new realm he called the Kingdom of Heaven.

Riff Raff

> As Jesus went on from there, he saw a man named Matthew sitting at the tax collector's booth. "Follow me," he told him, and Matthew got up and followed him. While Jesus was having dinner at Matthew's house, many tax collectors and "sinners" came and ate with him and his disciples. When the Pharisees saw this, they asked his disciples, "Why does your teacher eat with tax collectors and 'sinners'?" On hearing this, Jesus said, "It is not the healthy who need a doctor, but the sick. But go and learn

what this means: 'I desire mercy, not sacrifice.' For I have not come to call the righteous, but sinners" (Matthew 9:9–13 NIV).

If fishermen were near the bottom of Galilean society, their occupation was at least considered to be honest and respectable. Such was not the case with Matthew. Matthew was one of the tax collectors located in Capernaum, the person who collected the taxes and polls placed upon the livelihood of men like Peter, Andrew, James and John. Matthew was Jewish, but his place in the network of social relationships in Galilee was basically as a collaborator with the Romans. In order to maintain economic and political control throughout the empire, the Romans contracted out with local members of the subjugated peoples to carry out the menial tasks of minor administration and collection of all the various fees and taxes. Such tax collectors also oversaw the granting and payment of leases for the right to fish, or to transport the fish, or to process the fish in various ways. Each of these activities was regulated by Rome, as were other trades and aspects of trade and commerce. K.C. Hanson puts it bluntly:

> Galilee of the first century was ruled by Herod Antipas, a Roman client, and was therefore a form of what Kautsky calls an "aristocratic empire." Furthermore, it was an "advanced agrarian society" in terms of its form of production and technology. I mention here a few of the basic characteristics of political economies and infrastructures of such societies:
>
> 1. The primary functions exercised by aristocratic families are *tax-collection and warfare*: both of these functions serve the urban elites' interests.
>
> 2. While the small number of elites compete for honor and the right to control and tax peasant families, peasant families remain at *subsistence level*, reinforced by a sense of "natural" hierarchy.
>
> 3. These empires are *"exploitative"* in that peasants have no say in their control or taxation; and while the peasants are cognizant of their place in the rather rigid social hierarchy, they develop strategies to evade control through a variety of means (e.g., lying, hiding, protest).
>
> 4. Since much of the peasant families' produce (the so-called "surplus") is extracted by the aristocratic families in the form of labor, produce, and money (through the instruments of tithes, taxes, tolls, rents, tribute, and confiscation), *technological progress* is impeded, minimizing change; the

> exception to this is the technology of warfare, since it is subsidized by the aristocratic families to protect their power, privilege, and possessions.[2]

From this description, it becomes apparent as to why Jesus' call of Matthew posed such a scandal and raised so many objections. But the call of Matthew also represents a calling out from the political and economic relationships that defined the lives of the male disciples. Matthew would have benefited financially from the labor of men such as Peter, Andrew, James and John. Quite possibly there was antagonism between these men. In the liminal state of life as a disciple of Jesus, then, these men would find their lives redefined, their relationships revised, and their loyalties and hostilities rearranged, if not released.

Overturned Hierarchies

This change in political and economically-defined relationships is reflected in the controversies about status among the male disciples. Consider, for example, the following stories:

> Also, a dispute arose among them as to which of them was considered to be greatest. Jesus said to them, "The kings of the Gentiles lord it over them; and those who exercise authority over them call themselves Benefactors. But you are not to be like that. Instead, the greatest among you should be like the youngest, and the one who rules like the one who serves. For who is greater, the one who is at the table or the one who serves? Is it not the one who is at the table? But I am among you as one who serves (Luke 22:24–27 NIV).

> Then James and John, the sons of Zebedee, came to him. "Teacher," they said, "we want you to do for us whatever we ask."
> "What do you want me to do for you?" he asked.
> They replied, "Let one of us sit at your right and the other at your left in your glory."
> "You don't know what you are asking," Jesus said. "Can you drink the cup I drink or be baptized with the baptism I am baptized with?"
> "We can," they answered. Jesus said to them, "You will drink the cup I drink and be baptized with the baptism I am baptized

---

2. Hanson, "The Galilean Fishing Economy and the Jesus Tradition," 100. See also Kautsky, *The Politics of Aristocratic Empires*, and Lenski, *Power and Privilege*.

with, but to sit at my right or left is not for me to grant. These places belong to those for whom they have been prepared."

When the ten heard about this, they became indignant with James and John. Jesus called them together and said, "You know that those who are regarded as rulers of the Gentiles lord it over them, and their high officials exercise authority over them. Not so with you. Instead, whoever wants to become great among you must be your servant, and whoever wants to be first must be slave of all. For even the Son of Man did not come to be served, but to serve, and to give his life as a ransom for many" (Mark 10:35-45 NIV).

Then the mother of Zebedee's sons came to Jesus with her sons and, kneeling down, asked a favor of him.
"What is it you want?" he asked.
She said, "Grant that one of these two sons of mine may sit at your right and the other at your left in your kingdom."
"You don't know what you are asking," Jesus said to them. "Can you drink the cup I am going to drink?"
"We can," they answered.
Jesus said to them, "You will indeed drink from my cup, but to sit at my right or left is not for me to grant. These places belong to those for whom they have been prepared by my Father."
When the ten heard about this, they were indignant with the two brothers. Jesus called them together and said, "You know that the rulers of the Gentiles lord it over them, and their high officials exercise authority over them. Not so with you. Instead, whoever wants to become great among you must be your servant, and whoever wants to be first must be your slave—just as the Son of Man did not come to be served, but to serve, and to give his life as a ransom for many" (Matthew 20:20-28 NIV).

These three stories, probably all variants of the same incident, are packed with meaning for a male spirituality after the heart of Jesus. They are particularly illustrative of Jesus' heart because he specifically identifies what he understands his life-mission to be: to serve and to give his life as a ransom. To *serve* and to *give*. In a nutshell this describes the spirituality of Jesus. But Jesus describes it himself in direct contrast to the lines of power, privilege, domination and control as found in the world.

In the original Greek, the words Jesus uses are *katakyrieuousin* ("to act as lord over" or "to lord it over") and *katexousiazousin* ("to exercise power or authority over"). Now, the definitions I have just given make reference to power over. But the force of the Greek *kata* is actually more like "down upon." So the grammatical force of the Greek is much more in terms of someone who is over someone else, pressing down upon them, exerting or asserting force downward upon them. Indeed, Werner Foerster in his discussion of *katakyrieuousin* in *the Theological Dictionary of the New Testament* says, ". . . the word means the exercise of dominion against someone, i.e., to one's own advantage," and regarding *katexousiazousin*: ". . . the word implies the tendency towards compulsion or oppression which is immanent in all earthly power, and not merely in political."[3]

Jesus is engaging in a thorough critique and rejection of how power is used in human affairs to control, dominate and oppress other people. It is not just referring to the control one would have if one happened to be in a position of political authority or power. Few, if any, of his disciples would have ever had that opportunity to power, with the possible exception of Matthew, whose authority was merely derivative from being a hireling of the Roman empire. What Jesus does is basically to say this: "You are familiar with how political power is wielded in our world. You have experienced it used against you. You have seen how it oppresses and hurts and destroys. That is the opposite of what I am about. The power you have experienced presses people down. I have come to raise them up. The power you have experienced captures and enslaves people. I have come to ransom and set people free. The power you have experienced has been used by those in power for their own personal benefit. I have come that others may benefit from me."

Implications

Giving and serving are not concepts foreign to men. The participation of many men in the military is evidence of the willingness of men to give their lives to a cause. After all, it is not called "military *service*" for nothing. Volunteer fire departments all across the country and world are staffed by men who willingly leave the comfort and safety of work and home in order to confront the danger and threat out-of-control fires present to their communities. What Jesus does is to focus upon this impulse and raise it to a guiding theme for his followers.

This impacts men in specific ways. Instead of asking, "How will this action get me ahead in the world or raise me up a notch," we ask

---

3. Foerster, κατεακυριευω in *TDNT* 3:1098 and κατεξουσιαζω in same, 2:575.

ourselves, "How does this action serve others and help them get ahead, raise them up a notch, or provide for their welfare?" In the sphere of politics consider how the tone might instantly change from the triumphalist, no-holds-barred, winner-take-all, battle-front atmosphere of national politics to one that is based upon serious consideration of how to serve the lowest economic sectors of society. Or consider how differently business might be done if the bottom line of a company was not amassing profits for shareholders and exorbitant salaries for upper echelon executives, but how profits might be used not only to develop new products that actually served the needs of persons, but also were used to provide needed services to under-privileged communities?

Of course, stating it in this fashion immediately raises objections to the "pie-in-the-sky idealism" of all of this. That is precisely the point. What Jesus expected of these male followers was a radical and definitive break from "business as usual," in fact, from life as usual. The fact that Jesus chose people from different social and economic strata of society, brought them all together, and then expected them not only to get along but to act in ways that are not only completely different but also opposite from their conventional assumptions indicates the nature of his spiritual enterprise.

As each disciple left their accustomed life situation and gathered around Jesus, this new liminal state left the threads of hierarchy, power and domination unstitched and free. Whenever the old ways of knitting relationships showed up, he promptly unraveled the presumptions and taught a new set of knots. At one point he says, "No one sews a patch of unshrunk cloth on an old garment. If he does, the new piece will pull away from the old, making the tear worse. And no one pours new wine into old wineskins. If he does, the wine will burst the skins, and both the wine and the wineskins will be ruined. No, he pours new wine into new wineskins" (Mark 2: 21–22 NIV). What Jesus was doing was to weave a new way of being, and a new community out of entirely new cloth.

Significantly, Jesus did not set up a new hierarchy. Even when he says, "the last shall be first and the first last," this is qualified by his saying, "you shall not lord it over others." The idea of "being on top" is replaced with the ideal of serving others and contributing to their welfare. When the enculturated impulse to elevate oneself is replaced with the impulse to serve the needs of others, not as an imposition of a new hierarchy but as a freely chosen way of relating and being, a new form of freedom is at work. This freedom requires an act of will, and a conscious rearrangement of priorities, expectations and relationships.

In order to make this effective, however, requires living in community. The changes Jesus enacted were not done in isolation from a lived community. As discussed earlier, one of the spiritual practices Jesus engaged in was the formation of a new form of community. In this new community, his followers were to establish new ways of relating. Rank had no place. Economic privilege had no place. Jesus spoke with women in public, and welcomed them as disciples. Luke even indicates that several women followed Jesus and provided for him and the entire group of disciples—women and men—"out of their own means" (Luke 8:3 NIV).

As we endeavor to become men after Jesus' heart, we need to seek out the support of other men who are dedicated to this same path. It is not enough to gather with other men who are well ensconced in the hierarchies and ways of relating of our society. Instead, it will be necessary to gather with men—and women—who are dedicated to this new way of being in Jesus.

Application

Survey of Rank

The first thing to do in order to move into this new way of being is to recognize and identify the various forms of hierarchy that we each experience and in which we participate. In order to do this, we will engage in an exercise called a "Survey of Rank." Take the Life Map you started in Chapter 3 and in the Social arena, place your name in the middle of each of the life sequence boxes. List those who were "above" you in terms of having authority or responsibility over you. For example, our parents exert authority over us in the early years of our lives, but as we move through adulthood, that relationship becomes more equal, and even may shift in later years. List those who are under you. For example, in younger years, when we have little opportunity to exercise any form of power, we may have younger siblings that we have to look after or even be in charge of when our parents are absent. Perhaps this was a responsibility thrust upon us by the death of a parent or by having parents who were unable to offer us appropriate parenting, whether because of illness, work schedules, mental incapacity, or drug or alcohol addiction. Perhaps we were younger, but because we were male, assumed responsibilities and decision-making authority over our older sisters because this was the practice in our family or culture. Whatever the reasons and situations, label and diagram these rankings of authority and responsibility. They need not be considered to all be negative. Some hierarchies are highly effective ways to order families, groups and societies. What is important to recognize these rankings and to name them.

After you have made a list—and keep adding to this list as you become aware of more rankings—draw a line from each name or figure down to the Personal Arena and indicate not only the quality of that relationship, but some of the attitudes that you developed towards those persons, and towards that relationship. Did you resent being answerable to someone else, or did you resent being in charge? Did you come to think of everybody in the social class as being above you or below you? Did you bristle at the unfairness of these relationships, or did you experience joy or a sense of power in them? Take note of these relationships, your attitudes and arguments or justifications for each of them.

Again, it is not necessary to consider all such rankings as negative. Indeed, many are not. Parents must exercise authority. Teachers exercise authority in order to instruct students. Jesus even accepted the title "rabbi," even though he was never formally trained in any rabbinical school. However, he assumed the authority that his followers conferred upon him, because, as one of them said, "You have the words of life." This issue with hierarchies and rankings is how they are used, or abused, and how power is wielded. Who benefits from the ranking? In many situations, the highest ranked person is responsible for the care and welfare of the whole community, and does not gain financially or personally from that position. What is important in this exercise, then, is simply to acknowledge how these hierarchies impact our lives and the lives of those around us. Only then can we begin to carefully discern which tables need to be turned, and which should remain upright.

— 10 —

Son of Magnificat

Explication

A Mother's Touch

There is a saying that "the hand that rocks the cradle can topple empires." While this may not be literally true, it expresses a more cogent truth: the incredible influence of mothers upon their children. From conception on, a bond develops between a mother and her child that is deep beyond description and measuring. This bond is so profound that the Bible makes reference to it when describing God's love for humankind: "Can a mother forget the baby at her breast and have no compassion on the child she has borne? Though she may forget, I will not forget you!" (Isaiah 49:15 NIV). Think of who it was that spoke to you daily, calling you by name, soothing your hurts and pains, ministering to your injuries, guiding your footsteps, correcting your mistakes, setting the limits upon your play, teaching you to speak, punishing your misdeeds, encouraging your exploration, feeding you, bathing you, wrapping you in clothes, supervising your play, appraising your friends and so on. The chances are that it was your mother. Even if you had a very involved father, if your mother was still in your life, she was probably the primary influence upon your early development as a child. This is the case across virtually every human culture studied by scholars and visited by travelers. Children learn to see the world initially through their mother's eyes.

Explication

If it is true that mothers exert significant influence upon the early development of a boy's spirituality, then what might we learn about the beginnings of Jesus' spirituality that his mother might have nurtured? Of course we have very little in the way of actual recorded history of Jesus' early life apart from the stories surrounding his birth, which are found only in Matthew and Luke, and even these differ from one another due to the differing perspectives from which the Evangelists are writing. Of these, Luke gives us the most in-depth glimpse into the hopes, dreams, thoughts and commitments of Mary, the mother of Jesus. We can discern at least two main commitments that Mary has in the text: saying "yes" to God, and, growing out of that, realizing that God's intention for human society is radically different from the way human societies are usually structured. Let's look at how this is expressed in Luke.

> In the sixth month, God sent the angel Gabriel to Nazareth, a town in Galilee, to a virgin pledged to be married to a man named Joseph, a descendant of David. The virgin's name was Mary. The angel went to her and said, "Greetings, you who are highly favored! The Lord is with you."
>
> Mary was greatly troubled at his words and wondered what kind of greeting this might be. But the angel said to her, "Do not be afraid, Mary, you have found favor with God. You will be with child and give birth to a son, and you are to give him the name Jesus. He will be great and will be called the Son of the Most High. The Lord God will give him the throne of his father David, and he will reign over the house of Jacob forever; his kingdom will never end."
>
> "How will this be," Mary asked the angel, "since I am a virgin?"
>
> The angel answered, "The Holy Spirit will come upon you, and the power of the Most High will overshadow you. So the holy one to be born will be called the Son of God. Even Elizabeth your relative is going to have a child in her old age, and she who was said to be barren is in her sixth month. For nothing is impossible with God."
>
> "I am the Lord's servant," Mary answered. "May it be to me as you have said." Then the angel left her. (Luke 1:26–38 NIV)

Mary says, "Yes" to God. Of course, she has questions about what the angelic messenger is saying, but they serve to clarify how it is all to come about. She is a virgin, after all, so she needs some clarification about the agency of her conception. It is analogous to being told to go get groceries at the store, and then asking how it will be paid for. But once it is explained to her, she willingly signs on to the program. That she acts of her own free will in consenting to this cannot be overemphasized. Mary is not a puppet. She possesses freewill as does every human being, and she is free to choose, free to say "yes" or "no." It is in this freedom to choose, to align oneself with this or that program, to act according to this or that design, to throw one's lot in with this or that cause or group or way of life that spirituality is even possible. Simply put, without freewill choice, there is no possibility for spiritual growth or development, no possibility for testing or being tested, for failure or success, for learning or forgetting. This is the first principle of all Christian spirituality.

Mary says "Yes" to God. She agrees to sign on with God's program for human affairs. She essentially enters into a partnership with God by allowing God's Son to be conceived within her. This illustrates the second principle of Christian spirituality: partnership with God. From the moment of the first breath God breathes into humankind, humans embody the divine-human dance of relationship. Humanity can choose to ignore or even rebel against the leading of God, a fact that is reflected throughout the Bible. In spite of all this, the Divine Presence is ever-present.

Spirituality is about choice, and it is about the possibility of partnering with God to be the agents of God's work in the world. Thus, it is also about relationship. Freedom and relationship. The Spirituality of Jesus, based in free-choice partnership, forms the basis and model for all human relationships, and for men seeking to walk the Path of Jesus, it stands as the axial core around which all other considerations revolve. These two basic principles of freedom and partnership reverberate continually throughout this discussion of a male spirituality rooted in Jesus Christ. They define a major spiritual task for men in any relationship: to support and enable, if necessary, the exercise of freedom of the other person, indeed, of all persons.

This task is reflected in what Mary proclaims to be God's basic mission in the world: to humble the high and mighty and to exalt those who are put down, pushed down and pushed around. Just as in a musical play, where the plot is spotlighted in a song, so Mary bursts into song about what it means to say "yes" to partnership with God:

> My soul glorifies (or: magnifies) the Lord
> and my spirit rejoices in God my Savior,
> for he has been mindful
> of the humble state of his servant.
> From now on all generations will call me blessed,
> for the Mighty One has done great things for me—
> holy is his name.
> His mercy extends to those who fear him,
> from generation to generation.
> He has performed mighty deeds with his arm;
> he has scattered those who are proud in their inmost thoughts.
> He has brought down rulers from their thrones
> but has lifted up the humble.
> He has filled the hungry with good things
> but has sent the rich away empty.
> He has helped his servant Israel,
> remembering to be merciful
> to Abraham and his descendants forever,
> even as he said to our fathers." (Luke 1:46–55 NIV)

This magnificent song of Mary's is called the Magnificat after the first word in the Latin version of the Bible, which was the official version for centuries. Notice carefully how Mary describes God's program that she has signed onto. Mary first proclaims that God is conscious of her humble state. The Greek word in the original is *tapeinos* and refers to one's social status or position. James uses it when he says "the brother in humble circumstances may well be proud that God lifts him up; and the wealthy brother must find his pride in being brought low" (James 1:9–10 NEB). Echoes of the Magnificat! But if it is true that according to Christian tradition and the book of Acts that James is the brother of Jesus, then he was immersed in the Magnificat faith of his mother Mary from early on, which is reflected in his concerns for equal treatment of all persons regardless of social status or economic advantage or disadvantage (see James 2:1–13).

God is concerned about the social conditions of all persons, and how it is that human beings relate to one another and treat one another. This is affirmed for Israel in the teachings of Moses when he reveals to them God's nature and character: "For the Lord your God is God of gods and Lord of lords, the great God, mighty and awesome, who shows no partiality and accepts no bribes. He defends the cause of the fatherless and the widow, and loves the alien, giving him food and clothing" (Deuteronomy 10:17–18 NIV).

This same God, whose name is holy, knows the true order of things, in contrast to the proud, whose pretensions of status, privilege and power are simply constructions of their imaginations. This shows that, to God, social hierarchies are simply human inventions, but not the reflection of a Divine plan at all. Just because those who wield power over others claim that it is the "order of things," does not mean that it is God's order. Those in power always try to remain in power, and will interpret the course of events in order to justify their hold on power. It is a fact of human existence reflected in all the official histories of human empires and is repeated over and over again in the Bible.

But the Magnificat of Mary reveals God's plan in contrast: to put down the mighty from their thrones, to exalt those of low status, to feed those who are hungry, and those who are wealthy are sent away. Contrast these priorities of God with the priorities of contemporary society (which aren't really all that much different from the societies of the Roman empire of Jesus' time). Essentially, then, God's intention is to overturn patterns of social interaction that favor the few at the expense of others. God is not opposed to wealth *per se*, but rather God is opposed to how the concentration of wealth in the hands of a few serves to oppress other people, and how that concentration of wealth is viewed by them to be justification for or proof of their special status: "He has scattered the proud in the imagination of their hearts" (Luke 1:51b RSV).

Implications

The practical concerns that arise out of these priorities of God have direct bearing upon being a man after Jesus' heart. Namely, that if God is aware of the oppressiveness of human social and economic divisions, we need to be so mindful as well. If God is opposed to oppressive social and economic divisions, we need to be as well. If God's intention is to overturn and upset those oppressions and divisions, then that needs to be our intention as well. And if God sets out to change those oppressive divisions, then we should not stand in the way, but join in with God's program in whatever ways we can whenever we can.

This requires that men take careful stock of the nature of their relations with other persons in every aspect of their lives. If saying "yes" to God means aligning oneself with God's view of and intention for things, and if saying "yes" means entering into partnership with God, and if that partnership is founded upon the possibility and the practice of freedom, then the respect for every human being's freedom and its protection and even defense is of paramount concern for men. This also means to be ever vigilant for those who will try to co-opt the cause of freedom for their own political, personal or financial ends. In God's economy, no one's freedom is sacrificed for the private gain of another. Nor does the realignment of power relationships witnessed to by Mary in the Magnificat contradict human freedom. The exercise of human freedom is not an absolute end in itself. Its exercise always has a particular directionality to it, outward in relation to others. It can either be manifested in ways that build up others, promote their welfare, expand their spiritual awareness, and encourage the achievement of their God-given potential or it does the opposite, either directly or indirectly by indifference.

Applications

This is the situation of a male spirituality in the world today, just as it was in the time of Jesus. This is also the starting point for every man to examine in his own life. Where do I stand in my commitment to God? But more specifically, have I inclined my heart after Jesus' heart, have I aligned my priorities with His priorities? Have I said "Yes" to the God to whom Mary said "Yes," and have I made the Magnificat the theme song of my life? Am I, like Jesus, a Son of Magnificat?

The spiritual practices that arise out of the teachings of the Magnificat include social analysis, personal reflection and personal stock-taking. Social analysis in a spiritual mode is similar to the admonitions of John the Baptist when he addressed the cross-section of the populace that sought him out along the Jordan River.

> John said to the crowds coming out to be baptized by him, "You brood of vipers! Who warned you to flee from the coming wrath? Produce fruit in keeping with repentance. And do not begin to say to yourselves, 'We have Abraham as our father.' For I tell you that out of these stones God can raise up children for Abraham. The ax is already at the root of the trees, and every tree that does not produce good fruit will be cut down and thrown into the fire."
>
> "What should we do then?" the crowd asked.

> John answered, "The man with two tunics should share with him who has none, and the one who has food should do the same."
>
> Tax collectors also came to be baptized. "Teacher," they asked, "what should we do?"
>
> "Don't collect any more than you are required to," he told them. Then some soldiers asked him, "And what should we do?"
>
> He replied, "Don't extort money and don't accuse people falsely—be content with your pay." (Luke 3:7–14 NIV)

His admonitions may not seem terribly radical to us today, but they struck at the heart of the social inequities of the time. We will examine these further in the chapters that follow. But it is not enough simply to do social analysis. The work of spiritual transformation requires that we engage in those practices that will help us re-pattern our ways of thinking, change our attitudes, alter our values and reform our behaviors. This is what John is referring to when he talks about bearing "fruit in keeping with repentance." Of course, these practices operate in the personal, inter-personal and social arenas. In order to begin this process, the spiritual practice for this chapter is the Social Situation Inventory.

Every person is embedded in a particular constellation of relationships and social situations such as gender, ethnicity, economic class, education, employment or unemployment, leisure activities and so on. Usually we are quite unconscious of all these factors and how they influence our lives, attitudes, commitments and behaviors. The practice of doing a Social Situation Inventory serves to name and bring into consciousness all the forces, places, persons and experiences that have shaped the persons we are.

Personal Inventory

We will begin with a Social Situation Inventory at the Personal level. On a piece of paper, or two or three, make a list that includes at least the following items. Leave space after each item is listed. Go back after making the list and then fill in as much detail about the relationships, situations or experiences in your life that fit into each category. The items on your list should include, but are not limited to, the following:

- Your gender
- Your race/ethnicity

- Where you grew up
- Where your home was located in the town(s) in which you grew up
- Median income of that neighborhood (estimate)
- Where you live now (town/city as well as location in that town or city)
- Median income of that neighborhood (estimate)
- Your job
- Your income
- Where you went to school
- Did you attend college or vocational school? Where?
- Have you ever been jobless?
- Have you ever been homeless?
- Have you served in the military?
- Who would you place in your close circle of friends?
- Who are less close or merely acquaintances?
- In what sports or other recreational activities do you engage?
- What TV programs and movies do you watch?
- Where do you shop most frequently?

All these things say something about what has formed you and what has instilled in you the values, beliefs and life commitments you have. They also can give an indication of your social mobility. Many other things can be added to this list, and you are free to add your own items. The purpose of making such a list is to begin to acknowledge and recognize where it is that you fit in the "grand scheme of things."

Interpersonal Inventory

The next step is to extend the inventory into the interpersonal arena. For this you list your family members, your friends, co-workers and other significant relationships in your life. Next to each name, describe the nature and quality of your relationship with each of them. Use descriptive words, or perhaps use a color-coding system of your own devising.

Next to these descriptions, describe the nature and dynamics of power and authority between you and them. Do you supervise them, or they you? Are you an older or younger sibling? Is your relationship characterized by competition, sharing of tasks or activities, or general camaraderie?

In the next column describe the style of communication you have with each person. Would you characterize it as loving and supportive? Loving and parental? Joking and humorous? Confrontational? Competitive? Professional? Compassionate? Manipulative? Do you try to avoid that person? Describe the communication in any manner that seems true.

Social Inventory

The final step requires a large piece of paper, the size of a piece of newsprint or several feet of butcher-style paper. Lay the paper out. Draw a very small circle somewhere near the middle of the paper. Have that circle represent you. Then arrange everything you listed in the personal and inter-personal inventories in order of closeness and influence to you. Draw lines between you and the items and people listed. The lines can be color-coded or coded in whatever way speaks to you. On those lines write the descriptive comments about the relationship of that person or situation to you. What are your feelings about that relationship? What do you owe to that relationship? What did you gain or lose? What was the most influential part of that relationship? What would you like to change, if you could, about that relationship?

What will emerge is a schematic diagram, as it were, of who you are and where you are in the world, that is, what your social situation is. You will also begin to chart out all the forces that have shaped and continue to shape your life, your attitudes, your values and your behavior. But these factors merely shape and influence—they do not determine these things. Only you in your conscious, willful choices fully determine how you are as a person in the world. The purpose of diagramming your social situation is to graphically bring to the fore everything that will be addressed in the process of spiritual transformation. Each line you trace on the paper represents in turn the trace left upon your consciousness by that person or situation. Some of the traces feel more like scars from wounds, others may feel like gentle caresses or kisses.

After you have completed the inventories and diagram, place them on the floor or on a tabletop. They represent you in the world. Pray over them. Offer them to God for the Spirit's blessing. If anything has arisen in this process that you are ashamed of or sorry for, prayerfully consider what you might do to make amends or to change. If there are things for which you are grateful, persons who have made your life better or blessed, think of some way to acknowledge them or express your gratitude.

Lift everything in this process up to God. God is a God of transformation and blessing. The Psalmist reminds us that God forgives our iniquities, heals our diseases, redeems our lives and crowns us with steadfast love and mercy. God knows our frame and remembers that we are dust. We flourish like a flower and then the wind passes over us and we are gone. As far as the east is from the west, so far does God remove our sins and iniquities from us (Psalm 103).

God wants us to be transformed from all that the world has made us and marred us to be into what God knows we can be. So it is that as we set out to become men after Jesus' heart, we will find that God's Spirit is with us in the process, leveraging our every attempt toward change. Every movement toward healing of our memories and past experiences is salved by the balm of grace. God wants us to be whole persons. So, treat yourself as God wishes you to be treated: as another precious son.

— 11 —

Sorting Things Out
Tempting Jesus

OVER THE YEARS AS I have served various churches, I have had several occasions to move from one city to another. This has meant packing up all the household goods, loading them on a truck, driving to the new place, unloading and unpacking. An inevitable and helpful component of that process is sorting through the accumulation of the previous few years to find what is still useful and needed, and what can be disposed of. Far too often, however, things just get tossed in a box, and then everything is moved from one place to the next, the useful along with the no-longer-useful.

I find that I go through a lot of life that same way, still carrying around with me things from my past that are no longer serving me well: attitudes from the past, old hurts and grudges, behaviors I learned growing up or from my socialization, ideas and thoughts from things I've read or conversations I've had. What I need to do is to engage in a little internal housecleaning. I don't need to have a mental garage sale. The things that don't serve me well will not serve anyone else well either. I just need to do a dump run.

It is good for the soul and mental health to take stock of the things in our life from time to time. This is especially true when we set out on a new venture in life, or a new relationship, or at any point in which things just seem stuck. The stories in the Gospels telling how Jesus begins his ministry are instructive in this regard. In the first three Gospels (the "Synoptic" Gospels), Jesus is baptized in the River Jordan by John, and then goes to the wilderness for a period of prayer and fasting. During that time he sorted through the things in his life, choosing the things that would serve him well in his ministry and discarding the deterrents, detriments and detritus. This process of sorting is depicted symbolically and dramatically in the stories of being tempted by the devil.

Explication: Temptation

That Jesus is a Son of Mary's Magnificat is shown in the sermon he gives in Nazareth to inaugurate his ministry, which we will examine in the next chapter. Luke portrays this address as following upon a time in which Jesus spent forty days fasting and praying in the desert around Palestine. During this time the scriptures say he "was tempted by the devil." It is instructive to see what Jesus said "No" to before we look at what he said "Yes" to.

> Jesus, full of the Holy Spirit, returned from the Jordan and was led by the Spirit in the desert, where for forty days he was tempted by the devil. He ate nothing during those days, and at the end of them he was hungry.
> The devil said to him, "If you are the Son of God, tell this stone to become bread."
> Jesus answered, "It is written: 'Man does not live on bread alone.'"
> The devil led him up to a high place and showed him in an instant all the kingdoms of the world. And he said to him, "I will give you all their authority and splendor, for it has been given to me, and I can give it to anyone I want to. So if you worship me, it will all be yours."
> Jesus answered, "It is written: 'Worship the Lord your God and serve him only.'"
> The devil led him to Jerusalem and had him stand on the highest point of the temple. "If you are the Son of God," he said, "throw yourself down from here. For it is written:
> 'He will command his angels concerning you
> to guard you carefully;
> they will lift you up in their hands,
> so that you will not strike your foot against a stone.'"
> Jesus answered, "It says: 'Do not put the Lord your God to the test.'"
> When the devil had finished all this tempting, he left him until an opportune time. (Luke 4:1-13 NIV. See also Matthew 4:1-11 and Mark 1:12-13.)

The first thing to which he said "No" was the unbridled and unrestricted use of power. The devil specifically identifies him as the Son of God, as one who possesses all the power, privilege and prerogatives of divinity, and challenges him, indeed, *dares* him to use it to satisfy his hunger. Quoting Deuteronomy 8:3, Jesus parries the devil's thrust with a declaration that life is more than simply about eating and drinking, or satisfying one's real or perceived physical needs. It is about developing a life of character and integrity, of aligning one's desires and intentions with God's desires and intentions, of inclining one's heart toward God's. That is precisely what Jesus went into the desert to do. The practice of prayer and fasting, which Jesus undertook, is an ancient practice that provides the occasion to examine one's life and priorities closely. Going without food for an extended amount of time can draw attention to the dependence we have upon material things, and helps us to realize how we order our lives around material concerns. This can help us to recognize how we stake our self-worth and value in material gain and material measures of success and fulfillment. At whose expense have we gained what we have? When we undertake a fast in full mindfulness of what we have, who we are, and to what we have dedicated our time, energy and resources, and then drench that awareness in prayer before God, the power of the Spirit can do incredible things in our lives. This is precisely the situation in which Jesus began his ministry.

The priorities of Jesus were not for self-aggrandizement or for using his power for his own ends. In the parallel story of the temptation found in Matthew, Jesus' reply to the devil completes the quote from Deuteronomy 8:3: "It is written: 'Man does not live on bread alone, but on every word that comes from the mouth of God'" (Matthew 4:4 NIV). These are the priorities of a man who has made the will and way of God as his own—material needs are attended to, but do not control or shape his life. It is the word of God, the purposes of God, the intentions of God that shape a man to good effect.

The second thing to which Jesus says "No" is political power, dominance and absolute possession. It is interesting to notice that, in Luke, the exercise of political control is actually *given* to the devil, who then freely gives it to whom he wishes. The devil offers to give complete control and authority over things to Jesus in exchange for Jesus' worship of him. What is often overlooked in this story of the second temptation is how the devil treats the kingdoms of the world as a possession to keep or give away as he sees fit. This is a parable of human hubris in its most raw form: treating the lives of entire groups of people as toys and playthings.

Reading this story I can't help but think of how time and time again, people of power and position have sat down and drawn arbitrary lines across a map and said, "This is mine and that is yours." How can one possess an area of land? How can one possess an entire community or society or nation of people? The devil makes such a claim, and people in positions of power have done the same for millennia.

The devil is willing to turn it all over to Jesus if Jesus will worship him. If we remember that the act of worship means to proclaim the worth and value of something or someone, it is significant that Jesus refuses to place any value in the devil and his ideas of power, privilege and possession. In this act of rejecting the worship of the devil and his attitudes and philosophy of life, Jesus also rejects outright any notion of possessing people or entire populations as property, to use, abuse or dispose of as one deems fit. Slave-owners and traders, dictators, factory owners, tyrants and despots take notice. But also, husbands and fathers, bosses and managers take notice.

The final thing to which Jesus says "No" is what I like to refer to as "pulling rank." The devil places Jesus upon the highest place in Jerusalem and dares him to throw himself off. He is not only God's Anointed One, the Messiah, but he is also God's son (even the devil acknowledges this), under whom legions upon legions of angels and the whole heavenly host stand in readiness to serve (which is the thrust behind the Psalm passage, Psalm 91:11-12, that the devil quotes). Jesus is the highest ranking officer, the commander-in-chief, the *chef de guerre*, the Absolute Authority to whom all beings owe their allegiance. If he throws himself off, surely no one in heaven or on earth will allow him to die, let alone even bruise his feet against the stones below. In effect, the devil is telling him to pull rank.

"Pulling rank," of course, is a term derived from the military in which there is a hierarchical layering of authority, flowing in a downward direction. If someone higher in rank than you orders you to do something, you do it, regardless (usually). Just like membership in American Express, rank has its privileges, and more than one ranking officer, or business manager or executive, has utilized their position to get things done their way, or to their advantage. The expression, "to pull rank" refers to the practice of directing the resources, abilities and energies of others toward oneself for one's own personal benefit. This is in direct contrast to the proper role for persons in positions of leadership and authority, which is to direct the resources of the community for the welfare of the community and the benefit of others. This decision by Jesus and his commitment to exercise the proper role of leadership and authority characterizes the whole of his life and ministry, and leads him directly to the edge of Jerusalem, the seat of religious and political power for centuries in that part of the world. Jesus will be elevated at Jerusalem, but it will be upon the outstretched beams of a cross.

These are the things to which Jesus says "no." Even if we were to look at nothing else Jesus did, his response to the temptation and dares of the devil serves as a powerful critique of the systems of power and control in most of the world's societies. But the spirituality that Jesus embodies is not simply a negation of things as they are. Most significantly, it is an affirmation of life in its fullness, in all its possibilities, in its gloriousness. At one point he declares, "I came that they might have life and have it to the full" (John 10:10 NIV). This is his purpose, his mission statement, as it were. This is the focus of his time, energy and power. "In him was life, and that life was the light of humankind" (John 1:4 NIV).

Let's explore for a bit the implications of this sorting out that Jesus does in terms of the way of life and spirituality that he was going to teach and model for those who would become his followers and disciples.

Implications

When I reflect upon these stories of the temptation of Jesus to discern what they might say to my own life, I find it helpful not to think of the devil as a singular individual that skulks around the world trying to lead people down the path of eternal damnation. In the Jewish community of the time, the inherited tradition of the devil was more of a figure that serves as an adversary, like a prosecutor in a court of law. This is exactly how he is depicted in the book of Job, where he is called in Hebrew, *ha satan*, which literally means "the adversary." The history of the word "devil," sheds light on its deeper meanings. The modern English is derived from the Old English *dēofol* (related to Dutch *duivel* and German *Teufel*), via late Latin from Greek *diabolos* "accuser, slanderer." *Diabolos* was used in the Septuagint to translate Hebrew *ha satan* "the Adversary." Diabolos is a noun, derived from the Greek verb *diaballein* "to slander," from *dia* "across" + *ballein* "to throw." An accusation or slander, in this cluster of meanings, is that which is thrown across us, which serves to misdirect us or cause doubt and uncertainty, or to cause us to depart from the path we have chosen to follow.

By the time of the first century, the figure of The Adversary apparently had assumed greater symbolic and mythic proportions, and in the fashion of the Mediterranean world, was personified. In the stories of Jesus' temptation and in later Christian writings, the devil represents those forces and systems and ideologies that tried to prevent Jesus from fulfilling his mission, or convince him to embrace values that differed from those he understood to be God's. This is not hard to understand. We face the same seductions to power and privilege and personal gain that Jesus faced. This is why this story is so poignant.

If we understand the devil to be the representation and personification of all that is opposed to God and those who seek to do the will of God, in what ways can the exercise of political power and control be opposed to the will of God? One way is when its exercise mitigates or works against the exercise of the personal freedom of individuals. When I was growing up, I had a teacher who said that my freedom extended as long as my arm. In other words, when the exercise of my choices bumped up against the free choices of someone else, my freedom ended. At that point, compromise and negotiation were required. Of course, life is much more complex than that simplified example, but it served to illustrate the relativity of personal freedom.

If I am in a position of authority over others, the sphere of my choices and decisions overlaps the spheres of freedom of others. They may voluntarily surrender some of their freedom to me, such as in the military or in a job or some other joint endeavor. We do this as humans all the time. It is how we operate as social beings. But if I am in a position of authority and direct the actions of other people, I must then take their welfare into account as well as the requirements of the task that is being undertaken.

Jesus was going to be in a position of authority. He would be called teacher, master, lord, and acted as "one who had authority." How he wielded that authority would make all the difference. He chose not to utilize his charisma and the draw of his personality to mount a political campaign. He chose not to amass sums of money. He chose not to set up a cult that would provide hoards of willing sexual partners.

Perhaps the most significant way in which the desire for political power and control can work against the will of God is at the level of personal devotion. "If you worship me," the devil says. But what is worship, in this case? Today, we tend to think of worship as going to church, saying prayers, singing songs, and listening to a sermon or exposition of scripture. But the Greek word translated in this passage as "worship" actually refers to the act of prostrating oneself on the ground directly in front of one to whom you are declaring your loyalty and devotion. To bow down in that manner was to expose your neck to the one to whom you were expressing devotion, thus expressing that your life was truly in their hands, and that your devotion to them acknowledged that you were indebted to that person for your very life. This is what the devil requires of Jesus in order to receive political power and control.

The exercise of power and control expresses the devotion and dedication of our lives. To what ends do we direct our energies? Who will benefit from our actions and choices? If we have the power and ability to affect the conditions and welfare of other people's lives, to what end do we direct our energy and actions? What ideology, values, goals, and intentions inform, guide and determine our decisions and actions? Since our values and beliefs determine the direction of our life in a wide variety of ways, that to which we express our devotion and dedication will consequently and *necessarily* determine the course of our lives. Jesus knows this and says "No" to the devil's offer of political power and control.

What does this mean for men who are in positions of political power and control who still want to pattern their lives after the example of Christ, and breathe deeply of His Spirit? First off, it is essential to be completely realistic in acknowledging the origins of such power and recognize its daily seductions. The worship of God in the sense of prostrating oneself in absolute dependence and commitment to God is the obvious antidote to the lure of power and authority. Worship in this sense does not refer to a house of belief that one attends periodically, but rather to the house of decisions, loyalties, and actions in which one abides daily. Devotion to God entails a commitment to work for the welfare of all humanity as well as the rest of God's creation, which is the original created purpose of human beings (see Genesis, chapters 1 and 2).

Applications

I began this chapter talking about the process of sorting out those things that are helpful and serve us well in life from those things that are not helpful and that don't serve us well. Reading that, one might typically think in terms of getting rid of small annoying habits such as procrastination or lethargy, forgetting to put the cap on the toothpaste or not balancing the checkbook. However, when you read and ponder the issues Jesus dealt with in the temptation stories, it is clear that Jesus didn't sweat the small stuff. The things Jesus decided to challenge and jettison from his repertoire were foundational building blocks of major civilizations for several thousand years:

1. The exercise of power over others,
2. The domination of a person or a people by another person or group,
3. The idea that people are property or commodities to be possessed, bought, sold or disposed of at whim, and
4. The exercise of a privileged status to serve his own ends.

The issues of power and privilege face every man to this day. For most men, it is not an easy issue of simply deciding not to use the power that one possesses by virtue of being a man, or being born into privilege or achieving a position of power as a result of advancement or education. The question revolves more around how one is to use the power that one does have and to what end. In addition, given the fact that all human communities are created by humans, how might one use this creativity to fashion societies that operate on a different set of values? And as one decides to work toward a certain end, what are the means one chooses to achieve those ends? How do those means reflect the outcome one is intending?

Power Survey

A place to begin this process is just the sort of sorting out and taking stock of one's place in life that Jesus engaged in at the start of his ministry. This is a time of truth-telling and a careful evaluation and analysis of one's place in life. The exercise I am suggesting to assist with this process is called a Power Survey. To take a power survey you need a long sheet of paper and a pen or pencil. Take the paper and place your name squarely in the center of the paper. Above your name write the words: "Power over me" with an arrow extending from your name upward. Below your name write the words: "I have power over" with an arrow extending from your name downward. It should look like this:

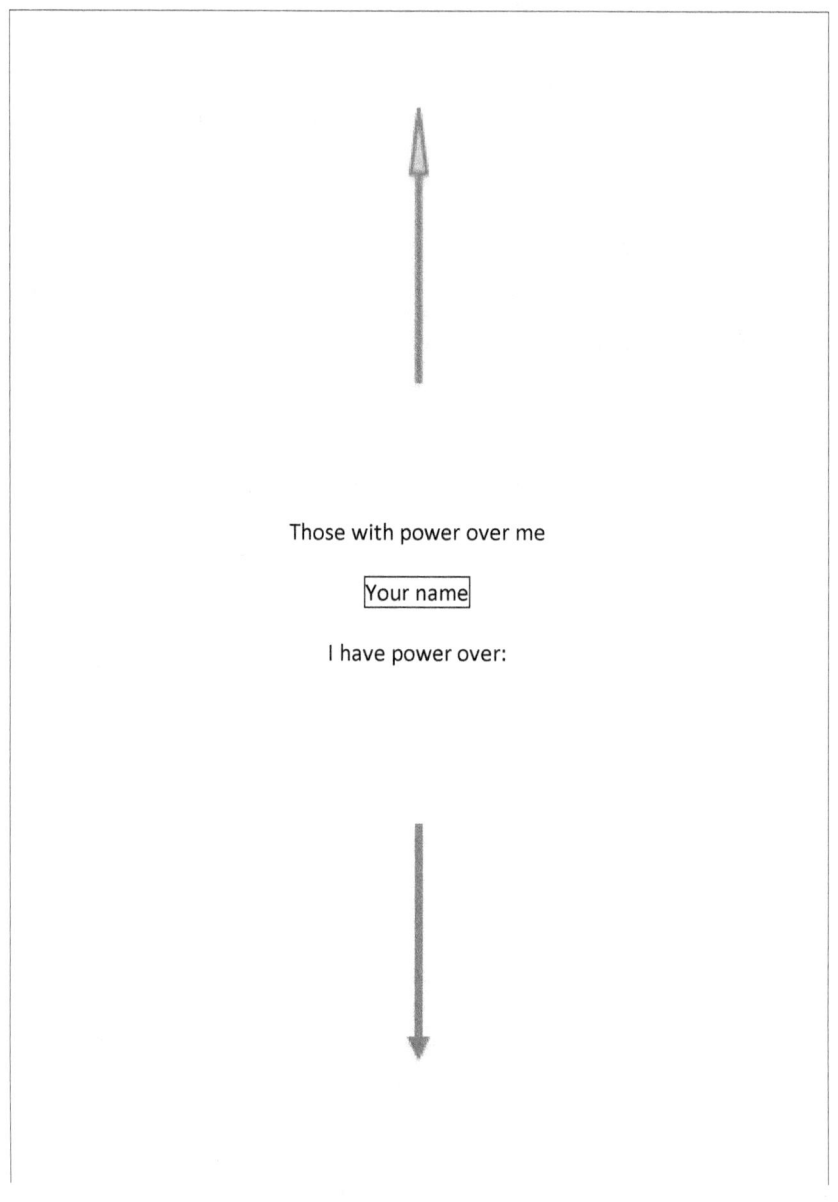

Figure 5 — Power Survey

Now, begin to name all the people or categories of people over which you have any form of influence, power or authority. Place them in relative position to you in the following manner: the more power you have over them, place them farther away. The more equal in power to you that they are, place them closer. Then name all the people or categories of people who have some form of influence, power or authority over you. Those with more power place farther away. Those who are more equal to you in power place closer to you. Name everyone: spouse, children, parents, siblings, store clerks, bosses, co-workers, subordinates, the President of the United States, I.R.S. agents, letter carriers, police officers, loan officers, insurance CEOs, students, little league players, Boy Scouts, etc. Include the things you make and design for use and consumption or entertainment of others, such as video games, movies, songs, books. Make the list as complete and as accurate as possible. Also, don't excuse away any power dynamic by saying, "It's a part of my job," or "I didn't create the system." That's not the point. The point is just to label and diagram out the relationships of power, influence and authority in your life. Pay attention to the flow of money, which is a means of wielding power. To whom are you obligated to pay money? Who owes you money? Who is in your care? Whose affairs are you managing? In whose finances or cases or life decisions do you have a significant say? All of these are ways of wielding power.

Also keep in mind that the issues associated with exercising power are not always negative or abusive. The point of this exercise is simply to see how power flows in our lives. How we choose to use the power that we have makes all the difference. Jesus did not preach against the existence of power. Rather, he was concerned with how it was used and to what ends.

Having diagrammed as fully as possible the lines of power in your life, circle the ones that you are in a position to influence how that power is used. What are the relationships in which you have a direct choice about the nature of your relationship and the manner in which you treat the other persons? This can range everywhere from the "Yes, sir!" subservience of the military to the long process of careful negotiating in order to reach consensus. Write adjectives next to the lines of power that describe the quality of relationship or flow of power.

Jesus never set out to topple Rome. He didn't attempt to enact a coup in Jerusalem. He didn't foment a revolution against Caesar, and when he confronted Pilate he was mostly silent. Instead, he worked with those closest to him, and those with whom he came in contact on city streets, in the countryside or in households and synagogues. The place to begin is our own sphere of influence.

— 12 —

"The Spirit Is Upon Me"
Jesus' Inaugural Sermon

EVERY FOUR YEARS IN the United States, a presidential election is held. Following that election, the newly elected (or re-elected) President is inaugurated into office. At that inauguration, it is traditional that the new president gives a speech in which he or she outlines his or her philosophy of governance and indicates the priorities to which he or she will attend while in office. Millions of people worldwide pay close attention to this speech, because it gives a glimpse into how history and the future may unfold, and how their lives may be affected.

In the Gospel of Luke we find just such an inaugural speech or sermon given by Jesus as he begins his ministry. It occurs immediately after his sojourn in the wilderness, having been tempted by the devil as discussed in the previous chapter. Now is the time in which he announces his intentions and defines what his mission and work will be.

Explication

So let us turn to a consideration of how Jesus affirms his commitment to the life and fulfilling of God's deepest purposes for human existence in the synagogue sermon in Nazareth.

Jesus returned to Galilee in the power of the Spirit, and news about him spread through the whole countryside. He taught in their synagogues, and everyone praised him.

"The Spirit Is Upon Me"

He went to Nazareth, where he had been brought up, and on the Sabbath day he went into the synagogue, as was his custom. And he stood up to read. The scroll of the prophet Isaiah was handed to him. Unrolling it, he found the place where it is written:
"The Spirit of the Lord is on me,
because he has anointed me
to preach good news to the poor.
He has sent me to proclaim freedom for the prisoners
and recovery of sight for the blind,
to release the oppressed,
to proclaim the year of the Lord's favor."
Then he rolled up the scroll, gave it back to the attendant and sat down. The eyes of everyone in the synagogue were fastened on him, and he began by saying to them, "Today this scripture is fulfilled in your hearing" (Luke 4:14–19 NIV).

Here Jesus uses the words of Isaiah 61:1&2 to express the thrust of his mission. Significantly, he does not say that he has come to expound a new philosophy or set of ethical teachings, nor even to reveal a new wisdom or teaching about the nature of reality and the universe (which is a concern that can be found in that set of writings that were not accepted into the canon of the New Testament by the early church).[1] His anointing by God is directed at how people's lives are affected by the social conditions and systems of power and privilege in which they find themselves. This is an inescapable reading of the text, especially when it is placed in its Gospel context following his experience of fasting and temptation in the desert. The things Jesus affirms by declaring himself to be the fulfillment of Isaiah's prophecy are the exact opposite of those things he rejects in the desert's temptations. He will direct his energy, teaching and power to those at the lowest levels of society: the poor, the imprisoned, the helpless, those on the margins of society, those without power or privilege, those whose lives are defined and circumscribed by those who have wealth or military, religious or political authority and control over them. This characterizes the entirety of Jesus' ministry. It is the expression of his own spirituality. It is the manifestation of his own set of values and his commitments. It is his "Yes" to God, and his partnership with the will of God for God's creation.

---

1. For an excellent treatment and discussion of these non-canonical gospels about Jesus, see Ehrman, *Lost Christianities*; Ehrman, *Lost Scriptures*; Meyer, *The Gnostic Discoveries;* Meyer, *Secret Gospels*; Pagels, *The Gnostic Gospels*; Pagels and King, *Reading Judas*; and Patterson, *The Lost Way*.

While it is certainly true that this passage can refer to spiritual poverty, blindness, imprisonment and oppression, the Gospels themselves give witness to Jesus dealing with the real social and material conditions of people's lives. Those conditions in a very specific sense can be understood to be the physical expression and external manifestation of the inward and spiritual blindness of people in this way: the oppressiveness of religious doctrines and the poverty of the human soul do find their expression in the human systems of social relationships. This is an example of the fact that every human phenomenon has an inner and an outer dimension: a physical manifestation (outer dimension) and a spiritual condition, relationship or conscious decision (inner dimension).

The Synoptic Gospels depict vividly that Jesus set about addressing the physical needs of people as well as addressing spiritual needs, the inner and the outer—often simultaneously. At one point in Luke's Gospel, there seems to be some question and uncertainty on the part of John the Baptist and his followers as to whether Jesus was the One for whom they were waiting. Jesus replies by means of his accomplishments.

> John's disciples told him about all these things. Calling two of them, he sent them to the Lord to ask, "Are you the one who was to come, or should we expect someone else?"
>
> When the men came to Jesus, they said, "John the Baptist sent us to you to ask, 'Are you the one who was to come, or should we expect someone else?'"
>
> At that very time Jesus cured many who had diseases, sicknesses and evil spirits, and gave sight to many who were blind. So he replied to the messengers, "Go back and report to John what you have seen and heard: The blind receive sight, the lame walk, those who have leprosy are cured, the deaf hear, the dead are raised, and the good news is preached to the poor. Blessed is the man who does not fall away on account of me" (Luke 7:18-23 NIV).

Jesus in these Gospel stories is directly concerned with the physical suffering and needs of the people around him. But these needs and sufferings did not arise in a vacuum. They were part and parcel of the structure of a social system that determined who had access to what sort of health care (such as it was in those days), who had access to what levels of nutrition, who had access to what sorts of housing, what sort of work one could engage in, and to what sorts of dangers one might be exposed. Those social systems also determined a person's status when they became ill or what would happen to persons when members of their family died, such as husbands or sons if they were women.

But there was the spiritual side of things as well. Alongside the acts of Jesus that are recorded, there are teachings that probe deeper levels of reality, as it were. It is quite possible that the preservation of the teachings of Jesus alongside the acts of Jesus reflects the Semitic understanding of the vital interrelationship between the material level of reality and the spiritual level. This view is distinct from a view that was also prevalent at that time (and still to this day) that the physical world was distinct from the more real and perfect spiritual or ideal world. In this view, spiritual knowledge and teaching pertained to this other realm, and dealt with how to achieve or access that realm in this life or how to achieve it after death. This view found expression in a variety of ways with a wide diversity of nuances and expressions, but can be found in the so-called Gnostic writings, in Plato, in Neo-Platonism and in some of the writings that made it into the New Testament as well as in the letters and sermons of Christian writers in all centuries.

But it is different from what is usually described as a Semitic worldview that understands the physical and spiritual realms to be two aspects of the same reality that are interrelated and vitally interconnected. One way you can see this idea played out is in the Gospel of Luke in which the Holy Spirit is continuously acting in the physical world to influence and affect the physical, social and historical circumstances of the time. A succinct listing illustrates this. In Luke, the Holy Spirit is involved in the following:

- The ministry of John the Baptist (1:15)
- The miraculous conception of Jesus by Mary (1:35)
- The recognition by Elizabeth that Mary bore the Lord (1:41)
- The song of praise sung by Zechariah at the birth of John (1:67)
- The song sung by Simeon when he witnessed the presentation of Jesus in the temple (2:25–27)
- An appearance to Jesus at his baptism in the Jordan (2:22)
- The Holy Spirit sends Jesus into the wilderness and accompanies him during his fasting and temptation (4:1)
- The Holy Spirit empowers Jesus to begin his ministry (4:14)

- Jesus claims the power of the Spirit in his own ministry when he reads from the Isaiah scroll in the synagogue in Nazareth (4:18–21)
- The Holy Spirit will inspire what the disciples will say when they are brought before rulers and magistrates (12:12).

When Jesus claims that it is the Spirit of God that has anointed him to do his work, he is affirming a Semitic and very Jewish notion that God is directly involved in the working of the world. The task of the spiritual life is to work in concert with God, manifesting, as it were, the will of God in the physical and social structures of this material existence.

Implications

This is the whole crux of spirituality, any spirituality, but especially a Biblical spirituality and specifically a spirituality embedded in Jesus Christ: the manner in which one's life is lived in the world directly reflects the commitments and decisions of the heart. To follow the path of Jesus in the twenty-first century, then, means to engage the world in the manner in which Jesus engaged it and to live according to the same set of priorities and commitments that Jesus lived.

There is no compartmentalizing spirituality away from religion away from personal beliefs away from morality away from ethics away from business decisions away from sexual behavior away from how one treats the members of one's family away from politics away from the causes one chooses to support. It is all of one piece. It is about the congruence Eugene Peterson spoke about in the earlier chapter on spirituality. Congruence and coherence. The book of James addresses this issue of coherence in this way:

> My brothers and sisters, do you with your acts of favoritism really believe in our glorious Lord Jesus Christ? For if a person with gold rings and in fine clothes comes into your assembly, and if a poor person in dirty clothes also comes in, and if you take notice of the one wearing the fine clothes and say, "Have a seat here, please," while to the one who is poor you say, "Stand there," or, "Sit at my feet," have you not made distinctions among yourselves, and become judges with evil thoughts? Listen, my beloved brothers and sisters. Has not God chosen the poor in the world to be rich in faith and to be heirs of the kingdom that he has promised to those who love him? But you have dishonored

the poor. Is it not the rich who oppress you? Is it not they who drag you into court? Is it not they who blaspheme the excellent name that was invoked over you?

. . . What good is it, my brothers and sisters, if you say you have faith but do not have works? Can faith save you? If a brother or sister is naked and lacks daily food, and one of you says to them, "Go in peace; keep warm and eat your fill," and yet you do not supply their bodily needs, what is the good of that? So faith by itself, if it has no works, is dead (James 2:1–7, 14–17 NRSV).

Because the spiritual and the physical are not separate things but are part and parcel of the same full reality, what one proclaims about the world and one's place in it must be matched by one's deeds. The work of Jesus on behalf of those who suffered physically, emotionally and socially illustrates his understanding of God's priorities in the world. It also illustrates the fact that in attending to the physical needs of persons, their emotional needs must be addressed as well, as must be their social circumstances. All things work and cohere together.

This might require a new way of looking at the world, especially in our modern world that views things strictly in material terms, or separates out spiritual teachings from political and social realities. It requires a much more integrated way of thinking and acting.

Additional Implication: Choosing Nonviolence

There is another implication that arises from this passage about Jesus' Inaugural Sermon. It relates to what Jesus left out when he read from the scroll of Isaiah. Here is the full reading of what we today refer to as Isaiah 61:1&2 (chapters and verses were not added until some time in the Middle Ages):

"The Spirit of the sovereign Lord is on me,
because the Lord has anointed me
to preach good news to the poor.
He has sent me to bind up the brokenhearted,
To proclaim freedom for the captives
And release from darkness for the blind (or the prisoners)
to proclaim the year of the Lord's favor
and the day of vengeance of our God." (NIV)

You should notice right away that Jesus chooses deliberately to end his reading before the line proclaiming the day of vengeance of God.

Clearly, he is signaling to his listeners that his anointing by the Spirit does not include vengeance, and by extension, the use of violence to achieve his mission. This is part and parcel of his rejection of the unbridled and unrestricted use of power. Although the Magnificat of Mary discussed in the previous chapter and this reading from Isaiah speak of a dramatic and even revolutionary reordering of society, it is clear that Jesus chooses not to use violent means to achieve these purposes. This choice has enormous implications for the course of his ministry, and for us as well today. There are virtually no credible Biblical scholars who claim that Jesus was anything but nonviolent. In fact, the earliest Christian communities made nonviolence one of their central tenets of belief and practice.[2] This was because Jesus practiced and taught the use of nonviolent means to achieve change. In a later chapter I will examine closely some of the practical methods of nonviolence that he taught.

The implications for us today are significant, especially in our culture that espouses and glorifies the use of violence in entertainment, foreign policy, and as a demonstration of supposed manhood. Jesus came to demonstrate a way of true personhood, and to show his male disciples a model of true manhood. His followers came to proclaim him as the Son of God, and if we so proclaim him today, then we must also admit that his life is indeed a model of true manhood for men today. If this man, the Son of God, chose to reject the use and ways of violence, then we must also. There are no two ways about it. Jesus' world was as dangerous, riddled with crime and evil acts as our world is today. And yet he chose to engage it nonviolently. If we proclaim him as Lord and Savior, or even just as Teacher, or perhaps Master, how can we do anything different?

Application

I invite you to spend some time in reflection upon your own life and priorities. Ask yourself the following questions as honestly and truthfully as possible:

1. What do I believe to be the things of greatest value in the world?
2. What am I doing to live according to them?

---

2. See Akers, *The Lost Religion of Jesus*; and MacGregor, "Nonviolence in the Ancient Church and Christian Obedience."

3. What are the points of congruence between my beliefs and my actions, and what are the points of incongruence?
4. What do I do with the majority of my time and energy?
5. What do I do with my "spare time" or "free time?"
6. In what positions of authority or responsibility do I find myself?
7. Who are all the people upon whose lives I have a direct effect?
8. What all can I do to make their life better?
9. How have I been injured so that I wish for retribution or vengeance?
10. How do I plan or wish to "get even" with those who have wronged me?
11. How often have I struck out with my hands or words when someone opposes me or doesn't obey me or disagrees with me?
12. If Jesus were in charge of my actions, what would change?

How you answer these questions provides a reflection of "how it is with your soul," in the words of John Wesley and the early Methodist Societies. Strictly speaking, there are no right or wrong answers to these questions. However, there is a wrong and a right *way to answer* these questions. The *right* way is simply to "tell it like it is," to "tell the truth, the whole truth and nothing but the truth."

This is an ancient Christian practice based upon the Bible. It is called "confession." Because knowing the truth will make us free, the practice of confession is essentially the practice of telling the truth—about ourselves to ourselves and to God. It is not done in order to make ourselves feel guilty or miserable, nor to beat up on ourselves. We tell the truth because doing so grounds us in the living reality of Jesus Christ, who declares that He is the Truth, the Way and the Life (John 14:6). As we seek to follow the path of Jesus in the twenty-first century, we align our hearts with his by living and speaking truthfully. Living and speaking truthfully guides us into living lives of congruence and coherence, especially as we seek to be guided by the same Spirit that guided Jesus and infused his life and teaching. That same Spirit can infuse our lives as well, and can work through us to bring healing and wholeness to a world that is torn apart socially, politically and physically.

As we probe our inner lives by asking these questions and examining our outer actions, we may come to realize how our actions are not congruent with how we would like to be in the world, and with what we proclaim as our faith. The act of confession brings to the surface the discrepancies and incongruities of our lives in order to bring our actions into alignments with our deepest beliefs, to align the outer aspect with the inner aspect of our lives.

Paul personally reflects on this human inability to live according to the way of God through an amazingly perceptive passage of self-examination found in Romans 7:15–25 (NRSV):

> "I do not understand my own actions. For I do not do what I want, but I do the very thing I hate. Now if I do what I do not want, I agree that the law is good. But in fact it is no longer I that do it, but sin that dwells within me. For I know that nothing good dwells within me, that is, in my flesh. I can will what is right, but I cannot do it. For I do not do the good I want, but the evil I do not want is what I do."

The one who rescues us from this dilemma is Jesus Christ. How? By applying the healing salve of God's love and grace to our tortured fear and guilt of failure. Whenever we attempt to do what is right and fail, or whenever we do what is wrong and then regret it and repent of doing it, there still linger about us the effects of our choices and actions. These operate at a spiritual and psychological level. Our relationships may be strained as a result of our actions, pain and hurt may punctuate our interactions with people, resentments may accumulate, even anger and hatred may be present because of violations, abuse or violence. All of these are the stings of sin, the deep wounds left behind as a result of humans falling short of the way of heaven. We need to be healed from these effects as much as from the effects of physical illness or injury. The inner eyes of our souls need to be opened as much as our eyes of flesh.

It is the pronouncement of Divine forgiveness and the unconditional love of God that heals these inner wounds. It is the eternal mercy and gracious forgiveness of God that ceases the inner turmoil that Paul describes so eloquently. To receive the benediction of God that we are loved by God regardless of our failures, of all the times we miss the mark, we can be relieved of the burdens of shame, guilt and self-recrimination.

Prayer

So how is it with your soul? To what does your heart incline? If you discern that your commitments are in need of realignment, or that you wish to commit your life to God and seek to live out God's will in your life, I invite you to pray the following prayer or one of your own composition:

"Gracious and loving God, I confess that my ways are truly not your ways, I confess that my heart is not right with your heart. I confess that I have chosen to exalt myself instead of you, and that this has been at the expense of others. I ask for your forgiveness, even as I ask the forgiveness of others. Give me a new heart, O Lord. Make it a heart after Jesus' heart. By the power of your Holy Spirit, make me the man Jesus would have me be. I pray this from the depths of my own being, and in His name. Amen."

— 13 —

Changing Our Minds

THERE USED TO BE a slogan that went around when I was younger. It roughly went something like this: "It's 10:00. Do you know where your children are?" When I was in college, the dorms on campus were hit with a rather bizarre rash of thefts where someone stole the furniture out of the dormitories. Pretty soon signs went up all over campus asking, "It's 10:00. Do you know where your dorm furniture is?"

The spiritual life begins with a very similar question that goes like this: "It's 10:00 (or any other time). Do you know where your heart and mind are?" A person's heart and mind devise their priorities, determine their loyalties, and direct their actions. It is a common expression to speak of appealing to the hearts and minds of people. During the Vietnam War, the U.S. Government under President Johnson frequently spoke about winning the hearts and minds of the Vietnamese people. The same language was used by the Bush administration in reference to the people of Afghanistan and Iraq during those military occupations. The basic idea is that the heart will commit a person to a cause or a program or even a person, and the mind will figure out what to do to achieve the purposes of that cause, program or person.

Moses understood this clearly. In the book of Deuteronomy, as he sums up the law for the people of Israel before they prepare to cross over the Jordan into Canaan, he does it this way: "Hear, O Israel: The Lord is our God, the Lord alone. You shall love the Lord your God with all your heart, and with all your soul, and with all your might" (Deuteronomy 6:4–5 NRSV). When he was asked to sum up the Law, Jesus cites this very same passage and adds, "And you shall love your neighbor as yourself"

(Matthew 22:39; cf. Leviticus 9:18). The heart provides the inclination, and the mind activates the action.

So here is the question: Where is your heart? Is your mind where your heart is? We may desire to follow Jesus, but where does our mind direct our activities and behavior? Of course, in normal human experience, heart and mind work in concert most of the time. The spiritual life is thus directed at carefully discerning to what we have directed our minds and dedicated our hearts. Jesus puts it this way: "Where your treasure is, there your heart will be also" (Matthew 6:21). What we spend our time and energy on or doing is an indication of where our heart is. Where we direct our attention is an indication of what we love. Where we invest our emotional and physical energy is a statement of what we value.

Explication

Jesus' statement above is taken from a larger passage in Luke that is a discourse on worry and anxiety:

> Then Jesus said to his disciples: "Therefore I tell you, do not worry about your life, what you will eat; or about your body, what you will wear. Life is more than food, and the body more than clothes. Consider the ravens: They do not sow or reap, they have no storeroom or barn; yet God feeds them. And how much more valuable you are than birds! Who of you by worrying can add a single hour to his life? Since you cannot do this very little thing, why do you worry about the rest? Consider how the lilies grow. They do not labor or spin. Yet I tell you, not even Solomon in all his splendor was dressed like one of these. If that is how God clothes the grass of the field, which is here today, and tomorrow is thrown into the fire, how much more will he clothe you, O you of little faith! And do not set your heart on what you will eat or drink; do not worry about it. For the pagan world runs after all such things, and your Father knows that you need them. But seek his kingdom, and these things will be given to you as well. Do not be afraid, little flock, for your Father has been pleased to give you the kingdom. Sell your possessions and give to the poor. Provide purses for yourselves that will not wear out, a treasure in heaven that will not be exhausted, where no thief comes near and no moth destroys. For where your treasure is, there your heart will be also (Luke 12:22–34 NIV).

Anxiety and worry are related to where the heart is. This is because the human heart is basically restless and seeks satisfaction. Augustine put it pointedly: "Our hearts are restless, O Lord, until they rest in thee." Because our hearts are restless, we seek some sort of resting, some sort of satisfaction. This takes many forms. Some people become obsessed with money and material comforts. Others are incessantly busy, working on that project or helping with this cause, not because it is an expression of what they are drawn to do, but because they are so uncomfortable with themselves that they hide from their restlessness in a blur of frenetic activity and busy-ness. Others seek the adulation of others or seek to become the envy of their neighbors. Others may drift from job to job, or community to community, never quite finding their niche or place. Still their hearts are restless and yearn for satisfaction.

The danger of a restless heart is that it lacks direction, particularly an internally-guided sense of direction. A restless heart all too easily becomes adrift in life, simply going where the flow and flood of society takes it. Therefore it is significant that at the start of his ministry, Jesus addresses the question of where people are headed in life. In the Gospels of Matthew and Mark, Jesus begins his ministry by calling people to repent: "From that time on Jesus began to preach, 'Repent, for the kingdom of heaven is near'" (Matthew 4:17; see Mark 1:15). This preaching was an extension of the message of John the Baptist, who was Jesus' cousin, and who baptized Jesus in the Jordan River.

> In those days John the Baptist came, preaching in the Desert of Judea and saying, "Repent, for the kingdom of heaven is near." This is he who was spoken of through the prophet Isaiah:
> "A voice of one calling in the desert,
> 'Prepare the way for the Lord,
> make straight paths for him.'
>
> John's clothes were made of camel's hair, and he had a leather belt around his waist. His food was locusts and wild honey. People went out to him from Jerusalem and all Judea and the whole region of the Jordan. Confessing their sins, they were baptized by him in the Jordan River.
>
> But when he saw many of the Pharisees and Sadducees coming to where he was baptizing, he said to them: "You brood of vipers! Who warned you to flee from the coming wrath? Produce fruit in keeping with repentance. And do not think you can say to yourselves, 'We have Abraham as our father.' I tell you that out of these stones God can raise up children for Abraham. The

ax is already at the root of the trees, and every tree that does not produce good fruit will be cut down and thrown into the fire.

"I baptize you with water for repentance. But after me will come one who is more powerful than I, whose sandals I am not fit to carry. He will baptize you with the Holy Spirit and with fire. His winnowing fork is in his hand, and he will clear his threshing floor, gathering his wheat into the barn and burning up the chaff with unquenchable fire" (Mathew 3:1–12 NIV).

Jesus carried on this call to repentance. But what exactly is repentance? In the Koiné Greek, the word for repentance is *metanoia,* which literally means to change one's mind, to change the direction of one's mind, and thus one's life. In fact, as you might recall from earlier chapters, *metanoia* more accurately translates as "beyond the (normal) mind," and the force of the verb indicates going beyond our normal consciousness or way of thinking into a deeper, bigger mind. Jesus calls out, "Repent! Redirect your mind!" But what does this mean? Perhaps it is best to think of metanoia as not just a turning, but also a *re-turning* of the heart to the way, the way that moves us into a bigger circle of consciousness. This can be illustrated by considering what it means to have a "way" as taught in the Hasidic Jewish tradition.

Martin Buber is one of the great religious and philosophical thinkers and writers of the last century. He is particularly famous for his interpretation of Hasidic stories, "examining and explaining the basic tenets of a way of life which lies near the center of Judaism." In his book, *The Way of Man: According to the Teaching of Hasidism*, Buber explains the centrality of searching the human heart in Hasidism.

> Every person born into this world represents something new, something that never existed before, something original and unique. 'It is the duty of every person in Israel to know and consider that he is unique in the world in his particular character and that there had never been anyone like him in the world, for if there had been someone like him, there would have been no need for him to be in the world. Every single man is a new thing in the world, and is called upon to fulfill his particularity in this world. For verily: that this is not done, is the reason why the coming of the Messiah is delayed.' Every man's foremost task is the actualization of his unique, unprecedented and never-recurring potentialities, and not the repetition of something that another, and be it even the greatest, has already achieved.[1]

---

1. Buber, *The Way of Man*, 16.

Hasidism teaches that each person has a way, or a path, that is unique for them. As important as following one's given way may be, it is not presented to us on a golden scroll at birth. It is a path that must be discerned by examining one's heart. "The decisive heart-searching is the beginning of the way in (human) life; it is again and again the beginning of a human way. But heart-searching is decisive only if it leads to the way."[2]

This heart-searching of which Buber speaks is the kind of "repentance"—or *metanoia*—that Jesus talks about. Repentance as *metanoia*, involves this searching of one's heart, in order to return to one's path, one's way. So, Jesus is saying, "Where are you going? Where is your heart leading you? Where is your treasure? What is the treasure that is calling out to your heart? Where are you going?" Repentance means to return to searching the heart, realizing that the purpose of searching one's heart is not to berate oneself for failures or for getting off the track, the path, but rather to *get back on* the path, that it is possible to return to the path, to the way. But it requires that searching, that asking of "Who am I? Where am I going? Where is my heart taking me? Where is my treasure?"

Implications

Early in my ministry the importance of knowing where one is going was impressed upon me by the story another minister told of a call he received in the middle of the night. The voice on the other end shook with fear. "This is Mary _____, my husband has a gun . . ." The pastor hurriedly dressed, got in his car, and drove several miles to the house of his parishioners. All along the way he prayed for God to give him the right words to prevent a possible tragedy. He arrived, prayed hurriedly again, went in the door and saw the wife and children huddled against the corner. He looked around and saw the husband standing in the middle of the room holding a shotgun on them. He didn't know where the words come from, but the first thing the minister said was, "John, where are you going?"

That simple question caught John off guard, but it was the central question, the most important thing John needed to hear. It suddenly put everything into perspective. John just thought he was angry. He was so caught up in his rage that all he could think about was that moment. He couldn't think about tomorrow, or a week later, or a year later. But

---

2. Buber, *The Way of Man*, 13.

the words of the minister reminded him: he is heading somewhere, and what he decided to do with that trigger would determine where he went. After a couple of hours of talking, John relaxed his finger, and put the gun down. But it was those opening words that set the scene: "John, where are you going?"

It's a question we all need to ask: "Where am I going?" Sometimes we get so caught up in our own personal darkness that we are only aware of this moment, this pain, this anger, this problem, that we forget that we are headed somewhere, and that we have a choice about what that direction is.

"Where am I going? If I continue going down the road I'm on, where will it take me?" One day while I was in college, I took a walk in a nearby park. The park was wet from the morning's rain shower, and as I turned a corner in the path, the sunlight reflected brilliantly off the glistening path. In fact, it looked as though the earthly substance of the path had been transformed into light. I paused and took in the scene. I turned around, and the path behind me was dark in comparison. Only the path ahead of me was filled with light.

Jesus says, "Repent! Turn around! Change the way you're going. Change your direction! Follow me!" So it is, if we wish to get out of the darkness and into the light, we need to change where we are headed. We all have some place of darkness in our lives, some aspect of our soul that is in need of light. In order to move out of the darkness and into the light, we may need to change our direction, and we may need to change what we are doing.

John the Baptist was very specific in the changes of life he suggested to the people who came to him for baptism: "The man with two tunics should share with him who has none, and the one who has food should do the same." To the tax collectors he said, "Don't collect any more than you are required to," and to the soldiers he said, "Don't extort money and don't accuse people falsely—be content with your pay." Each of these admonitions is predicated upon the idea that a change of heart requires a change of life, a change in what one does. The heart provides the inclination, and the mind activates the action.

Application

In an earlier chapter, I had you sketch out maps for the personal, interpersonal and social realms. Now is the time to return to those maps and consider them carefully. Where is your life headed at this time? What sort of trajectory has the combination of your decisions and circumstances in your life set up for you? If your life continued in this course, or according to its present pattern, where will you end up? This sort of question relates to the "change your direction" definition of *metanoia*.

But the deeper definition of *metanoia* which speaks of going beyond the normal mind into an expanded consciousness takes this level of self-examination to a higher and deeper level. This is possible only if you expand your mind beyond the conventional way of thinking into an enlarged territory of consciousness. And we do this through the processes of prayer, meditation and contemplation. In prayer, we come before God bringing with us the deepest longings of our hearts. The greatest prayer we can pray is "God, show me your ways. Make me like your Son, Jesus. Let me have the mind which was in him." God will grant that prayer, because it is the highest human aspiration possible. In meditation, we can sit with the teachings of Jesus and turn them over in our minds. We practice quieting the busy-ness of our "monkey minds" and let the teachings of Jesus expand our thinking. In prayer and contemplation, we move into deeper connection with God.

In Chapter 6, I spoke about how prayer is a way of attuning our wills to the will of God. This sort of prayer goes beyond the kind of prayer in which we ask God to do certain things for us. The deeper, contemplative prayer seeks to align our minds with the mind of Christ, and to be changed according to his mind. It involves a close and careful reading of the Bible, especially the Gospels to discern what that mind is and how it thinks and directs our actions. The process called Lectio Divina, which will be discussed in detail in Chapter 14, is the best way to enter deeply into a place of listening for the Divine Voice to speak to the deepest places in our hearts. The following exercise will give you an example of this process of prayerfully listening to scripture and contemplatively aligning your mind with that of Christ.

In your Bible, turn to the passage we just looked at in Matthew 3:1–12. Pause for a moment to sit in silence. In this silence pray to God: "What is it you have to say to me today?" Perhaps say this slowly several times.

Turn to the passage. Read it over once.

Now read it again, but this time out loud. Listen as if the words were being spoken especially to you.

Now close your eyes and picture the scene you have just read. See the Jordan River, the willows and olive trees along the banks, a small crowd of people huddled on the river banks. Where do you stand in the crowd? Are you among the Pharisees and others? Do you stand at the edge of the crowd? When John speaks, does he look right at you, eyes ablaze? What does he say to you? What are the fruits you must bear that befit repentance? What changes will you need to make in order to enter this new life? What is the chaff within you that needs to be burned away?

Listen.

Listen as if to the rush and flow of the river.

When Jesus came to the Jordan, the heavens opened and flooded him with an immense love, almost liquid like the river. Let this same love wash over you.

Then sit in silence. Sit in this flood and flow of love.

Let this love seep into the nooks and crannies of your mind and soul.

Those places in need of the fruits of which John spoke? Let this love flow there, and begin its work.

— 14 —

Counting the Cost

When I decided to buy a house several years ago, it was because of a happy coincidence of several factors: low mortgage rates, a favorable buyer's market, and a salary that allowed me to consider buying. In addition, I was renting a house at the time and really wanted to put that money into my own home. So, I sat down with a realtor and looked at all the various considerations that I, as a first-time buyer, should consider. We looked at how much I could pay in monthly mortgage installments, which then helped me figure the price range I could afford. But I also had certain needs concerning the number of bedrooms, location, how much work I would need to put into the house, size of yard, etc. Then I added up the costs, and went looking. Eventually my daughter and I found a place that met both of our needs and dreams.

Jesus speaks about the importance of counting the cost before starting out on any venture, but especially the venture of following him:

> Suppose one of you wants to build a tower. Will he not first sit down and estimate the cost to see if he has enough money to complete it? For if he lays the foundation and is not able to finish it, everyone who sees it will ridicule him, saying, "This fellow began to build and was not able to finish."
>
> Or suppose a king is about to go to war against another king. Will he not first sit down and consider whether he is able with ten thousand men to oppose the one coming against him with twenty thousand? If he is not able, he will send a delegation while the other is still a long way off and will ask for terms of peace. In the same way, any of you who does not give up everything he has cannot be my disciple (Luke 14:28–33 NIV).

Following Jesus is not an easy thing. It is not for the faint of heart, nor for those who seek the adulation of popular society or the lure of fame and fortune. It also is not simply a Sunday morning activity—some place to go for a few hours and be entertained, perhaps mildly challenged, and then to be forgotten or ignored until the following Sunday. No, Jesus was clear: there was a cost to consider when following him. This cost might set you at odds with your family, former friends, even those in power over you. It was a new way of looking at the world, at yourself, and at the very purpose for being alive.

Explication

Are you beginning to see the overwhelmingly radical nature of the spirituality Jesus taught and demonstrated? Jesus certainly understood how it threatened and challenged the systems of power and domination of his time, both religious and political:

> They were on their way up to Jerusalem, with Jesus leading the way, and the disciples were astonished, while those who followed were afraid. Again he took the Twelve aside and told them what was going to happen to him. "We are going up to Jerusalem," he said, "and the Son of Man will be betrayed to the chief priests and teachers of the law. They will condemn him to death and will hand him over to the Gentiles, who will mock him and spit on him, flog him and kill him. Three days later he will rise" (Mark 10:32–34 NIV).

Not only is he predicting his own death and resurrection here, which is the usual interpretation of this passage, but he is also impressing upon the men following him the full implications of life in the Realm of Heaven. In order to follow Jesus, his disciples must dispossess themselves of any pretensions to power over anyone else, and must surrender their desire to exercise authority over others. They must live as Jesus did, seeking the ways that benefit others spiritually, physically, socially, and psychologically. When Jesus sends the disciples out into the surrounding countryside, "he gave them power and authority to drive out all demons and to cure diseases, and he sent them out to preach the kingdom of God and to heal the sick" (Luke 9:1–2 NIV). This echoed exactly the form of his own self-giving ministry.

> Jesus went through all the towns and villages, teaching in their synagogues, proclaiming the good news of the kingdom and healing every disease and sickness. When he saw the crowds, he had compassion on them, because they were harassed and helpless, like sheep without a shepherd. Then he said to his disciples, "The harvest is plentiful but the workers are few. Ask the Lord of the harvest, therefore, to send out workers into his harvest field" (Matthew 9:35–38 NIV).

Those workers at first were the disciples he had chosen. Luke also recounts that he later sent out an additional seventy or seventy-two persons to carry on this work. It was a work of compassion, of "feeling-with" and identifying with all those who were oppressed and beaten down by the economic, political and social systems of his time. It is not possible to read the Gospels any other way and remain true to the life, ministry and teaching of Jesus.

What Jesus did was to take his disciples out of the social, economic and political systems of their day, and invest them with a new form of power—power that was not to be accrued or hoarded for its own sake, but power that was to be used for the well-being, liberation, healing and wholeness (which is what salvation means in its Greek original) of all who were at the bottom of the social heap.

So, when James and John, or their mother, go to Jesus and ask to sit in the seats of honor, it is clear that they haven't fully understood what Jesus is about (see Chapter 8). They are still operating with assumptions of political power as manifested in the world around them. They are still being shaped by a spirituality modeled after economic and political power.

What also is significant is the fact that in each of the three gospels that contain this story (Luke 22:24–27; Mark 10:35–45; Matthew 20:20–28), these stories of greatness and servanthood are placed *after* Peter confesses (presumably on behalf of the other disciples) Jesus to be the Messiah—the Anointed One of God. There is also a direct reference back to the fact that even though Peter has confessed Jesus to be the Messiah, it is clear that his understanding of Messiahship is different from Jesus' understanding of the same.

> Jesus and his disciples went on to the villages around Caesarea Philippi. On the way he asked them, "Who do people say I am?"
>
> They replied, "Some say John the Baptist; others say Elijah; and still others, one of the prophets."
>
> "But what about you?" he asked. "Who do you say I am?"

Peter answered, "You are the Christ [Messiah]."

Jesus warned them not to tell anyone about him. He then began to teach them that the Son of Man must suffer many things and be rejected by the elders, chief priests and teachers of the law, and that he must be killed and after three days rise again. He spoke plainly about this, and Peter took him aside and began to rebuke him. But when Jesus turned and looked at his disciples, he rebuked Peter. "Get behind me, Satan!" he said. "You do not have in mind the things of God, but the things of men" (Mark 8:27–33 NIV).

Consider the Cost

There is a boldness and courage in the spirituality of Jesus that is both its attraction and its terror. It is not a religion for the fainthearted or the halfhearted. Those who are to follow it must count the cost (Luke 14:28), set their sights straight ahead and not look back (Luke 9:62), and be prepared to encounter resistance and opposition from those who wish to preserve the status quo. Because the spirituality that Jesus taught overturned the tables so thoroughly, he knew it would encounter opposition. He warns his followers to anticipate this.

> Then he called the crowd to him along with his disciples and said: "If anyone would come after me, he must deny himself and take up his cross and follow me. For whoever wants to save his life (or soul) will lose it, but whoever loses his life (or soul) for me and for the gospel will save it. What good is it for a man to gain the whole world, yet forfeit his soul? Or what can a man give in exchange for his soul? If anyone is ashamed of me and my words in this adulterous and sinful generation, the Son of Man will be ashamed of him when he comes in his Father's glory with the holy angels" (Mark 8:34–38 NIV).

To a person living during the time of the Roman Empire, his allusion here is unmistakable: the cross was an instrument of social and political control. It was used as a means of executing those who opposed Roman rule in any way, or who disrupted the tenuous peace of the time. Crosses often lined the major highways with the condemned left to die in full view of passersby as a reminder of the penalty for insurrection, social disruption, or economic interference. To pick up one's cross indicated that one had been tried by the Roman authorities and found to be guilty either of banditry or of being in opposition to the governing authorities. It did not mean, as we have watered down its force, merely to put up with whatever our lot in life is. Quite the contrary. To pick up one's cross meant to understand the consequences of the new way and life that Jesus was teaching and living, and to daringly forge ahead in full expectation of those consequences.

The early church experienced those consequences. The writings and records of the early martyrs of the church record how willingly the early followers of Jesus went to their death rather than renounce their faith.[1] When they declared Jesus to be Lord, they were proclaiming that Caesar was not, which was a crime punishable by death. But it was not simply a matter of a difference of political opinions. To proclaim Jesus as Lord meant that one's life was to be formed according to the values and spirituality taught and demonstrated by Jesus, not according to the values and spirituality of Rome.

This tension had existed in Palestine for decades, particularly evidenced when Roman commanders or procurators attempted to bring in Roman standards with their images into the precincts of the Temple. For example, in 4 BCE, a large image of an eagle had been erected over the main gate of the Temple in Jerusalem. This incensed many among the Pharisees, who helped foment demonstrations that resulted in its being torn down. Many were put to death for this. Many Jews also considered the military standards bearing images of the emperor as idolatrous, and at one point camped out in protest outside Pilate's residence at Caesarea Maritima.[2] Many such actions occurred and are examples of what the Jewish population understood to be at stake: the integrity of their life lived in covenant with God as revealed in the Torah. God had revealed a specific way of life to their ancestors, and when they had been faithless to that way, so their prophets admonished them, they had been taken into exile. The lesson had been learned, and instead of capitulating completely to Roman and Greek culture, they steadfastly maintained the integrity of their religious life and all its social and cultural practices. This is what brought them into conflict with the Roman authorities.

When Jesus speaks of taking up one's cross and following him, it is framed within this context. A life lived in faithful covenant with God

---

1. Accounts of these early martyrs can be found in works such as van Dam, *Glory of the Martyrs*; Mursurillo, *The Acts of the Christian Martyrs*; Hardy, *Faithful Witnesses*; Forbush, *Fox's Book of Martyrs*.

2. Cohn-Sherbok, *The Jewish Heritage*, 51.

often is at odds with the prevailing culture. At one point after the death and resurrection of Jesus, the early disciples come into conflict with the local authorities and they flat out declare, "We must obey God rather than men" (Acts 5:29 RSV), an act that earns them a severe beating. It did not matter. Jesus had shown them a Way that was Truth and Life. They could do nothing else.

Implications: Doing Nothing Else

With every pun intended, this, then, is the crux of the matter. The spirituality that Jesus taught and demonstrated for his male followers was one in which they ultimately could do nothing else. It was more than just a bunch of good ideas and clever sayings, it was a way of being in the world that required their all, their whole selves. It required that they sacrifice all that they had understood about the world and its way of operating. They had to abandon their preconceptions, prejudices and enculturated ways of being and behaving and enter into a whole new realm of thinking and acting. It felt like death.

Jesus told them that it was basically just that: a death. But it was a death that led to new life. "For whoever wants to save his life will lose it, but whoever loses his life for me will find it" (Matthew 14:25 NIV). This message was the hardest for his male disciples to hear and comprehend, and it is just as difficult and incomprehensible for men today. The closest experience we may have of its demands upon us is military service. When one enters the military, one surrenders direct control over one's life to the government. The military asserts control and possession of the minds, the bodies and even the souls of their soldiers. Through basic training soldiers are equipped physically, mentally and emotionally to be in peak condition, and to learn how to kill. Normal human psychological resistances to killing other humans are overcome through operant training and conditioning exercises. Submission to authority is drilled and pounded into recruits physically and mentally. Loyalty to one's fellow soldiers, one's unit and ultimately to the cause for which one is fighting is demanded. And this training regimen is highly effective. If you have ever served in the military, you know firsthand the experience I am describing. When you enter the military, you die to your world back home in order to enter a completely different world. Life is never the same again.

This is precisely the situation Jesus is describing to his male followers. None of them were being asked to be soldiers—in fact they were entering a world that was diametrically opposed to the assumptions and methods of military control. But the same totality of demands was made upon the lives of his followers. They were to die to the world they knew in order to enter the completely different world of the Realm of Heaven. Life would never be the same again.

Jesus poignantly describes this to Nicodemus in the Gospel of John. Nicodemus is a member of the Pharisees who is deeply interested in what Jesus is all about. He has recognized that Jesus has come from God, so he seeks Jesus out for further conversation and teaching under the cover of night. Jesus begins the conversation by stressing the totality of change that is required: "I tell you the truth, no one can see the kingdom of God unless he is born again" (John 3:3 NIV). Life will have to start all over for Nicodemus. It will be like a new birth, a new chance, a whole new world. Even though it may feel like death, it also has the positive aspect of being a life that is new, changed, completely different.

For most of Jesus' male followers the full implications of this new life were only realized after his death and resurrection, which only makes sense. When Jesus was arrested, the Gospels tell us quite plainly that he was betrayed by one of his closest associates, and that all the rest fled. "I will strike the shepherd and the sheep of the flock will be scattered" (Matthew 26:31). Peter, who had professed so much loyalty, even denied knowing Jesus three times. This is the effect of the old life, the life to which they had to die. Only the women and John followed him to his trial and execution.

After his crucifixion and entombment, the disciples hid in fear and huddled in bewilderment. Peter was distraught to his core over his cowardice. The others were shocked by the betrayal of Judas. Everyone was traumatized by the cruelty of what had just happened. Even though the Gospels depict Jesus as having warned and prepared them for these things, the raw brutal realization of his words still speared their hearts, even as Jesus' side had been pierced. What they didn't realize is that they had just entered into the most liminal aspect of their threshold time with Jesus. Just as Jesus had died, now they also were entering into their own death—but theirs was to be a death to their old world. The new birth about which Jesus spoke with Nicodemus was upon them. They were, in fact, in its labor pains.

What Jesus had done, in fact, was to dramatically and efficaciously enact what he had taught his disciples: in order to enter into the life of the Realm of Heaven, you have to die. Before the crucifixion, it was only words, the sort of platitude the pious and learned were always mouthing. It was the religious thing to do, to say these sorts of things. But on the hill of Golgotha Jesus powerfully demonstrated that he was not just turning clever phrases. The spirituality Jesus lived and embodied is life-demanding, life-surrendering, and ultimately, death-defying.

After death comes new life or rebirth. This was Jesus' message to Nicodemus, and this was his teaching to his disciples. On the Sunday morning following his brutal execution he demonstrated it. And forty-eight days later at the feast of Pentecost he made possible this new world in the lives of the faithful who had gathered in Jerusalem.

> When the day of Pentecost came, they were all together in one place. Suddenly a sound like the blowing of a violent wind came from heaven and filled the whole house where they were sitting. They saw what seemed to be tongues of fire that separated and came to rest on each of them. All of them were filled with the Holy Spirit and began to speak in other tongues as the Spirit enabled them (Acts 2:1–4 NIV).

Peter suddenly recognized the significance of this event, that indeed, a new era and a new world had been born:

> Then Peter stood up with the Eleven, raised his voice and addressed the crowd: "Fellow Jews and all of you who live in Jerusalem, let me explain this to you; listen carefully to what I say. These men are not drunk, as you suppose. It's only nine in the morning! No, this is what was spoken by the prophet Joel:

> « ‹In the last days, God says,
> I will pour out my Spirit on all people.
> Your sons and daughters will prophesy,
> your young men will see visions,
> your old men will dream dreams.
> Even on my servants, both men and women,
> I will pour out my Spirit in those days,
> and they will prophesy.
> I will show wonders in the heaven above
> and signs on the earth below,
> blood and fire and billows of smoke.
> The sun will be turned to darkness

and the moon to blood
before the coming of the great and glorious day of the Lord.
And everyone who calls
on the name of the Lord will be saved'" (Acts 2:14–21 NIV).

Pentecost is more than simply a story of the birth and empowerment of the new Christian movement. It was a powerful enactment of the teaching to Nicodemus. It was a rebirth that was empowered by God, a spiritual transformation so powerful that it was, in essence, a passage through death into new life. Such a transformation is possible only on the terms of the One who affects the transformation, however. This was the final lesson that Jesus taught his disciples, and which he teaches us. Peter, James, John and the others wanted to bring in the Kingdom of Heaven under their own power and according to their dictates. Jesus upbraided them: "From the days of John the Baptist until now the kingdom of heaven has suffered violence, and the violent take it by force" (Mathew 11:12 NRSV). Anything seized by means of violence was not the Realm of Heaven about which Jesus preached. The Realm of Heaven that Jesus made possible was opened to those who renounced their hold on power and their positions of prestige:

> "Do not be afraid, little flock, for your Father has been pleased to give you the kingdom. Sell your possessions and give to the poor. Provide purses for yourselves that will not wear out, a treasure in heaven that will not be exhausted, where no thief comes near and no moth destroys. For where your treasure is, there your heart will be also" (Luke 12:32–34 NIV).

In order to be transformed spiritually, Peter and the others needed to let go of their death grip on their old world. It required a rearranging of their internal world. But the ultimate paradox is that this internal rearranging could only be brought about through the action of God in the Holy Spirit. This is the meaning of Pentecost. And it is illustrated in Jesus' comment to Nicodemus: "you must be born again." The Greek word translated as "again" can also mean "from above." Jesus makes use of a word that has a double meaning to illustrate that the new birth, the new life of the Realm of Heaven is self-empowered—it can only be entered on its own terms and under its own power. The coming of the Holy Spirit at Pentecost dramatized this. God enables the inner spiritual transformation that is necessary for us to enter the new world of the Realm of Heaven. It is the very action of God that inclines our hearts toward God's heart, and enables us to persevere on the path of Jesus in the twenty-first century.

But God will never force this life and this change upon us. It is presented to us as an invitation and free gift. But it remains our choice to take it or leave it. In this we are instructed by the example of Mary, the mother of Jesus who responds to Gabriel's invitation: "Let it be to me according to your word."

Application: Self-Examination and Reflection

Following the path of Jesus in any century is by no means an easy proposition. Jesus makes this clear. It requires a thorough examination of our attitudes, our values, our presumptions about things, and our motivations. It is tough internal work. It flies in the face of most of what we have been taught by our culture as to what it means to be a man, and what matters most in life.

The spiritual practices that can help with this are taking a spiritual inventory, and spiritual reading of the Bible. A spiritual inventory is a much deeper form of self-examination than that in which we engaged at the end of the last chapter. One way to take a spiritual inventory is to sit down at the end of a day and write down as completely as you can everything you did and said during the day. Recall as completely as you can your conversations and your decisions. Take special note of your feelings, emotions, reactions and motivations. Make the list as complete as possible. Then look at every item on that list and ask one simple question: "Why did I do or say this?" Be surgically honest.

What you will discover is that the pattern of events, activities and thoughts throughout a single day sketches out the rough contours of the world in which you live. It is not only a physical world, but more importantly, it is a world of ideas, values, memories, expectations, assumptions and demands. It is a world created by the culture in which you live. It is a world that lives in your dreams, in your intellect, in your emotions and in your imagination. But it is not a given. It is human-made. Being human-made, it can be unmade, and that is spiritual work. Taking a spiritual inventory helps us to define the normal operating parameters of our world. In order to prepare us for the spiritual shift into the new world that is the Realm of Heaven, we need to provide our inner world with the building materials that God will use to construct this new world. We gain these materials by means of spiritual reading.

I gave an example of a spiritual reading in the previous chapter. This process is called Lectio Divina, and is an ancient Christian spiritual practice. I will describe the basic format that has been followed by people for centuries who wanted their hearts and minds to be shaped by what they came to understand as the Word of God, speaking to them.

Spiritual reading is a way to read scripture in a way that speaks deeply to heart and soul. There are basically four steps: Recitation, Reflection, Rumination and Resting. Begin by setting aside uninterrupted time for this. Settle yourself down in an attitude of prayer and openness. Offer the time to God. Ask for the Holy Spirit to speak to you through the words of scripture. Then proceed with the following steps:

- **Recitation.** In this step you read the scripture text. It is often best to read it aloud. Reading it aloud impresses upon you the fact that it is through this text that God is endeavoring to speak to you, and to provide the spiritual building materials for your new life. Do not read a lot. Concentrate on just a few verses at a time. Repeat the recitation if you wish.

- **Reflection.** In this step you focus your thoughts upon the reading. What are the words used? What is said? How does it sound to your ears? What are the images it provides?

- **Rumination.** This step is just what it sounds like: chewing upon the text. This is a form of prayer in which you turn the words over in your mind again and again and allow them to speak to the deepest yearnings and questions of your heart. What questions or challenges arise for you? What resistance do you encounter? Let a conversation emerge within you between the text and your own inner voices. Offer the conversation at all times to God.

- **Resting.** Finally, at the end of each period of spiritual reading, sit in silence as if in the presence of God. Sit as one who is greatly beloved of God. Sit as a child in the presence of the most loving parent you can imagine. Do not seek to do anything or change anything. Simply be. Allow God to be with you as well. Close out the time with a simple prayer of thanksgiving.

I recommend that you choose the text of the Sermon on the Mount for this exercise. It is found in the Gospel of Matthew, chapters 5–7. Do not hurry your way through this process. Also do not underestimate the power of this practice. Many people have found that God has spoken through a single verse to them, and their lives have never been the same.

Prayer

O God, search me and try me.
You know the desires of my heart, and the chains upon my feet.
You know what has shaped and molded me, and for what purposes.
You are the true potter, I am the clay.
Remold me, remake me, fit me for your Way.
Amen.

— 15 —

Family

I GREW UP THE oldest of eight boys in Boise, Idaho. As the oldest I was expected to set the example for my younger brothers at home as well as at school and church. I was a good student, and we developed a reputation as a family for being good students. My parents also had certain standards of behavior that they assiduously cultivated in me and my next younger brothers, which we were expected to cultivate in our younger brothers. And we did just that. They certainly weren't going to get away with anything we couldn't get away with. For a non-military family, my mother certainly had a clear grasp upon how discipline flowed down through the ranks. My father was less in charge of discipline for the simple fact that he was away at work during the day. I also sense he was a bit more reticent to dispense with discipline, preferring more to share with his sons the important things about being male, such as how to use a pocketknife, how to bait a hook, how to cast a rod and clean a fish. He was active in our scouting programs, and he enjoyed taking us on hikes whenever we needed to do something for a merit badge or advance in our rank. He also taught us the even more important things such as being scrupulously honest, treating others with kindness and respect (especially our mother), and how to provide for your family.

My mother has mused that I was a child of a large family who would have preferred being an only child. That is quite possible, although I cannot imagine to this day not having any of my brothers. But I suppose that that might be the psychological malaise of many of us who are oldest children—who recall at some deep subconscious level the fact that at one point in history, we were the sole subject of our parents' affections and attention. But then along came younger usurpers of that attention, through no fault, choice or action on our part. That said, the pictures of me in our family album of that time indicate that I was an enthusiastic big brother, and it was nice to have built-in playmates in the family.

Nonetheless, by the time I was a teenager, I began to chafe against my role as babysitter, surrogate parent, trailblazer, and enforcer of family standards. Because my mother and I have very similar personalities, we clashed frequently. It reached the point that when I was ready to graduate from high school my mother told me that I would need to either find my own apartment or go on to college and live in the dorm. She was not being unkind in this. She simply recognized that I needed to be out on my own, and being away from home would preserve our relationship. I agreed with her.

There is much more to this story, but I begin with this anecdote as a means to begin this chapter's reflections upon the roles family and friends play in the spirituality Jesus demonstrated to his male followers. The more I study the teachings and life example of Jesus, the more convinced I am that his spirituality was not so much propositional in character as it was relational. Because of this, a central key to understanding his spirituality is found in how he related to the people in his life—his family, his friends, the men and women he encountered, and those who opposed him.

Explication

At first reading, the relationship Jesus has with his family doesn't seem to fare very well. The only story we have in the Gospels of his adolescence depicts him remaining behind in Jerusalem after Passover in order to converse with the rabbis at the temple. He neglects to inform his parents of his whereabouts, and when they discover him, he is scolded by his mother, "Son, why have you treated us like this? Your father and I have been anxiously searching for you" (Luke 2:48 NIV). His reply is often thought to foreshadow the ministry he would commence nearly twenty years later: "Why were you searching for me?" he asked. "Didn't you know I had to be in my Father's house?" (Luke 2:49 NIV).

The interesting thing about this story is how it demonstrates that already in adolescence Jesus was beginning to separate his identity from the formative influences of his family and to expand his identity into a larger context. The story does not indicate rebellion, such as I experienced in my own life. Rather, the fact that Jesus refers to the temple—the place on earth where the Presence of God was thought to be most manifest—as his Father's house indicates that his definition of family was becoming expansive.

I have known people for whom the description of God as a Father repels them from religious faith. I have heard some say, "If God is anything like my father, I don't want anything to do with Him." Clearly this was not the case for Jesus. Instead, Jesus adopted a much more familial description of God, which undoubtedly reflected the nature of his relationship with God. Instead of referring to God as a king or ruler, he unfailingly used the term "Father." Even when using the term "Kingdom of Heaven" or "Kingdom of God," Jesus referred to God as Father. Consider the following examples:

> "Be merciful, just as your Father is merciful" (Luke 6:36)

> "I praise you, Father, Lord of heaven and earth, because you have hidden these things from the wise and learned, and revealed them to little children. Yes, Father, for this was your good pleasure" (Luke 10:21 NIV)

> "When you pray, say: 'Father, hallowed be your name, your kingdom come" (Luke 11:2).

> "If you then, though you are evil, know how to give good gifts to your children, how much more will your Father in heaven give the Holy Spirit to those who ask him!" (Luke 11:13 NIV).

> "Do not be afraid, little flock, for your Father has been pleased to give you the kingdom" (Luke 12:32 NIV).

> And, of course, "Father, if you are willing, take this cup from me; yet not my will, but yours be done" (Luke 22:42 NIV).

These, of course are just a few examples and they are taken from just one of the Gospels, but they are illustrative of how he expanded his sense of family to universal proportions. This expansion of identification had at least two aspects to it. The first involved separating himself from his family of origin, and the second involved externalizing the love he had experienced in his family of origin into a ministry of compassion, mercy and beneficence.

Let's look first at the process of separation and what that suggests for a male spirituality. The first act we see Jesus do before beginning his ministry is to travel to the Judean desert to be baptized by his cousin John in the Jordan River. John protests, "I should be baptized by you!" For centuries people have puzzled over his reply found in Matthew, "Let it be so now; it is proper for us in this way to fulfill all righteousness" (Matthew 3:13-15 NIV). Why should Jesus need to do this in order to fulfill all righteousness? I would suggest that Jesus submits to baptism in order to symbolize and effectively enact a formal break with his former life in order to begin his new life. Baptism is a ritual enactment of dying and rebirth. It was practiced by members of the Qumran sect at the time, and was also utilized, at least in a modified form, when Gentile proselytes converted to Judaism. John's baptism was dramatic in that it took place in the River Jordan. This was the very river that, according to tradition, the ancient Israelites crossed about one thousand years previous at the end of their forty years' wilderness pilgrimage. In essence, the Jordan marked the threshold and boundary between the old life and a new identity. When the Israelites set foot in the Jordan under the command of Joshua, their identity instantly shifted from wandering nomads to invading settlers. In their self-understanding, this symbolized the fulfillment of a promise given by God to their ancestors. Crossing the Jordan was the culminating act that effectuated the covenant's promise. There was no turning back. Significantly, then, Jesus likewise goes to that river that was pregnant with meaning and significance. And it should not be missed that his name, Jesus, is the Greek form of the Aramaic Yeshua, or Yehoshua in Hebrew: Joshua.

As he is baptized and emerges up out of the water, he receives a vision of heaven and sees the Holy Spirit descending upon himself. A voice declares, "This is my Son, whom I love; with him I am well pleased" (Matthew 3:17 NIV). In Mark and Luke Jesus is addressed directly: "You are my Son, whom I love; with you I am well pleased" (Mark 1:11 and Luke 3:22 NIV). Here as Jesus treads "the verge of Jordan" his identity shifts and is transformed. He is now a member of the family of his Universal Father, whose realm and reign he will soon proclaim. He breaks from his family of origin in order to take his place in his family of promise.

Implications

In the Gospels of Matthew, Mark and Luke, this significant ritual act is immediately followed by a period of prayer and fasting in the wilderness.

The family of promise is a spiritual family, and it is not enough simply to be baptized and be done with the old. This is the significance for male spirituality. The old life with its expectations and demands, its presumptions about the place of men in the family, the culture-bound definitions and expectations of privilege and power as well as the burdensome responsibility to be in charge or be the head of the family—all these hold sway over our lives and assert control over our decisions, our emotions and our behaviors. Although we cannot totally rid ourselves of these things, we can live out of a different set of standards and principles. We can set aside the power that the expectations of our culture and family upbringing have over us in order to embrace the life that is based upon the spirituality of Jesus.

This doesn't mean abandoning our families. Far from it. In fact, what it means is to set aside the cultural burdens placed upon the family in order to become the *sources of blessing* for our families that is the goal and purpose of the spirituality Jesus taught. These burdens vary from person to person. Some of us need to be healed and released from the burdens of abuse, or demeaning talk. We may have witnessed our fathers belittle or continually criticize our mothers. We may have had mothers who were tyrants themselves or expected us to be their virtual slaves. We may have had fathers who ruled the roost like barons. We may be racked with the anxiety of being measured according to how well we provide financially for our families. All of these are the burdens we have received from our families of origin and our culture. These have to be abandoned in order to receive the gift of our families as a blessing, and to be sources of blessing in return.

But how does one abandon these things in order to move into a new life, a new way of being? Obviously it is not easy to simply change overnight. For instance, if you grew up in a family in which violence was a constant presence, you will need to confront head-on how it was that you internalized that violence. You will need to become self-aware of where you may respond violently and angrily to situations that you wish to control, or that don't go the way you wish. You will need to acknowledge that the use of violence, whether it is physical, emotional or psychological, is a means of having power and control over others. As a child you may have felt helpless and powerless, and observed how violent words and actions seemed to confer power. You may also notice that that sort of behavior gives you an adrenalin rush or makes you feel powerful or in control. This may feel good to be in control of your home atmosphere even if the rest of the world is out of control. That need to assert control over your family, and its history within your own family of origin is precisely the sort of thing I am talking about. This need to control others is, in fact, controlling you. You are not a free person. You are still under the sway of whoever it was that used violence to keep you in line.

It may be that violence or abuse are not the primary issues in your life. Instead, you may be under the thumb of expectations around money. I can relate at a deep level to the scripture that says, "The love of money is the root of all evil" (1 Timothy 6:10 KJV). It doesn't say that *money* is the root of all evil, rather the *love of money*. To love money means that it has an inordinate control over my thoughts and motivations, my hopes and anxieties. I may find myself patterning my own behavior after its dictates. Whether we have a lot or very little, money can still exert control over us.

The spirituality of Jesus is all about freeing us from whatever it is that has control of our lives, be it the chokehold of our past or the ongoing snares of society. Jesus said, "You will know the truth and the truth will make you free"(John 8:32 NRSV). The truth that frees us has two parts. First, we must be totally honest about our lives, about our past, and about the person we have become. In order to be set free from bondage to our past we have to name that past and tell the truth about it. The people who came down to the Jordan to be baptized by John came down for a baptism of repentance. But what is repentance? It is one of those words that has acquired a bad taste for many of us, or has become a religious caricature.

The original Greek word that we translate as "repentance" is *metanoia,* which literally means to change one's mind. But it doesn't simply mean to change your opinions or ideas about something. It refers to a change or transformation of your whole way of thinking and reacting. It refers to the whole system of thoughts, values, motivations, patterned reactions, emotional reflexes, and reasons you think and do certain things. The mind is the whole complex of hopes, dreams, imagination, learned behavior, intellectual reasoning, and creative impulses. It is like a ship that is headed one direction and needs to be reoriented in another direction. Some things may need to be thrown overboard. The sails will need to be trimmed differently. The rudder will need to be moved in a different manner (or perhaps even be replaced!) We may find that we have actually run aground and will need to totally re-equip ourselves.

Application

This is all the work of repentance, or of receiving the expanded consciousness, the New Mind, the Mind of Christ, as Paul calls it (see Philippians 2:5–11). And it all begins with a careful, surgically honest self-assessment of where we have come from, where we are right now, and where we are going. In order to move into the life of freedom and blessing that Jesus offers, we need to ask ourselves, "What of our past do we need to abandon? What needs to be washed away in the waters of Jordan? What needs to be left on the shore and never picked back up?"

You may need to work with a counselor to identify some of these issues. You may also need to work through the spiritual dimensions with a minister you trust or someone who is clearly committed to following the Jesus Path for the twenty-first century as I have described it in this book. There is an ancient Christian practice called *confession*. Confession is simply "telling it like it is." There is no need to hide things from God. We don't need to keep family secrets from God, or preserve anybody's reputation. God knows the truth of our lives, and wants us to tell the truth so we can acknowledge and confront our own lives. Having someone who can receive and hold that truth with us as we tell it is extremely important, and very helpful to the process.

From the Heart of Compassion

The second part of the truth that sets us free is that we will see ourselves for who we truly are in the eyes of God, and we will look upon others as God sees them as well. This is the root of compassion, and is the other side of self-examination and confession. Having abandoned the old, we have to replace it with the new. Having run aground and left the ship, we need to re-provision and set sail in a new direction in a new boat. It is absolutely vital that we substitute new patterns of behavior and ways of thinking for that which we are leaving behind.

But there are things we can do in our everyday lives that can manifest a spirituality of compassion. I call these things *Living from the Heart of Compassion*. For example, we can manifest great compassion for our life partners, our children and our friends and co-workers. As fathers, we can manifest this compassion for our children through listening deeply and carefully to them. If they make a request of us we can listen completely to what they are asking, and try to discern the greater need beneath the request. When I have been able to listen carefully to my own daughters without immediately dismissing their request, I have found that they know what they need, and that it is usually not unreasonable. If I'm not able to provide it, in my best moments I try to explain carefully and respectfully why. We reason it out together. If they are disappointed, instead of getting angry or defensive, I can try to sympathize with their disappointment. I have had many disappointments, and I know how it feels. I also know what it feels like to feel alone in my disappointment. Sympathizing with our children's disappointment expresses our love for them, and reassures them that we are not rejecting them or their request.

When I instead react angrily or act like a tyrant or "pull rank" simply because I am the "one in charge," I can sense my children shut down and shut me out. To parent from a heart of compassion means that I set aside the need I have inherited from my old way of being that says I have to be right or be in charge. Instead I try to sense and feel what will benefit the other person most in a situation. Often it is simply to know that someone cares, and that they will not be rejected outright without a hearing. Sometimes our families simply want to be seen and acknowledged by us for who they are, not as we think they should be. This is how God sees them, and that is the gift we can give them as well.

It is written about Jesus that he looked out upon the crowds and was moved to compassion within himself. By looking upon our families through a heart of compassion, we manifest the spirituality of Jesus. The next time you are in a conversation with your spouse or child, think to yourself, "What would bless them just now? What is the greater need being expressed? Is it possible for me to release them from something that has hold of them, like a fear or the effects of an unkind word? Do I need to make an apology and confess something I may have done to hurt them? How can I listen past this immediate emotional display to the cry for love, or comfort or affirmation?"

To react from a heart of compassion requires that we set aside our own emotional reaction for the moment and attune our heart and feelings to those of the other person. But in order to do this, we may need to pay attention to our own immediate reaction as well.

Be Forewarned: It Won't Be Easy

Jesus demonstrates the rigor of this change in identity several times. One incident sounds harsh unless we understand that the spirituality of Jesus is based in a God-infused life.

> Now Jesus' mother and brothers came to see him, but they were not able to get near him because of the crowd. Someone told him, "Your mother and brothers are standing outside, wanting to see you."
> He replied, "My mother and brothers are those who hear God's word and put it into practice" (Luke 8:19–21 NIV).

At another point, Jesus directs the crowd's attention away from genealogy and human patterns of inheritance and value.

> As Jesus was saying these things, a woman in the crowd called out, "Blessed is the mother who gave you birth and nursed you."
> He replied, "Blessed rather are those who hear the word of God and obey it" (Luke 11:27–28 NIV).

The woman in this passage reflected the cultural values of her time that considered a woman's worth was measured by having sons, and how well those sons fared in the world. Jesus rejects this value, and indicates that each person's source of blessing resides in her or his relationship with God. The spiritual life of Jesus rearranges all our priorities and sources of self-worth and value. In our baptism, or in our entry into the spirituality of Jesus, we are each touched by the Spirit of God, and receive the words spoken to Jesus, "you are my son, my beloved. I am well-pleased with you." Our blessing and worth comes from the love of God, not our bank account or the positions we hold in society. To seek the way and word of God is of far greater value than a thousand Rolls Royces in our garage.

Make no mistake, the call and lure of the patterns of behavior and ways of thinking that we have received from family and culture will continue to call out to us. We will continue to be tempted to gauge ourselves according to the standards of success of our society. We will continue to hear the voices of our families telling us we aren't quite measuring up or that we are failures. These voices, these patterns of behavior, these ways of living and acting all have to be left behind if they hinder us from the life of being the spiritual blessings that are the goal of being a man after Jesus' heart. This is illustrated in this incident:

> As they were walking along the road, a man said to him, "I will follow you wherever you go."
>
> Jesus replied, "Foxes have holes and birds of the air have nests, but the Son of Man has no place to lay his head."
>
> He said to another man, "Follow me."
>
> But the man replied, "Lord, first let me go and bury my father."
>
> Jesus said to him, "Let the dead bury their own dead, but you go and proclaim the kingdom of God."
>
> Still another said, "I will follow you, Lord; but first let me go back and say good bye to my family."
>
> Jesus replied, "No one who puts his hand to the plow and looks back is fit for service in the kingdom of God" (Luke 9:57–62 NIV).

Jesus is not urging abandonment of family or family responsibilities. Rather, he is demonstrating the radical break from the old patterns of relationship that his spirituality represents. In fact, it is important to remember that as he hung dying on the cross, one of his last acts was to entrust his mother's care into the hands of his disciple, John (John 19:26–27). Clearly, Jesus had not abandoned his family, nor had they abandoned him. Rather, his love for his family was transformed by being folded into his spiritual mission of being a blessing to the world. The same can be true for us as we seek to become men after Jesus' heart—we can become a source of blessing to our families. Can there be anything greater in life than this?

— 16 —

Women

THE MOST SIGNIFICANT AND socially complex relationships men have are with the women in their lives. The reason for this complexity lies in the fact that while there are notable biological differences between men and women, there is much more that they have in common. Skills, abilities, intelligence, aesthetic pursuits, athletic abilities and interests all are represented in both genders. It is this tension between similarity and difference that defines the often-troubled relations between the genders.

Any study of the roles assigned in societies to men and women as well as the opportunities available to men or women to make meaningful contributions to their societies or communities reveals wide variability from one culture to the next, as well as wide variability from one time period to the next. The changes have not proceeded in a linear fashion: women in some eras have exerted greater influence and had greater freedom in some earlier eras than later.

The relationships and interactions between Jesus and the women with whom he came in contact were no less complex. However, the Gospels depict these interactions as being characterized by a quality that was striking enough in its originality and uniqueness that the Gospel writers frequently make allusions to it. The best way to describe it is to say that his interactions with women and men were characterized by a spiritual and social egalitarianism. By that I mean to say that Jesus did not differentiate nor discriminate between men and women when someone approached him for healing, advice, teaching, or even to become a disciple or apostle. If a person had a need, or showed true willingness to learn,

Jesus delivered to them just what they needed in order for their life to be made better or to grow spiritually.

In this chapter we will look at several paradigmatic stories in which Jesus has significant interactions with women in order to see what they might show us concerning the complex, important and often problematic relationships between men and women.

Explication 1: Each Person Shall Be Blessed

It has frequently been noted that Jesus broke social norms of his day by speaking with women and by treating them as equals. This was not something peculiar to his personality. Rather it was part and parcel of his spirituality. Jesus proclaimed as a statement of his mission that "I came that they might have life, and have it abundantly" (John 10:10 NRSV). As such, the spirituality of Jesus was manifested in his treating each person in the way that benefited and blessed them the most. This was as true of the women as of the men.

Jesus' encounter with the woman at the well in Samaria is illustrative of this.

> Now he had to go through Samaria. So he came to a town in Samaria called Sychar, near the plot of ground Jacob had given to his son Joseph. Jacob's well was there, and Jesus, tired as he was from the journey, sat down by the well. It was about the sixth hour.
>
> When a Samaritan woman came to draw water, Jesus said to her, "Will you give me a drink?" (His disciples had gone into the town to buy food.)
>
> The Samaritan woman said to him, "You are a Jew and I am a Samaritan woman. How can you ask me for a drink?" (For Jews do not associate with Samaritans.)
>
> Jesus answered her, "If you knew the gift of God and who it is that asks you for a drink, you would have asked him and he would have given you living water."
>
> "Sir," the woman said, "you have nothing to draw with and the well is deep. Where can you get this living water? Are you greater than our father Jacob, who gave us the well and drank from it himself, as did also his sons and his flocks and herds?"
>
> Jesus answered, "Everyone who drinks this water will be thirsty again, but whoever drinks the water I give him will never

> thirst. Indeed, the water I give him will become in him a spring of water welling up to eternal life."
>
> The woman said to him, "Sir, give me this water so that I won't get thirsty and have to keep coming here to draw water."
>
> He told her, "Go, call your husband and come back."
>
> "I have no husband," she replied.
>
> Jesus said to her, "You are right when you say you have no husband. The fact is, you have had five husbands, and the man you now have is not your husband. What you have just said is quite true."
>
> "Sir," the woman said, "I can see that you are a prophet. Our fathers worshiped on this mountain, but you Jews claim that the place where we must worship is in Jerusalem."
>
> Jesus declared, "Believe me, woman, a time is coming when you will worship the Father neither on this mountain nor in Jerusalem. You Samaritans worship what you do not know; we worship what we do know, for salvation is from the Jews. Yet a time is coming and has now come when the true worshipers will worship the Father in spirit and truth, for they are the kind of worshipers the Father seeks. God is spirit, and his worshipers must worship in spirit and in truth."
>
> The woman said, "I know that Messiah" (called Christ) "is coming. When he comes, he will explain everything to us."
>
> Then Jesus declared, "I who speak to you am he." (John 4:4–26 NIV)

Several things are significant in this passage. First, Jesus speaks with the woman and expresses his need of water to her. It was the custom of his time for men not to speak with women in public, and it was further the custom of Jews not to fraternize with Samaritans. There was longstanding antipathy between the two groups such that neither acknowledged the other in public, nor risked being rendered unclean through contact. The Jews observed the same treatment of other gentile groups, although that practice was hard to observe strictly in Galilee. But here Jesus transgresses both boundaries. In order to live out his spirituality of blessing, he relates to this woman as a fellow human being rather than as a particular gender or ethnic group. It is not that her gender or ethnicity was insignificant. Jesus simply looked straight to the human person at the core.

The second thing of significance is that he was willing to have her minister to his needs before he ministered to hers. This is not to be overlooked. It is not uncommon for people in the helping professions to be unable or hard-pressed to receive the assistance or care of others. This can be a problem especially for men. Call it ego or pride, the fact of the matter is that refusing the care someone else wishes to give us or is able to give us sets us apart from them and works against the possibility for entering into meaningful relationship. Relationships of blessing are based upon relationships of meaning, and require the establishment of relationship first. Jesus establishes such a relationship with the woman at the outset by addressing her in her full humanness.

The third thing of significance is that he is free and ungrudging with what he offers her. He is not concerned that she might not be worthy or receptive. He has come that she might have life and have it abundantly. So he offers spiritual counsel and teaching in such a way that her life is touched and blessed.

Explication 2: Learning from the Other

Of course, this story should be compared to another similar incident in which Jesus appears to behave differently.

> Leaving that place, Jesus withdrew to the region of Tyre and Sidon. A Canaanite woman from that vicinity came to him, crying out, "Lord, Son of David, have mercy on me! My daughter is suffering terribly from demon-possession."
>
> Jesus did not answer a word. So his disciples came to him and urged him, "Send her away, for she keeps crying out after us."
>
> He answered, "I was sent only to the lost sheep of Israel."
>
> The woman came and knelt before him. "Lord, help me!" she said.
>
> He replied, "It is not right to take the children's bread and toss it to their dogs."
>
> "Yes, Lord," she said, "but even the dogs eat the crumbs that fall from their masters' table."
>
> Then Jesus answered, "Woman, you have great faith! Your request is granted." And her daughter was healed from that very hour (Matthew 15:21–28 NIV).

At first glance this passage appears to be a case in which Jesus is called to task for his own cultural insensitivity and ethnic prejudice. And it may indeed be a case in which Jesus was taught by a woman who was also a Gentile (the text says she was a Canaanite). If such is the case, then it is all the more instructive for us in that the word we need to hear may come from places and people we may disregard or count of little worth.

But it is also possible that it was a situation that served to drive home a lesson that Jesus had just taught his disciples. As it is recorded in Matthew this story appears immediately following a lengthy dispute with the Pharisees concerning what truly defiles a person: what goes in a person, or what comes out.

> Jesus called the crowd to him and said, "Listen and understand. What goes into a man's mouth does not make him 'unclean,' but what comes out of his mouth, that is what makes him 'unclean.'" Then the disciples came to him and asked, "Do you know that the Pharisees were offended when they heard this?"
>
> He replied, "Every plant that my heavenly Father has not planted will be pulled up by the roots. Leave them; they are blind guides. If a blind man leads a blind man, both will fall into a pit."
>
> Peter said, "Explain the parable to us."
>
> "Are you still so dull?" Jesus asked them. "Don't you see that whatever enters the mouth goes into the stomach and then out of the body? But the things that come out of the mouth come from the heart, and these make a man 'unclean.' For out of the heart come evil thoughts, murder, adultery, sexual immorality, theft, false testimony, slander. These are what make a man 'unclean'; but eating with unwashed hands does not make him 'unclean.'" (Matthew 15:10–20 NIV)

Given this context it is possible that in his encounter with the Canaanite woman, Jesus was giving an example of how words and attitudes can defile a person more than contact with a supposedly "unclean" or undesirable person. By allowing himself to be "shown up" by the Gentile woman, Jesus demonstrated the humility that is part of his spirituality as well as reminded his disciples that his way was not the way of their culture of birth. Over and over again, Jesus pressed this point home.

Explication 3: Women as Providers

Another thing that was unusual in the ministry of Jesus was that he welcomed women within his ranks not only as followers and disciples, but also as economic providers. Mary Magdalene, Joanna (wife of Chuza, steward to Herod), Susanna and many others are specifically mentioned as following Jesus and providing for his ministry out of their own means

(Luke 8:2–3). Think of what it must have looked like to see this band of men and women traveling with Jesus, and when someone asked to speak with his "business manager" he referred them to Joanna or Mary Magdalene! Clearly Jesus did not believe that women were incapable of managing businesses, nor did he support the idea of strictly separated roles for men and women, contrary to the teaching of many religious people both then as well as today.

Explication 4: Worthy to Receive Teaching

One of the great divides in many cultures and time periods has been the access of women to education and religious instruction. The situation in Jesus' time was mixed. Boys tended to be the ones who were taught to read and write in villages in formal settings, but girls might be taught the same at home. Many women became skilled in business dealings, which is indicative of access to education. So it is important not to make too sweeping a generalization in this regard. The variation in education may also reflect differing attitudes from one family to the next.

Much of what Jesus did as he traveled around Galilee and Judea was to teach. These teachings appeared to have been primarily spiritual in nature, although he also gave advice from time to time concerning how to apply spiritual principles to social and political situations, usually by applying nonviolent tactics to conflict situations. As he engaged in such teaching, it is evident that he allowed women to receive the same teaching as men. It is possible that the presence of women disciples among his followers was to provide such teaching to groups of women in each community, with the men instructing the men. Whatever the formal practice was, there were times in which women were present with Jesus' approval during his teaching session.

> As Jesus and his disciples were on their way, he came to a village where a woman named Martha opened her home to him. She had a sister called Mary, who sat at the Lord's feet listening to what he said. But Martha was distracted by all the preparations that had to be made. She came to him and asked, "Lord, don't you care that my sister has left me to do the work by myself? Tell her to help me!"
>
> "Martha, Martha," the Lord answered, "you are worried and upset about many things, but only one thing is needed.

Mary has chosen what is better, and it will not be taken away from her" (Luke 10:38–42 NIV).

Mary and Martha and their brother, Lazarus, were friends of Jesus, perhaps from younger days. There are stories in the Gospels that take place with Jesus staying at their home. When Jesus came, presumably with several disciples in tow, Middle Eastern rules of hospitality would inevitably be followed. This would involve many preparations to make the guests feel comfortable, including washing their feet and providing refreshment. Sleeping arrangements would be made, and special meals would be prepared, often at great expense. Thus, when Jesus arrived, it placed a great burden upon his friends in Bethany. Thus, the exasperation of Martha with her sister should not only be understandable to us, it should almost be expected.

Jesus' reply is not meant to berate Martha for upholding the rule or practice of hospitality. Rather, he is honoring the deep spiritual hunger that Mary displayed, powerful enough to overcome the socialization of her upbringing. Mary at this time apparently desired to hear the words Jesus spoke and to learn from him. There is no indication that any of Jesus' Bethany friends were able to travel with him, so his visits were occasions of special note, and special opportunity. Jesus respected this, and responded to it. That which provided blessing and improvement of life—contributing to the abundant life—always trumped every other concern for Jesus.

It is important also to point out that Mary and Martha do not represent two different spiritual types or personalities as is sometime maintained. Martha was as spiritually aware as Mary. In fact, it is Martha who, in John's Gospel, first makes the declaration of faith that came to epitomize the fullness of faith in Jesus. This occurs upon the occasion of the death of Lazarus, who Jesus raises from the dead:

> On his arrival, Jesus found that Lazarus had already been in the tomb for four days. Bethany was less than two miles from Jerusalem, and many Jews had come to Martha and Mary to comfort them in the loss of their brother. When Martha heard that Jesus was coming, she went out to meet him, but Mary stayed at home.
>
> "Lord," Martha said to Jesus, "if you had been here, my brother would not have died. But I know that even now God will give you whatever you ask."
>
> Jesus said to her, "Your brother will rise again."

> Martha answered, "I know he will rise again in the resurrection at the last day."
>
> Jesus said to her, "I am the resurrection and the life. He who believes in me will live, even though he dies; and whoever lives and believes in me will never die. Do you believe this?"
>
> "Yes, Lord," she told him, "I believe that you are the Christ, the Son of God, who was to come into the world" (John 11:17–27 NIV).

Clearly, Martha had also had occasions to "sit at Jesus' feet" and receive instruction. This is what is most important to glean from these stories.

Explication 5

Not all of the stories that we find in the Gospels are found in all four Gospels. For instance, the birth stories of Jesus appear only in Matthew and Luke. The Temptation stories are only in the Synoptics, Jesus changing water into wine at Cana is only found in John. The Feeding of the 5000 families is found in all four Gospels, as is the crucifixion story. The cleansing of the temple is found in all four, although it occurs earlier in Jesus' ministry according to John. Curiously, the story of the resurrection of Jesus is only found in Matthew, Luke and John. Mark leaves us with an empty tomb.

If a story appears in all four, we can assume that not only is it based on true events, but also that it was significant to all the various Christian communities that preserved the teachings of and stories about Jesus. Let's look at Luke's telling of the following incident, which is the occasion when a woman, sometimes identified and sometimes not, comes into a house where Jesus is teaching, and anoints him with a costly perfumed oil. We will look at Luke 7:36–50. The parallel stories can be found in Mark 14:1–9; Matthew 26:6–13 and John 12:1–8.

> One of the Pharisees asked Jesus to eat with him, and he went into the Pharisee's house and took his place at the table. And a woman in the city, who was a sinner, having learned that he was eating in the Pharisee's house, brought an alabaster jar of ointment. She stood behind him at his feet, weeping, and began to bathe his feet with her tears and to dry them with her hair. Then she continued kissing his feet and anointing them with the ointment. Now when the Pharisee who had invited him saw it, he said to himself, "If this man were a prophet, he

would have known who and what kind of woman this is who is touching him—that she is a sinner." Jesus spoke up and said to him, "Simon, I have something to say to you." "Teacher," he replied, "speak." "A certain creditor had two debtors; one owed five hundred denarii, and the other fifty. When they could not pay, he canceled the debts for both of them. Now which of them will love him more?" Simon answered, "I suppose the one for whom he canceled the greater debt." And Jesus said to him, "You have judged rightly." Then turning toward the woman, he said to Simon, "Do you see this woman? I entered your house; you gave me no water for my feet, but she has bathed my feet with her tears and dried them with her hair. You gave me no kiss, but from the time I came in she has not stopped kissing my feet. You did not anoint my head with oil, but she has anointed my feet with ointment. Therefore, I tell you, her sins, which were many, have been forgiven; hence she has shown great love. But the one to whom little is forgiven, loves little." Then he said to her, "Your sins are forgiven." But those who were at the table with him began to say among themselves, "Who is this who even forgives sins?" And he said to the woman, "Your faith has saved you; go in peace." (Luke 7:36–50 NRSV)

Luke's version of this story pulls together several elements that not only illuminate Jesus' treatment of women, but also his non-hierarchical approach to faith and spirituality. Let's look at these elements closely.

The first element of significance is that the woman is declared by the Pharisee to be a "known sinner." It is not indicated what her sins supposedly are, but over the centuries she has most commonly been described as a prostitute. Most famous of those who have made this declaration was Pope Gregory the Great in the Sixth Century who conflated three different women in the bible and declared that Mary Magdalene and Mary of Bethany were the same woman who was the "known sinner," and was a prostitute. This has besmirched Mary Magdalene's reputation for centuries for reasons not based upon historical facts, nor directly based upon the scriptural evidence. Curiously, it is not specified in Luke's text just what sins she was guilty of. What is curious about this is the propensity of theologians, preachers, and other male church leaders over the years to identify these sins as being sexual in nature. This propensity reveals an underlying tendency for these male leaders to view women in terms of their sexuality or as sexual objects, rather than as whole persons with complex intellectual capacities, spiritual depth, rich emotional lives, and tremendous moral decision-making abilities. Jesus, on the other hand, viewed women in their wholeness, and addressed them in those terms. Significantly, he does not grill this woman to learn of her sins. Instead he perceives that she is coming to a resolution concerning some undesignated personal inner turmoil and has come to Jesus to express her gratitude.

Not only does he acknowledge the fruitfulness of this inner struggle, he identifies the source of forgiveness and salvation as being her own spiritual work. When he proclaims that she has been forgiven, he is acknowledging what has already occurred within her: "her many sins have been forgiven—for she loved much." When people grumble about this pronouncement, he returns to the woman to clarify the situation for all to know: "Your faith has saved you, go in peace."

"Your faith has saved you." This declaration occurs several places in the Bible whenever people want to attribute wonder-working power to Jesus. Instead of reveling in the adulation and glory being heaped upon him, Jesus directs the attention to the moral agency and spiritual work that each person is accomplishing in their own life. For instance, we do not know the details concerning this woman or her supposed sins. But Jesus has sensed her inner struggle, and whereas the Pharisees and others—quite probably all men—viewed her in the terms of their sexually-vectored moral worldview, Jesus honors and acknowledges her struggle towards wholeness.

In addition, when Jesus declares that it is her faith that has saved her, he removes salvation from any sort of priestly hierarchy. Nor is it based upon male approval. She does not need to seek absolution from anyone. She does not need to go to the temple and offer sacrifices. She is fully capable of affecting her own salvation through her own faith, spiritual actions and moral decisions.

Then there is the whole issue of being anointed in the first place. In the other Gospels, Jesus proclaims that she has anointed him in preparation for his burial, which would seem odd to people of the time, since he did not appear close to death. This explanation seems to me to smack of a certain interpolated utilitarianism that seeks to explain such an apparently extravagant act as having some useful purpose: preparing Jesus' body for his burial. Instead, I believe that Jesus is embracing her act as not only an act of gratitude, but also as an act of beauty. Anointing with oil is not only a way of honoring a person, but also of doing something delightful for them. If the oil is perfumed, as in this case, there is the great aesthetic pleasure of the aroma, that delights all who smell it, especially the person anointed. By embracing this act of beauty, Jesus makes an important statement for his male disciples to learn, and for us to heed. Far too often, men undervalue the importance of beauty and aesthetics in life, often disparaging the ways women will seek beauty in their homes and lives. Although Jesus truly lived a simple life, this story reveals that he appreciated the beautiful things in life, and did not deprecate the practice of beauty.

One final point is important to make about this passage. In this passage, no women speak. The woman says nothing. The controversy and discussion occurs between men. The issue of the woman's status ("known sinner") and the issue of her behavior toward Jesus (anointing him with oil) are created and framed entirely by men. Jesus addresses this directly through his pronouncement that her faith has saved her and brought her forgiveness. This is related directly to the relationship between men and women in which men define and circumscribe a woman's worth, purpose and moral agency in the world. When Jesus says, "Your faith has saved you," he returns moral agency to her, and by accepting her acts of beauty and devotion he uplifts and sanctions aesthetic expression as a mark and practice of the spiritual life. This spiritual work of beauty is also an expression of love: "for she has loved much."

Implications

These five stories reveal a pattern to the way Jesus related to the women in his life and those he encountered every day: he related to them all as persons in their wholeness and integrity; he found ways that their individual concerns could be addressed and their lives be blessed; he taught women and humbled himself to learn from them; and he honored their acts of love, devotion, moral decision-making, and even their acts of beauty. He did not regard them as sexual objects, but as persons in their wholeness. He set a new standard in the relationship between men and women.

It is a fact of history that the standards of Jesus remained in practice just a few short generations. Very soon, hierarchies developed first by a division of labor between table servers (deacons) and elders who devoted themselves to teaching, and then with the development of overseers, or bishops, who were at first chosen for their experience and wisdom, but soon grew into an office of power and decision-making over other Christians. When the church became sanctioned by the Emperor Constantine and made the official religion of the empire, then the imperial hierarchies were superimposed on the Church, and the concerns of the Empire became identical with the concerns of the Church. This took place across several centuries, of course, but it led to the erosion of the vision and practice of Jesus.

The status and treatment of women suffered a similar fate wherein women might be forbidden to speak in church assemblies, or were not allowed voice in decision-making, or remained subject to the decisions of the men in their lives. Frequently, as Christianity spread across the world, the social mores and customs of the new peoples concerning the place and treatment of men and women remained unchanged by the teachings of Jesus. In fact, this continues to this day. Hiding under a thin veneer of putative morality, male religious leaders continue to view women as sexual objects, controlling their behavior and removing the potential for moral decision-making as responsible agents. This is frequently enacted in the public and political sphere. All too frequently, women who find themselves in abusive relationships are encouraged to remain in them by male religious leaders, often citing scripture to encourage them to consider their trials as a share in the suffering of Christ, or as their own "cross to bear." Too often that advice results in women being seriously injured and even killed. Such thinking and treatment of women is heretical to the teaching and example of Jesus. It is the antithesis and negation of all that Jesus said and did. There is no excuse for it, and any man who seeks to live in the way of Jesus must do everything in his power to oppose and end such treatment of women.

Applications

The implications of the teaching and practice of Jesus concerning men's relationship with women may be unsettling to you. This may be all the more so if you grew up in a household in which your father treated your mother disrespectfully, or emotionally and/or physically abused her. You may be seeking a different way of relating to your partner or spouse. It is important to seek out professional counseling with a counselor skilled in dealing with domestic violence. This is also the place for the spiritual practice of confession and repentance—and the practice of relating empathetically with your spouse or partner. How do they feel when you speak a certain way or do certain things? The way of repentance—*metanoia*—means to move into the larger mind, the mind that causes you to be aware of the feelings and needs of other persons, and causes you to act in ways that benefit and bless them on their own terms, not your terms. This practice is vital in our relationship with our families and the women in our lives.

Find ways to advocate for women in your workplace and in society, including politically. It is not enough that women struggle on their own to achieve equal treatment in the workplace and equal access to the health care they need. All too frequently they face cadres of men unsympathetic to their situation. But if men rose up to speak on behalf of women, society would change. Laws would change. Attitudes would change. This is men's work. We must begin to speak out to other men. We must teach our sons and the boys in our realm of influence what it means to treat women in the same manner in which Jesus treated them.

Further Application: Ending Domestic Violence

One of the reasons that I am writing this book is because of my association over the years with domestic violence shelters and crisis centers. In addition, I have had many parishioners who have experienced domestic violence or abuse in their families. I have seen the psychological damage done, and the devastation that results when trust and love are betrayed. Jesus came to show us the abundant life, a life that is flooded with love, compassion, mercy, gentleness and peace. The way of Jesus can make our homes to be shelters of shalom. However, many families do not experience home to be a shelter of shalom but instead find it a place of psychological intimidation, of sexual coercion, emotional bullying or physical injury and danger. Here are some unsettling statistics:

The Facts: Domestic Violence Statistics[1]

The National Coalition Against Domestic Violence compiled the following statistics concerning domestic violence:

---

1. These statistics were compiled in 2020 and found online at https://www.ncadv.org/statistics.

- On average, nearly 20 people per minute are physically abused by an intimate partner in the United States. During one year, this equates to more than 10 million women and men.
- 1 in 4 women and 1 in 9 men experience severe intimate partner physical violence, intimate partner contact sexual violence, and/or intimate partner stalking with impacts such as injury, fearfulness, post-traumatic stress disorder, use of victim services, contraction of sexually transmitted diseases, etc.
- 1 in 3 women and 1 in 4 men have experienced some form of physical violence by an intimate partner. This includes a range of behaviors (e.g. slapping, shoving, pushing) and in some cases might not be considered "domestic violence."
- 1 in 7 women and 1 in 25 men have been injured by an intimate partner.
- 1 in 10 women have been raped by an intimate partner. Data is unavailable on male victims.
- 1 in 4 women and 1 in 7 men have been victims of severe physical violence (e.g. beating, burning, strangling) by an intimate partner in their lifetime.
- 1 in 7 women and 1 in 18 men have been stalked by an intimate partner during their lifetime to the point in which they felt very fearful or believed that they or someone close to them would be harmed or killed.
- On a typical day, there are more than 20,000 phone calls placed to domestic violence hotlines nationwide.
- The presence of a gun in a domestic violence situation increases the risk of homicide by 500%.
- Intimate partner violence accounts for 15% of all violent crime.
- Women between the ages of 18–24 are most commonly abused by an intimate partner.
- 19% of domestic violence involves a weapon.
- Domestic victimization is correlated with a higher rate of depression and suicidal behavior.
- Only 34% of people who are injured by intimate partners receive medical care for their injuries.

Rape

- 1 in 5 women and 1 in 71 men in the United States has been raped in their lifetime.
- Almost half of female (46.7%) and male (44.9%) victims of rape in the United States were raped by an acquaintance. Of these, 45.4% of female rape victims and 29% of male rape victims were raped by an intimate partner.

Stalking

- 19.3 million women and 5.1 million men in the United States have been stalked in their lifetime. 60.8% of female stalking victims and 43.5% men reported being stalked by a current or former intimate partner.

Homicide

- A study of intimate partner homicides found that 20% of victims were not the intimate partners themselves, but family members, friends, neighbors, persons who intervened, law enforcement responders, or bystanders.
- 72% of all murder-suicides involve an intimate partner; 94% of the victims of these murder suicides are female.

Children and Domestic Violence

- 1 in 15 children are exposed to intimate partner violence each year, and 90% of these children are eyewitnesses to this violence.

But if these statistics aren't enough to concern you, the response of religious communities and their leaders should. Frequently the victims of domestic violence turn to their pastor or priest or rabbi or imam and receive counsel to remain in relationship with their abusive partner and "try to work it out." Some women have even been advised that their suffering is redemptive, or it shares in Christ suffering so is a good thing. Some may be told that it is a sin to leave their partners, so they return to home to face possible reprisals for seeking out help, continued violence or psychological bullying or domineering control over their life. Some even face death. If they choose to ignore such destructive advice and summon up the incredible courage necessary to leave their abusive partners, their chances of being killed by their partners skyrockets.

Places that should be shelters of shalom, of peace, of blessing and wholeness, of compassion, love and trust become instead places of fear, hurt, injury, and oppression. Even churches can be complicit in the perpetuation of domestic violence and abuse in families—either by what they teach or by their silence in the face of violence and abuse.

I know from my own experience that it is hard to speak up against behavior that is abusive or even violent. It can be terrifying to confront someone on their behavior, or to risk involvement by phoning the police. It is especially difficult if the offender is a friend, a prominent person in the community, or a member of your congregation. The bonds of friendship or relationship may feel strained or threatened. We might even be paralyzed by fear that we might suffer violence. Silence and turning a blind eye feels safer.

But Paul reminds us that we are all members one of another, and the well-being of one person depends upon the active engagement of everybody. As Martin Luther King, Jr. phrased it, "We are caught in an inescapable network of mutuality, tied in a single garment of destiny. Whatever affects one directly affects all indirectly." It is not enough to retreat into the safety of our own homes, if they are such places, and deplore the behavior of "those people over there." The entire fabric of society is disrupted and torn by the effects of domestic violence.

And so what can we do? How can we become communities, churches and homes that are shelters of shalom, places wherein no one shall hurt or destroy? What can we do on behalf of all victims of domestic violence—both male and female? What are some ways that we can make the unrestricted and unlimited love of God very concrete and real for people who are victims of domestic violence?

One way is theological. We must never equate the undeserved suffering of victims of domestic violence with the torture and crucifixion of Jesus Christ. The death of Jesus on the cross was a one-time sacrifice that was for all, and was to be the end of all such sacrifices, suffering and cruelty. His was the death to end death, the suffering to end suffering, and the freely-chosen submission to violence that was to put to an end, once and for all, our addiction to violence.

We can be supportive of victims in ways that are helpful to them, and hold the abuser accountable. Groups that work with domestic violence victims suggest the following ways to support those who have suffered from violence:[2]

- Listen to the victim and believe them. Tell them that the abuse is not their fault, and is not God's will.
- Tell them they are not alone and that help is available.
- Let them know that without intervention, abuse often escalates in frequency and severity over time.
- Seek expert assistance. Refer them only to specialized domestic violence counseling programs, not to couples counseling. Help them find a shelter, a safe home or advocacy resources to offer them protection. Suggesting that they merely return home places them and their children in real danger.
- Hold the abuser accountable. Don't minimize their abusive behavior. Support them in seeking specialized batterers' counseling to help change their behavior. Continue to hold them accountable and to support and protect the victim even after they have begun a counseling program.
- If reconciliation is to occur, it can be considered only after the above steps have taken place.

There are also things we can do regarding our own behavior and attitudes. Here are several suggestions adapted from "A Few Ways Any Adult Can Make Ending Domestic Violence His or Her Business.":[3]

- Cultivate a respectful attitude toward women in your family and at your workplace. Avoid behaviors that demean or control women.
- When you are angry with your partner or children, respond without hurting or humiliating them. Model a nonviolent, respectful response to resolving conflicts in your family. Call a domestic violence

---

2. This list is derived from material found on the website of the Faith Trust Institute at www.faithtrustinstitute.org.

3. From the National Resource Center on Domestic Violence, http://www.nrcdv.org/, and the National Domestic Violence Awareness Project, http://dvam.vawnet.org/.

or child abuse prevention program for their help if you continue to hurt members of your family.
- If you have a friend or co-worker who is afraid of their partner or who is being hurt, offer them your support and refer her to the 24-hour, local hotline, in your area.
- Learn about the domestic violence services in your community. Contribute your time (volunteer!) resources, or money.
- Call the police if you see or hear violence in progress.
- Examine your own life for violence and oppressive behaviors. Try to live a violence-free life.

In Psalm 139:23–24 the writer says, "Search me, O God, and know my heart; test me and know my anxious thoughts. See if there is any offensive way in me, and lead me in the way everlasting." (NIV) We internalize the violence we experience, that we see perpetrated and that we see condoned by our society. The way of God is not a way of violence. The way of Jesus Christ is not a way of violence. But our culture does condone violence. When we examine what we have internalized within ourselves, when we look closely at what we allow as normal or acceptable, and when we confront that which is an "offensive way," which the way of violence is, then we have made an important step towards building a shelter of shalom.

This may be the greatest thing we can do as men: to create a world that is safe and free from violence for our spouses and partners, our families, our communities, and ourselves. We need to gather with other men committed to ridding the world of violence in ourselves, in our families and world. It is long past the time to fully embrace the Way of Jesus and to make it a reality in our world.

— 17 —

Friends

It is common and even expected to speak about the people who followed Jesus and learned from him as being his "disciples." As a disciple, one submits oneself to the instruction and leadership of another person. There is an immediate inequality of relationship, which a person freely takes on in order to receive information that the teacher possesses. Because the teacher has mastered a certain skill or body of knowledge or way of doing something, the apprentices acknowledge this status by referring to their teacher as "master." Jesus' followers frequently referred to him this way. Thus, there was always a certain imbalance in the relationship between Jesus and his associates. They were his disciples, after all. Jesus began his ministry by choosing people to join him, inviting them, "Follow me." Significantly, he never says, "Come join me." Throughout the Gospels, there is a gradation of knowledge, power and authority between Jesus and his disciples, and because of that there was always a distinction between them. This is reflected in the terms used to refer to Jesus—master, lord, teacher, rabbi, savior, messiah—and those used to refer to his followers—disciples, apostles (i.e., those "sent out" by Jesus), servants, etc. This all changes the evening that Jesus gathers with his closest associates in the upper room of a house in Jerusalem during his last Passover trip to Jerusalem.

Explication: New Commandment and New Way of Being

In John's Gospel, we are given a close and intimate inside look at what happened during the last meal that Jesus shared with his followers before he was arrested, tried and crucified. John gives us a detailed account of what Jesus said and did during that meal. The entire account is found in John, chapters 13–17. Because of the length of these chapters, I will refer you to your own Bible in order to read these chapters carefully. The basic sequence of the story is as follows:

1. Everyone gathers in the upper room, and Jesus washes their feet. He tells them, "I have set you an example that you should do as I have done for you" (13:15 NIV).

2. Jesus speaks about his betrayal (by Judas Iscariot) and Peter's upcoming denial of knowing Jesus (13:21–38).

3. Jesus speaks of being the truth, the way and the life, and that he is showing the way to the Father. He is the "Way" because he is in the Father and the Father is in him (14:1–14).

4. Jesus promises to send the Advocate, Spirit of Truth, Holy Spirit to dwell within them and lead them into truth (16:12–15). Their love for one another and for Jesus will fold them into the interconnected life of love that Jesus shares with the Father, which is mediated and made possible by the Holy Spirit (14:15–31).

5. Jesus elaborates upon this spiritual interdwelling by referring to himself as a vine and the disciples as branches of that vine. Their spiritual practice is to "abide" or remain spiritually connected to him, and thus to the Father by continuing to do what they have been taught and commanded by him (15:1–11).

6. Jesus gives them a new commandment: "love one another as I have loved you." In this relationship of love, they are no longer servants but friends (15:12–17).

7. This new identity and relationship with Jesus and the Father and Holy Spirit removes them from the political and cultural systems that dominate and control the world. When Jesus leaves (dies), the Holy Spirit will come and carry Jesus' work forward, continuing to teach new generations and empower them to live a transformed life not based upon the world's system of power and domination but upon an interconnected, love-based system of relationships that can best be described as "inter-abiding." This inter-abiding is rooted in and empowered by the presence of the Holy Spirit (15:18—16:28).

8. Jesus then prays to God that all this may come to pass and be fulfilled (17:1–26).

Clearly, this is an extremely significant section of the Gospels. Jesus is not only wrapping up his ministry and mission in the Roman province of Palestine, he is setting up the momentum for his work to continue and spread across the face of the earth. In these few chapters, Jesus makes it clear that his work cuts against the grain of the world in which his followers find themselves. He is showing them a way of being and of living in community that is based not in the love of power, but in the power of love, (to borrow a turn of phrase attributed to Jimi Hendrix). The communion and love shared between the Divine Reality that Jesus calls "Father" and Jesus himself is the model for a transformed human community, and is achievable by seeking after the spiritual presence of God, and is lived out in the way of life that Jesus taught his followers—men and women alike.

Jesus calls his disciples, "friends," a new designation. It is a new ordering of their relationship. Even though Jesus remains a figure of authority, he changes the nature of their relationship from servant/master to friend/friend. This continues the pattern begun at his Inaugural address of overturning hierarchical power relationships and substituting what is best described as a dynamic flow of interconnected relationships in which the welfare of each person is cared for and their spiritual potentials are maximized by having their physical, emotional and social needs addressed. This has been the pattern of Jesus' ministry, and he commands that it continue. This new community that he has worked to establish is not to be based upon a hierarchical ranking of power and privilege, but instead consists of a community of friends who are to serve one another, and love one another to the extent of laying down their lives for one another. He dramatically and ritually enacts this new community of love by washing the feet of his followers. There he is, the one they call "lord" and "master," at their feet doing the humblest of acts—washing their dirty, dusty feet. This act, of course, is not casually considered. In fact, by setting it in the context of his commandment and commission to love one another with self-giving love, he frames the context for his upcoming crucifixion as an extreme act of self-giving love.

This form of self-giving love is called *agapê* in Greek, and was distinguishable from the other two forms of love called *eros* and *philia*. Dr. Martin Luther King Jr., in his 1956 speech, "Facing the Challenge of a New Age," describes the differences between the three kinds of love, and how this distinction was crucial in the work to build a new form of community based on goodwill and brotherhood—what Jesus intends for his followers when he calls them "friends":

> The Greek language has three words for love. First it speaks of love in terms of Eros. Plato used this word quite frequently in his dialogues. Eros is a type of esthetic love. Now it has come to mean a sort of romantic love. I guess Shakespeare was thinking in terms of Eros when he said "Love is not love which alters when it alteration finds, or bends with the remover to remove." It is an ever fixed mark that looks on tempest and is never shaken. It is a star to every wandering bark . . . This is Eros. And then the Greek talks about philia. Philia is a sort of intimate affectionateness between personal friends. It is a sort of reciprocal love. On this level a person loves because he is loved, then the Greek language comes out with another word which is the highest level of love. It speaks of it in terms of agape. Agape means nothing sentimental or basically affectionate. It means understanding redeeming goodwill for all men. It is an overflowing love which seeks nothing in return. It is the love of God working in the lives of men. When we rise to love on the agape level we love men not because we like them, not because their attitudes and ways appeal to us, but because God loves you. Here we rise to the position of loving the person who does the evil deed while hating the deed that the person does. With this type of love and understanding goodwill we will be able to stand amid the radiant glow of the new age with dignity and discipline.[1]

Although Dr. King was referring to a new age of race relations in the United States, it applies to the new age—what many call the "Christian Era"—that Jesus inaugurated. But Dr. King's vision of a New Age in race relations, which he called the Beloved Community, was solidly rooted in the New Age that Jesus opened up. Indeed, Dr. King saw that the new form of community, based upon this self-giving *agapê* love commanded by Jesus had yet to be fully realized.

The early church, however, recognized the power of this kind of love, and how it is rooted in divesting ourselves of all power and prerogatives of privilege in order serve one another and do those things that benefit others. In his letter to the Philippians, Paul, in about the third decade after Jesus' death, quotes from what was already a hymn circulating among the first Christians:

> If then there is any encouragement in Christ, any consolation from love, any sharing in the Spirit, any compassion and sympathy, make my joy complete: be of the same mind, having the

---

1. King, Jr., "Facing the Challenge of a New Age."

same love, being in full accord and of one mind. Do nothing from selfish ambition or conceit, but in humility regard others as better than yourselves. Let each of you look not to your own interests, but to the interests of others. Let the same mind be in you that you have in Christ Jesus,
who, though he was in the form of God,
> did not regard equality with God
> as something to be exploited,
but emptied himself,
> taking the form of a slave,
> being born in human likeness.
And being found in human form,
> he humbled himself
> and became obedient to the point of death—
> even death on a cross.
Therefore God also highly exalted him
> and gave him the name
> that is above every name,
so that at the name of Jesus
> every knee should bend,
> in heaven and on earth and under the earth,
and every tongue should confess
> that Jesus Christ is Lord,
> to the glory of God the Father.
(Philippians 2:1–11 NRSV).

This great hymn of the early church looks to the Incarnation of Jesus as being the great example of humbling oneself in order to do that which benefits others. Paul's admonitions parallel directly Jesus' commandments to his disciples, whom he calls friends. But it is clear from all of this that Jesus is not glibly slapping them all on the back and acting like some "good old boy." No, this sort of friendship risks death for others. This sort of friendship comes from having, as Paul says, the "mind of Christ"—a *metanoia*-induced higher consciousness, that looks not to one's own narrow self-interests, but to the interests of others, because one has come to realize that all humans are bound together, members one of another as Paul says, woven into the same garment of destiny, as Dr. King said. This consciousness comes, of course, through inter-abiding in one another, like vines in the One Great Branch.

Application

This higher consciousness of inter-abiding can only be achieved through the coupling of an active prayer life with direct service to others all while being actively engaged in a spiritually-supportive community. The mind of Christ is not achieved by merely wishing it into being or through the intellectual act of agreeing with theological or doctrinal statements. No, Paul echoes Jesus in this: it is achieved by how we treat one another, and how we orient our lives for the welfare of others. This is why Jesus openly engaged in acts of compassion and love as well as acts of mercy and justice. Doing these things—feeding the hungry as well as working to see that the conditions that caused them to be without food were corrected, visiting the sick as well as working for healthy living conditions and making the arts of healing available to all, working as a blessed peacemaker—are the mark of a true follower of Jesus. These "doers of the word" are the ones will enter into the joy of life in Christ, because as we do it to the least among us, we have done it to Jesus (Matthew 25:31–46). This is a function of the greater consciousness, the mind of Christ. And it can only be achieved through actions.

Find a community that understands this way of opening up into the higher mind of Christ through engagement with the needs of society. Find a community that understands they are not in a position of judgment or condemnation of others, but are there to serve, like Jesus washing the feet of his friends. Find a community that exists not to succeed according to the standards and dictates of the society round them but rather to transform that society by the example of divine self-giving love. And after you have found that community and have become an active participant in its outreach of love into the wider community around you, continue to nurture your spirit through prayer, study and contemplation.

Being a friend of Jesus, and friends with others, is holistic, involving our hearts, our minds, our souls and our fully embodied strength. Everything is unified and integrated together in word and deed, proclamation and performance, belief and action.

— 18 —

Foes

FAR TOO OFTEN, MEN'S worlds can be divided into three camps: those they are *with,* those they are *for,* and those they are *against.* Take sports, for instance. A common experience for men as they are growing up is to play on a sports team of some sort. As a member of a team, they are *with* one another, pitted *against* the other team. They develop a sense of camaraderie and bondedness. When they get older and no longer play in an organized sport, frequently that love of sports translates into watching sports on television or in person. There they will cheer *for* the team they favor, and sneer at the team they are *against.* Or take military service, for example. Soldiers are psychologically cultivated to bond together *with* their buddies in their unit in preparation to fight *against* whatever enemy they may face. Soldiers who face intense danger together also become so closely bonded emotionally that their relationship to one another assumes the nature of a family, and sometimes supplants their families—whether of origin or of choice.

Politicians, seeking support for military action against other countries will tap into this tendency to separate into opposing camps. The political leader will urge people to be *for* his or her plan, and to join *with* them in order to stand up *against* the enemy that is supposedly threatening them. Sometimes an enemy will even be created where there is no real threat in order to rally the citizenry around that leader or their party or political or religious group in order to assert their own agenda. The language of *for/against/with* is very powerful, and even primal.

This is because the emotions and behavior associated with these three categories are connected to the most primitive parts of our brains that are concerned with survival and emotional bonding to a group for survival. Deep within the brain, the structures that we share with reptiles and other mammals—brainstem, medulla, pons and parts of the cerebellum—are responsible for determining if there is a threat requiring an immediate response, or if there is safety in the current situation. This brain center is responsible for the fight or flight response to danger. In mammals, the limbic system of the brain connects the basic perceptual information we are constantly receiving in our waking experiences with an emotional tag that is also processed by the primitive part of the brain that determines if there is a threat or not in the information being perceived. As humans, that information is further processed by various portions of the cerebral cortex which analyze the perceptual information, categorize it in a number of ways, assign abstract labels or descriptions of what is being perceived, and confirms or counteracts what the primitive brain has determined to be a threat or not, and may then issue a command modifying a behavior or reaction initiated by the primitive brain. This complex of activities is responsible for our tendency to separate into the *for/against/with* camps. *For/against/with* are conceptual categories that the labeling functions of our brain associate with the more primal experiences of threat or safety. The emotional bonding that the limbic system makes possible provides the feelings of warmth and pleasure of being with other humans that form the experiential component of the conceptual category *with*.

Even though this bifurcation—or trifurcation, if you will—of experience is part of our neurological make-up, it is subject to our conscious control and molding. All the responses and neurological pathways of the brain are subject to adaptation, change and reshaping or reforming. This is how we learn behaviors, and it is how we change our behaviors. It is also why any change we want to instigate in ourselves, any sort of repentance or *metanoia*-based amendment of life needs to involve specific embodied practices that are repeated constantly. Old behaviors need to be replaced with new behaviors precisely because the brain needs to establish new neural pathways that will control what we say and how we react to situations.

Jesus understood the need for this. As he taught his followers a new way of being, he always coupled his teachings with actions and ways of relating that not only modeled a new form of consciousness, but also helped instill it in people neurophysiologically. We have already considered how Jesus overturned hierarchies of power and domination, and provided new ways of relating to family, women and friends. One of the other groups that he dealt with was anything that one might consider a foe or enemy—anything that a person experiences as being *against* them. Jesus dealt with those not only on the conceptual level, but also on the practical level of how to deal with the various conflicts in our lives in a nonviolent manner. Put simply, the teachings of Jesus are anti-belligerent and non-pugnacious, extolling nobleness in mercy, kindness, and altruism. Let's look at how this works out.

Explication

It is inevitable that we all will find ourselves in conflict with someone. This may range from minor disagreements to life-threatening situations. How we choose to move through these situations is not only an issue of survival, it is an issue of what we contribute to the world as our legacy. Jesus also left a legacy in terms of how to move through conflict. Basically, Jesus taught his followers how to: rehumanize the enemy; transform enemies into friends; and engage one's opponents nonviolently by confronting power with love.

Rehumanize Our Enemies

Many of Jesus' teachings concerning the new Way of Heaven that he came to inaugurate can be found in the so-called Sermon on the Mount in Matthew. One of the issues he addresses in this is how to relate to those who oppose us:

> You have heard that it was said, "Love your neighbor and hate your enemy." But I tell you: Love your enemies and pray for those who persecute you, that you may be children of your Father in heaven. He causes his sun to rise on the evil and the good, and sends rain on the righteous and the unrighteous. If you love those who love you, what reward will you get? Are not even the tax collectors doing that? And if you greet only your brothers, what are you doing more than others? Do not even pagans do that? Be perfect, therefore, as your heavenly Father is perfect (Matthew 5:43–48 NIV).

When we divide into "us against them" there is a tendency to define ourselves over against whoever is "them," and frequently to depict "them" as less than "us," less than human, as it were. Nowhere is this more frequently expressed than in times of war. In London, England, one of the more intriguing museums to visit is the Imperial War Museum. In this museum, you find the collected accouterments and paraphernalia of the First and Second World Wars. One entire section is devoted to that venerable tool of government propaganda: the War poster. In these posters, the enemy, usually German, is depicted as being non-human, bearing fangs, horns, cloven hooves, in short, basically like an ogre or troll or some Satanic beast would look as depicted in popular children's stories. Never is the enemy depicted with the same humanity as the home troops.

The names we give the enemy are likewise designed to lessen their humanity. For example: Krauts, Japs, Nips, Geeks, Monkeys, towelheads, etc. Governments at war always try to depict the enemy as being less than human. Why do we dehumanize the enemy? The answer is at once simple and profound. We dehumanize the enemy because it makes it easier to kill them. This is a basic psychological principle. Once we realize the full humanity of the person who is arrayed against us, we suddenly identify with them out of our shared humanity. This makes it terribly difficult to kill them.

John Donne put it this way: "No man is an island, entire of itself; every man is a piece of the Continent, a part of the main; if a clod be washed away by the Sea, Europe is the less, as well as if a Promontory were, as well as if a Mannor of thy friends or of thine own were; any man's death diminishes me, because I am involved in mankind; and therefore never send to know for whom the bell tolls; it tolls for thee..."[1] By killing another person, somehow, we also kill a part of ourselves. As a religious leader, this is what concerns me deeply. When we engage in war, there is a sort of soul death that happens in people as well.

This is why one of the most demoralizing things to an army is to come into close contact with the enemy and discover the things they have in common as human beings. An example of this was featured in a story in *The Oregonian*, Tuesday, January 22, 1991, which told of a raid by a U.S. Navy frigate on 11 Iraqi oil platforms in the Persian Gulf during the so-called Persian Gulf War. 23 Iraqi soldiers were taken prisoner. I quote:

> Many on the frigate said nothing had been more sobering than seeing Iraqi prisoners of war face to face. As long as the Iraqis remained on the oil platforms, they were the enemy, the crew

---

1. Donne, "Meditation XVII."

said. Once on board, however, perceptions changed. "I had an image of fierce, ruthless fighters, but, really, these men weren't different than you or me," said Coast Guard Lt. j.g. Walter Westin, 28, of Richmond, Va. "When I started working with the first prisoner, I saw the fear in his eyes and saw him shaking. I think I would have had the same fear if I was in his situation. Here's the enemy, but for me, at that time, it wasn't. It was a life."

"It was a life." Once we realize the full humanity of the person who is arrayed against us, we suddenly identify with them out of our shared humanity. This makes it terribly difficult to kill them. That soldier couldn't have described better the Christian response to the dehumanization of war. The basic Christian response, and I will say this unequivocally, is to rehumanize the enemy, never to let the enemy's humanity be sacrificed.

Let me explain how we know this. The basic command of Jesus is to love. This is a command—not a nice thought, not a suggested form of behavior, but a command. Jesus actually left very few commands. Baptism and communion or Eucharist are two things he said to do, but most importantly he said to love:

- When asked what the greatest of the commandments is, he replies, "'You shall love the Lord your God with all your heart, and with all your soul, and with all your mind.' And a second is like it, 'You shall love your neighbor as yourself.' (Mark 12:29–31 NRSV)"

- In the Upper Room, Jesus says to his disciples-become-friends, "A new commandment I give to you, that you love one another; even as I have loved you, that you also love one another. By this all people will know that you are my disciples, if you have love for one another" (Jn. 13:34–35 RSV)

Someone has once said that it is the easiest thing in the world to be a Christian when things are easy and everything is sunlight and warmth. But when darkness descends and the tempest rages—that is the time when faith is put to the test. War puts us to the test. Racial prejudice puts us to the test. Racial and ethnic profiling puts us to the test. How we treat any immigrant or foreigner puts us to the test.

As W.H. Auden put it, "To do what is difficult all one's days as if it were easy, that is faith."[2] The core of the Christian faith is to do that which is most foreign, most difficult for human beings: to love one's

---

2. Auden, *For the Time Being*. (Quoted from the personal script of the author.)

enemy and to pray for those who are arrayed against us. As we pray for those who are against us, we cannot help but elevate them to a place of full humanity. We recognize that they are imperfect human beings just as we are, with the same needs, desires, fears and joys that we experience. They have families and loved ones, homes and beloved countries just as we do. As we pray for them, we begin to open our hearts to the great Love that permeates the universe and to expand into the mind of Christ, who came that all of the world might be transformed by God's love. As we pray for those we perceive to be against us we come to realize that they are also part of the world that God so loved that he sent his only son into in order to save (John 3:16). As we pray for those who oppose us, the dividing lines of "us" and "them" dissolve into a greater circle of "us." The more we do this, the bigger that circle grows, until it encompasses the whole world.

Transforming Enemies into Friends

We can experience opposition and confrontation with people who are close to us or who may be our associates even. Conflicts are bound to arise between us and those who are around us, leading to a rift in our relationship. It is easy at this time to slip back into the categories of *with* and *against*. This certainly occurred among Jesus' disciples, and in the early church. Many of Paul's letters address conflicts and disagreements among those early communities. Jesus addressed this on several occasions:

> You have heard that it was said to those of ancient times, 'You shall not murder'; and 'whoever murders shall be liable to judgment.' But I say to you that if you are angry with a brother or sister, you will be liable to judgment; and if you insult a brother or sister, you will be liable to the council; and if you say, 'You fool,' you will be liable to the hell of fire. So when you are offering your gift at the altar, if you remember that your brother or sister has something against you, leave your gift there before the altar and go; first be reconciled to your brother or sister, and then come and offer your gift. Come to terms quickly with your accuser while you are on the way to court with him, or your accuser may hand you over to the judge, and the judge to the guard, and you will be thrown into prison. Truly I tell you, you will never get out until you have paid the last penny. (Matthew 5:21–26 NRSV).

> If another member of the church sins against you, go and point out the fault when the two of you are alone. If the member listens to you, you have regained that one. But if you are not listened to, take one or two others along with you, so that every word may be confirmed by the evidence of two or three witnesses. If the member refuses to listen to them, tell it to the church; and if the offender refuses to listen even to the church, let such a one be to you as a Gentile and a tax collector. (Matthew 18:15–17 NRSV)

Disagreements and grievances are to be talked out as friend-to-friend, equal-to-equal, outside of the adversarial court system if at all possible. As Jesus points out, going to court, i.e., proceeding as adversaries, only ruins us financially, and gains us little. But more than that, it keeps us in the mindset of "us" and "them," the *for/against/with* way of thinking.

There is something interesting about the word "adversary." In the Bible, the title "The Adversary" refers to the figure of the Devil. In the book of Job, the figure called Satan literally means "the adversary" (*ha satan*) in Hebrew. This type of adversary is based upon the model of a court with an accuser or prosecutor bringing charges against someone. It is this figure who confronts Jesus in the wilderness, who comes *against* him. But how does the Devil oppose Jesus? By trying to deflect him from his mission and purpose in life. Jesus came to show the Way of God, the way of love, compassion, and unity to the world. That was his goal—the abundant life. Nothing was going to defer him from achieving that goal. That same goal exists for each of us. This is what Jesus means when he says "Be perfect as your Father in heaven is perfect." Being "perfect" means achieving the goal of seeking after the abundant life that the way of Jesus makes possible. When we continue to think in adversarial terms, it is a situation analogous to the situation Jesus faced at the start of his ministry. Our way of thinking is preventing us from achieving the goal of coming into the mind of Christ, of becoming men after Jesus' heart. Our way of thinking becomes our chief adversary.

Jesus taught the way to reconciliation between those who find themselves at odds with or in opposition to one another. In the next chapter we will explore closely how the work of forgiveness facilitates reconciliation. But the point here is that forgiveness aims at reweaving relationships that have been broken or strained. It moves according to the idea of making enemies into friends, opponents into allies.

Engaging Our Opponents Nonviolently by Confronting Power with Love

Throughout this book, I have made the argument that Jesus criticized the use of power to dominate anyone else, and that he especially taught his male disciples a way of life that is based on mutuality, love and service to one another. The fact remains, however, that power continues to be brandished violently in our world, and is routinely used to rob people of their property or rights, to make them acquiesce to economic systems or injustices that diminish their humanity or dignity. It is not enough simply to offer a critique of power, or to grumble and growl about how power is wielded by others against you. Power needs to be confronted and engaged somehow. New Testament scholar Walter Wink has done an in-depth analysis of how Jesus not only criticized the systems of power and dominance of his time but also articulated and demonstrated a non-violent response. The following comments are indebted to his argument and research.[3]

When Jesus gathered his disciple around himself to teach them this way of spiritual transformation, he was faced with the same problem that faces each of us today: living in the midst of an entire culture based upon the use of violence—or the threat of violence—as a means of maintaining order or as a means to challenge that order. It was, like our world today, what Walter Wink calls a "Domination System." We are familiar with this system—it is a system of hierarchies of power and privilege. It is where the very wealthy 1% of society control the lives of the rest of society through the economic and management decisions they make, it is where men exercise power over women, earn more than women when doing the same work, it is domestic violence, it is child abuse, it is the idea that one country can send in their military to ensure their unlimited access to that other country's resources, it is sending in the military or police SWAT teams to quell popular dissent, it is when any segment of society exercises political power to prevent any other segment or immigrant from exercising their rights or having access to medical care or basic services. In Jesus' day it was expressed through the presence and power of the occupying Roman forces. It created a system of oppression

---

3. This analysis is found particularly in the following books and articles: Wink, *Engaging the Powers*; *Jesus' Third Way*; *The Powers That Be*; *Jesus and Nonviolence*; "The Third Way;" "Neither Passivity nor Violence;" and "Beyond Just War and Pacifism."

and hardship that kept the rural peasantry in poverty leading lives of quiet desperation.

Only some people were not so quiet. Militant resistance groups were active, seeking to overthrow the Romans, and carrying out assassination campaigns. The group we know the most about was called the Zealots. There is evidence that Jesus was looked upon as a possible leader of a violent overthrow of the Romans. But he had other plans, and another path to teach people. And this other path is what Walter Wink has called the Non-Violent Third Way of Jesus.

The Domination System is based upon what seems to be only two choices available to people to confront oppression: either violently overthrow it or acquiesce to it. Either duke it out or become a doormat. Fight or flight. The problem with acquiescing, of course, is that it destroys human dignity and eats away at the soul. If we are created in the image of God, but continually live in grinding poverty, are constantly under someone else's thumb, or have our choices severely curtailed because of our gender, sexual or ethnic identity, religious faith or economic or class status—then that status or classification becomes our identity and image—not God's. On the other hand, it is continually the pattern that those who overthrow their oppressors violently soon become the new oppressor, who then hold on to power using the very forms of violence they fought to overthrow. "Meet the new boss: same as the old boss," is how *The Who* put it in their song, "Won't Get Fooled Again." Over against both of these options, Jesus taught a Third Way.

This Third Way is found throughout the Gospels. In fact, we have been examining its basis throughout this book. But Jesus also offered a few practical suggestions that were aimed at addressing specific situations. However, because those original contexts are no longer understood, many of his teachings have been misunderstood, and often misapplied. Look closely at the following section from the Sermon on the Mount:

> You have heard that it was said, 'An eye for an eye and a tooth for a tooth.' But I say to you, Do not resist an evildoer. But if anyone strikes you on the right cheek, turn the other also; and if anyone wants to sue you and take your coat, give your cloak as well; and if anyone forces you to go one mile, go also the second mile. Give to everyone who begs from you, and do not refuse anyone who wants to borrow from you. (Matthew 5:38–42 NRSV).

Jesus addresses various commandments found in the scriptures or in the received tradition of his time and reformulates the commands according to the new way that he taught. This section addresses not only issues of revenge and retaliation, but also how to stand up to the use of power without losing your dignity and without doing violence.

He begins by quoting from the book of Leviticus in which various punishments for offenses against one another are spelled out. The force of the principle of "an eye for an eye" was actually to limit the severity of punishment in terms of the original offense. In a culture that sought to avenge insults and injuries with ever-escalating violence, the principle of an eye for an eye helped to curb bloody reprisals.

But Jesus takes it a step further and actually urges his followers to give up the desire to "render accounts" and even up the score. The practice of nonviolent resistance seeks to live by a deeper law of love, which in essence means to give up the urge for revenge. It also means not stooping to the terms of engagement that the Domination System lays down in order to keep people in subjugation, as well as to keep people accepting the rule of violence in society. Jesus urges his followers, therefore, to give up the urge to seek revenge or respond with violence.

However, Jesus is not saying to acquiesce to evil when he says "do not resist an evil person." The word "resist" in the original Greek, *antitistênai*, actually translates best as "stand up against," and refers specifically to a soldier standing up against a foe (violently). Therefore, he is saying, do not *violently* resist anyone who does evil to you, otherwise you will be transformed into the evil you oppose. This sets the terms of engagement. Resist evil, but do not acquiesce to its modus operandi.

"If anyone strikes you on the right cheek, turn the other also."

This takes a bit of acting out to comprehend the full force of this command. A normal slap by a right-handed person strikes the opponent on the left cheek. For a right-handed person to strike someone on the right cheek requires that person to do it back-handedly. Wink explains the significance of this: "A backhand slap was the usual way of admonishing inferiors. Masters backhanded slaves; husbands, wives; parents, children; men, women; Romans, Jews. We have here a set of unequal relations, in each of which retaliation would be suicidal. The only normal response would be cowering submission."[4] What Jesus is referring to in this

---

4. Wink, "Beyond Just War and Pacifism."

passage was a particular situation in which someone is being humiliated and assaulted by someone who is considered by society to be a superior.

But when Jesus says to offer the other cheek instead of cowering in submission is to affect a change in relationship. By offering the other cheek, in this case the left cheek, the person being struck is in effect saying, "If you are going to strike me, strike me as an equal." This action robs the oppressor of the power to humiliate. What this does is to slowly change the terms of engagement. The poor and powerless would no longer participate in their own oppression.

Part of the work of nonviolence is to counteract the psychological violence that robs people of their basic self-esteem, and sense of humanity and dignity. This injunction provided a creative and nonviolent way for the underling, as it were, to remind their overlord that they were, in fact, human beings of equal worth and dignity. As Gandhi taught 1900 years later, "The first principle of nonviolent action is that of noncooperation with everything humiliating."

"If anyone wants to sue you and take your coat (outer garment), give your cloak (or undergarment) as well."

Wink explains this admonition in detail:

> Indebtedness was endemic in first century Palestine. Jesus' parables are full of debtors struggling to salvage their lives. Heavy debt was not, however, a natural calamity that had overtaken the incompetent. It was the direct consequence of Roman imperial policy. Emperors had taxed the wealthy so stringently to fund their wars that the rich began seeking non-liquid investments to secure their wealth. Land was best, but it was ancestrally owned and passed down over generations, and no peasant would voluntarily relinquish it. Exorbitant interest, however, could be used to drive landowners ever deeper into debt. And debt, coupled with the high taxation required by Herod Antipas to pay Rome tribute, created the economic leverage to pry Galilean peasants loose from their land. By the time of Jesus we see this process already far advanced: large estates owned by absentee landlords, managed by stewards, and worked by tenant farmers, day laborers, and slaves. It is no accident that the first act of the Jewish revolutionaries in 66 C.E. was to burn the Temple treasury, where the record of debts was kept.
>
> It is to this situation that Jesus speaks. His hearers are the poor ("if anyone would sue you"). They share a rankling hatred

for a system that subjects them to humiliation by stripping them of their lands, their goods, finally even their outer garments. [5]

Giving the undergarment would have resulted in the person being sued leaving the court stark naked. In Jewish culture at that time, dishonor and shame came upon the person forcing or viewing nakedness, not from being naked oneself. In the shame and honor culture of the Middle East, this could then become a powerful force to assert one's dignity, even when the rules and laws were arrayed against you. Nonviolence substitutes positive, creative and constructive actions—practices—for actions that have served to degrade, humiliate and disempower.

Application

In the Beatitudes, which form the introduction to the Sermon on the Mount in Matthew, Jesus proclaims, "Blessed are the peacemakers, for they will be called children of God" (Matthew 5:9 NRSV). Jesus as the preeminent Child of God shows us the way to make peace. There are many groups in existence today that seek to bring peace to the world by reconciling people and groups that have ancient enmities and current conflicts. Seek these groups out and read their publications to gain deeper and broader perspectives about cultures and religions and nations that are foreign or you may consider to be an enemy—perhaps because the media or your government depicts them to be "against us." One of the oldest such peacemaking groups is the Fellowship of Reconciliation that was founded after the First World War by a German pastor and an English pastor to bring about reconciliation between the former enemies. The Fellowship of Reconciliation has "walked the talk" about peace and justice for nearly 100 years now, and they have been significantly involved in efforts around the world for oppressed communities to seek liberation and justice using nonviolent means. For example, Dr. Martin Luther King, Jr., contacted the Rev. James Lawson of the Fellowship of Reconciliation to come down and do nonviolence training for the Montgomery bus boycott, and subsequent protests and marches conducted by the Civil Rights Movement. Rev. Lawson had gone and worked with Gandhi in India, so he was well-acquainted with the use of nonviolence.

In addition to the Fellowship of Reconciliation, many faith groups have peace and justice associations or fellowships that seek to overcome

5. Wink, "Beyond Just War and Pacifism."

divisions and injustices that break down human community, trust and peaceful affiliation. These include Pax Christi in the Catholic Church, The Methodist Federation for Social Action, Ansar as-Salam (Muslim Peace Fellowship), Jewish Peace Fellowship, Alternatives to Violence Project and many others. The Fellowship of Reconciliation website[6] has links to many affiliate organizations and a long list of faith-based groups seeking to work for peace, justice and reconciliation between peoples. These groups provide support communities and training for people who seek to become peacemakers from a standpoint of various faith communities. As we seek to walk the Path of Jesus in the twenty-first century, we must take seriously his call to be blessed peacemakers, in the world, in our communities and in our families. Joining with like-minded and open-hearted people will further you on this journey.

Another practice to explore has to do with how we communicate with those closest to us as well as those with whom we associate or work. Dr. Marshall Rosenberg developed a system of communication he calls Nonviolent Communication, NVC.[7] NVC begins by assuming that we are all compassionate by nature and that violent strategies—whether verbal or physical—are learned behaviors taught and supported by the prevailing culture. NVC also assumes that we all share the same, basic human needs, and that each of our actions are a strategy to meet one or more of these needs. The goal of NVC is for people to find greater authenticity in their communication, increased understanding, deepening connection and conflict resolution. Nonviolent communication is one means to develop a communication style based upon compassion and connection. What is significant about NVC is that it is a practical method that a person can learn and apply in everyday situations.

It is possible that you are uncomfortable with these suggested applications of the teachings of Jesus. You may be uncomfortable about getting involved with groups that seem overtly political, or who may advocate a position that is different from one you currently hold, or perhaps may be advocated by your church. I invite you to read carefully the teachings of Jesus and see which positions and practices most closely align with his way. Remember that as Jesus ate his final meal he warned the disciples that "the world" and its system of domination, violence and injustice would hate them as it had hated him. As we seek to follow Jesus on his Path and

---

6. Website: www.forusa.org
7. Website: www.cnvc.org.

become men after *his* heart, we must continually look to our own hearts, and discern what is shaping our values, attitudes and behaviors.

We may need to die to some if not many of our preconceptions and former political beliefs and attitudes as we follow Jesus, and as we walk the road of reconciliation. Jesus lived and died in order to affect reconciliation—between God and humankind, and between persons all around the world. The Apostle Paul recognized the centrality of Jesus' life and death in this work:

> Therefore, if anyone is in Christ, the new creation has come: The old has gone, the new is here! All this is from God, who reconciled us to himself through Christ and gave us the ministry of reconciliation: that God was reconciling the world to himself in Christ, not counting people's sins against them. And he has committed to us the message of reconciliation. We are therefore Christ's ambassadors, as though God were making his appeal through us. We implore you on Christ's behalf: Be reconciled to God (2 Corinthians 5:17–20 NIV).

Following in the Way of Jesus is to become a new creation. As we follow after Jesus, old things will need to give way to the new things that God is working to instill within us. This is the Holy Spirit's work. It is a work that takes courage, and it takes commitment. But it is a work that God intends to bring about in the world, and God needs people such as you through whom to work.

"Blessed are the peacemakers because they will be called children of God."

— 19 —

Mending the Strands
Forgiveness

Forgiveness: What It is and Isn't

There was a man who loved dogs. He served as a speaker in various civic clubs to benefit the SPCA. He was known far and wide as a dog lover. One day his neighbor observed as he poured a new sidewalk from his house out to the street. About the time he smoothed out the last square foot of cement a large dog strayed across his sidewalk leaving footprints in his wake. The man muttered something under his breath and smoothed out the footprints. He went inside to get some twine to string up around the sidewalk only to discover dog tracks in two directions on his new sidewalk. He smoothed those out and put up the twine. About five minutes later he looked out and the footprints indicated that the dog had cleared the fence, landed on his sidewalk and proceeded as he desired. The man was mad now. He troweled the wet concrete smooth again. As he got back to the porch he saw the dog come over and sit right in the middle of his sidewalk. He went inside got his gun and came out and shot the dog dead. The neighbor rushed over, "Why did you do that?" he inquired, "I thought you loved dogs." The man responded as he cradled his gun in the crook of his arm. "I do, I do like dogs, in the abstract, not in the concrete."

I wonder if it might not be the same with forgiveness. We love it in the abstract, but when we really have something to forgive, we hate it in the concrete. Jesus' comments are not abstractions. They are rooted in the very nature and design of the Universe. So we pay very close attention to them as to what they teach us about the way the universe is put together, and we pay attention to them so as to discover what they tell us about ourselves. Therefore, it is significant that Jesus talks about forgiveness 37 times in the New Testament. If something is mentioned that many times in the Bible, it indicates that it is important.

Before we look closely at what Jesus said about forgiveness, let's first consider what forgiveness isn't and what it is. We'll begin with what forgiveness *is not*:

1. Forgetting: deep hurts can rarely be wiped out of one's awareness. The expression "forgive and forget" is a psychological impossibility. Forgiveness involves how we choose to deal with our memory and consciousness of injury or offense. It is an act of our will, but it is not an act of willed amnesia.

2. Reconciliation: reconciliation takes two people, but an injured party can forgive an offender without reconciliation. Sometimes the other party is gone or has died and true reconciliation cannot be achieved. Forgiveness then becomes something we do to affect healing within our own minds and hearts.

3. Condoning: forgiveness does not excuse bad, hurtful, immoral or illegal behavior. Forgiveness expects and requires true change of behavior, if the other person asks for forgiveness, but if there is no true repentance or modification of behavior, forgiveness becomes a cynical game played by the perpetrator.

4. Dismissing: forgiveness involves taking the offense seriously, not passing it off as inconsequential or insignificant.

5. Pardoning: a pardon is a legal transaction that releases an offender from the consequences of an action, such as a penalty. Forgiveness is a personal transaction that releases the one offended from the interpersonal indebtedness of the offense. When one person commits an offense against another, they incur an obligation to right the wrong they have committed. This is a debt toward the offended party borne by the offender. The offended can make room for the possibility to receive the request from the offender to make amends and set things right. What the offended does in offering forgiveness is to set aside the interpersonal indebtedness that has accrued.

What forgiveness is:

1. Socially restorative: We are made to be in community with each other, and interpersonal offenses and injuries strain the fabric of community, tearing its strands and weakening it. Forgiveness works to mend those strands.

2. An act grounded in the character of God—Jesus taught his followers to ask and give forgiveness as part of their regular prayer life: when we pray the Lord's Prayer we say, "... forgive us our trespasses as we forgive those who trespass against us." Because we all miss the mark and fall short of that person we should be and we don't do those things that we ought to do, or do those things we shouldn't do (to paraphrase an ancient prayer of confession and repentance), we need forgiveness to help us get back on track.

3. Psychologically and spiritually necessary—it is necessary in order for the human soul to be healthy. This works both ways—for the offended as well as the offender. As indicated above, when an offense is committed, there is an interpersonal debt established. Releasing someone from their indebtedness frees them to rebuild relationships without the emotional baggage of guilt, shame or remorse.

4. A necessity of the Christian community—The God revealed by Jesus is a God of startling, unimaginable compassion and the community based upon the presence of this God must be steeped in that same spirit. God's forgiveness is merciful and overflowing—there is never too much forgiveness. Because there is too little expressed in human relationships, it becomes vital for the followers of Jesus to demonstrate its practice to the world.

Explication: On Earth as in Heaven

Now that we have considered what forgiveness is and isn't, let's look closely at some of the things Jesus said about forgiveness, and how he practiced and offered forgiveness. We will begin with something I've already mentioned, the guide to prayer he taught his disciples:

Luke's version:

He said to them, "When you pray, say:
Father,
hallowed be your name,
your kingdom come.
Give us each day our daily bread.
Forgive us our sins,
for we also forgive everyone who sins against us.
And lead us not into temptation" (Luke 11:2-4 NIV

Matthew's version:

This, then, is how you should pray:

"Our Father in heaven,
hallowed be your name,
your kingdom come,
your will be done
on earth as it is in heaven.
Give us today our daily bread.
Forgive us our debts,
as we also have forgiven our debtors.
And lead us not into temptation,
but deliver us from the evil one."
For if you forgive men when they sin against you, your heavenly Father will also forgive you. But if you do not forgive men their sins, your Father will not forgive your sins (Matthew 6:9-15 NIV).

The form of this prayer establishes how forgiveness is rooted in the character of God. We begin by acknowledging the absolute holiness of God, and profess that even to invoke God's name is to call forth God's holiness. God is so much grander than we are and God's ways, encompassing the universe as they do, are so far vaster than anything our sciences, arts and imaginations can begin to describe or conjure. And yet, we are told to invite God's realm, or kingdom, to become the pattern for our own world, our own life. But it is not just in our individual lives, we ask that God's will be done *on earth*, which invokes God's Way to find expression in all the communities and processes of our world. It is actually a form of a very ancient expression or idea: "as it is above, so shall it be below." There is a very old idea, found in many cultures, religions and even philosophies, most notably Plato, that this world is a reflection or shadow of an ideal realm, symbolically envisioned as being above us in the heavens. This ideal realm is the pattern or model for the reality we experience here on earth, but in a muted or partial sense. The prayer asking that God's will be done on earth as in heaven is a plea that the imperfect expressions of God's realm and way that we experience everyday be more and more conformed according to God's reality.

This reveals all the more powerfully the connection between the practice of forgiveness and the realm where God's will is fully expressed. Because we are in a world in which humans only partially manifest the intentions and purpose for which we were created, we will always fall short of what we could be—our potential, or goal, or target. But this potential is not held up against us in order to ridicule us or burden us with shame or guilt or to become shackles upon our souls. The forgiveness of God is such that it fully celebrates our creatureliness and sets us free from every snare and entanglement we encounter so that we might grow up into the fullness of our created potential, without impediments. But this growth is not done in a vacuum. It is done in the context of the human community. The community of the followers of Jesus is to be such a community that is modeled after the pattern of the realm of God. Paul recognized this goal of human existence when he proclaimed:

> The gifts he gave were that some would be apostles, some prophets, some evangelists, some pastors and teachers, to equip the saints for the work of ministry, for building up the body of Christ, until all of us come to the unity of the faith and of the knowledge of the Son of God, to maturity, to the measure of the full stature of Christ. We must no longer be children, tossed to and fro and blown about by every wind of doctrine, by people's trickery, by their craftiness in deceitful scheming. But speaking the truth in love, we must grow up in every way into him who is the head, into Christ, from whom the whole body, joined and knit together by every ligament with which it is equipped, as each part is working properly, promotes the body's growth in building itself up in love. (Ephesians 4:11–16 NRSV).

Our goal is to be knit together that we might manifest better God's realm in the world as revealed and embodied by Jesus, the "fullness of Christ." Forgiveness is just that sort of practice that keeps those ligaments soft, supple, and strong and working conjointly.

Explication: How Many Times?

Naturally, if forgiveness is an important part of keeping a community of people working well together, the question arises, "How often do I need to forgive someone?" Peter addressed this question directly to Jesus:

> Then Peter came to Jesus and asked, "Lord, how many times shall I forgive my brother when he sins against me? Up to seven times?"
>
> Jesus answered, "I tell you, not seven times, but seventy-seven times.
>
> "Therefore, the kingdom of heaven is like a king who wanted to settle accounts with his servants. As he began the settlement, a man who owed him ten thousand talents was brought to him. Since he was not able to pay, the master ordered that he and his wife and his children and all that he had be sold to repay the debt.
>
> "The servant fell on his knees before him. 'Be patient with me,' he begged, 'and I will pay back everything.' The servant's master took pity on him, canceled the debt and let him go.
>
> "But when that servant went out, he found one of his fellow servants who owed him a hundred denarii. He grabbed him and began to choke him. 'Pay back what you owe me!' he demanded.
>
> "His fellow servant fell to his knees and begged him, 'Be patient with me, and I will pay you back.'
>
> "But he refused. Instead, he went off and had the man thrown into prison until he could pay the debt. When the other servants saw what had happened, they were greatly distressed and went and told their master everything that had happened.
>
> "Then the master called the servant in. 'You wicked servant,' he said, 'I canceled all that debt of yours because you begged me to. Shouldn't you have had mercy on your fellow servant just as I had on you?' In anger his master turned him over to the jailers to be tortured, until he should pay back all he owed. "This is how my heavenly Father will treat each of you unless you forgive your brother from your heart" (Matthew 18:21–35 NIV).

In all fairness, Peter had the right to think that he had done something good in deciding to forgive someone seven times. But he surely must have been taken aback when Jesus said you must forgive seventy times seven. Of course, the point is not to keep a tally. Seventy times seven invokes the ancient idea of the jubilee, in which all debts were to be canceled and all slaves released after a period of 49 years.[1] Jesus is saying that we are to constantly live in a jubilee frame of mind.

---

1. Read about the jubilee laws in Deuteronomy 15:1–18, Exodus 23:10–11, and

Then Jesus proceeds to tell a story to press the point home. There was a certain king who had a day of reckoning for his servants. He found one who owed him 10,000 talents and, because he could not pay, he was about to have him thrown into jail and his wife and children sold into slavery. Now, it is important to keep in mind that a talent was worth several years' wages. In essence, the servant owed his master the equivalent of 100 million denarii. The talent was the highest monetary denomination, 10,000 was the highest figure in which arithmetic was calculated. You can think of the man's debt as being equivalent to the national debt to get a sense of what Jesus is depicting here. In response to the man's pathetic pleadings, however, he forgave him the entire debt. Whereupon that forgiven servant went to a fellow servant who owed him 100 denarii, a very small sum of money, and demanded payment. He pleaded for extra time, an extension, but the man would not hear of it and he had him thrown into jail. This story got back to the king who went into a rage. He called in the forgiven servant and said that because of his conduct, he was now to be thrown into jail. His original debt was reinstated.

Jesus says that the same will happen to us if we do not forgive those who are indebted to us in any way. This admonition echoes his instructions in the Lord's Prayer about forgiving others when we pray to God. Our own forgiveness is contingent upon the forgiveness we demonstrate to others. Since we are most likely to be in as much need of forgiveness as anyone else, the only way we will experience the forgiveness we need is to express forgiveness as freely as God is willing to express it, which is constantly. That is truly a jubilee way of living and thinking. This idea is reinforced in the following teaching found in Luke:

> Do not judge, and you will not be judged. Do not condemn, and you will not be condemned. Forgive, and you will be forgiven. Give, and it will be given to you. A good measure, pressed down, shaken together and running over, will be poured into your lap. For with the measure you use, it will be measured to you (Luke 6:37–38 NIV).

You have heard it said that to err is human, to forgive is divine. This is not just a cute saying. It is profound theology. William Willimon writes: "The human animal is not supposed to be good at forgiveness. Forgiveness is not some innate, natural human emotion. Vengeance, retribution, violence, these are natural human qualities. It is natural for

---

Leviticus 25:1–55.

the human animal to defend itself, to snarl and crouch into a defensive position when attacked, to howl when wronged, to bite back when bitten. Forgiveness is not natural. It is not a universal human virtue."[2] Forgiveness is possible precisely because it is in the nature of God to forgive, and we are shaped by the power of the Holy Spirit according to that nature.

God is not some cosmic scorekeeper. But, as Jesus points out, we are still held accountable for our actions. If we claim to be followers of Jesus Christ, and if Jesus revealed the great forgiveness of God, then we are also to bear that forgiveness to the world. If we don't forgive, then we will forfeit forgiveness ourselves. What this means is that our own emotional, psychological and spiritual health is intimately bound up with the health of others, and we contribute to the health of others. What Jesus is telling us is that forgiveness is not an individual matter. The Christian faith is not simply an individual matter. We are all joined together.

Explication: Humility and Sincerity

To some who were confident of their own righteousness and looked down on everybody else, Jesus told this parable:

> "Two men went up to the temple to pray, one a Pharisee and the other a tax collector. The Pharisee stood up and prayed about himself: 'God, I thank you that I am not like other men—robbers, evildoers, adulterers—or even like this tax collector. I fast twice a week and give a tenth of all I get.'
>
> "But the tax collector stood at a distance. He would not even look up to heaven, but beat his breast and said, 'God, have mercy on me, a sinner.'
>
> "I tell you that this man, rather than the other, went home justified before God. For everyone who exalts himself will be humbled, and he who humbles himself will be exalted" (Luke 18:10–14).

It is easy to mouth the words, "I forgive you," and not mean it. Likewise, it is easy to ask for forgiveness with no intention of changing our behavior or desire to make amends. It is also possible to wear forgiveness on our sleeves like a badge we've earned or as a charitable donation we bestow upon the "less fortunate." Forgiving and receiving forgiveness should keep us humble. But unfortunately, there are those who believe

---

2. Willimon, *Pulpit Resource*, 44.

they are entitled to forgiveness just as they feel entitled to all the world's riches and benefits, to the exclusion of others. This sense of entitlement seems to go hand in hand with hypocrisy, greed and covetousness, and self-righteousness. It is to this sort of self-righteousness and miserliness that Jesus directs this parable.

Humility and generosity go hand in hand. They are based in the fact that we plain and simply cannot claim responsibility for more than a small fraction of the things we accomplish in life. Not a single wealthy person has earned their wealth by the actual sweat of their brow. If they haven't inherited their wealth to begin with, they are certainly indebted to the hard work of many people under them as they climb their way to the top of their professions. They are indebted to the many teachers and professors who taught them to read and write and do arithmetic and to the many people who have built their buildings, paved their roads, and cruised their streets making sure no burglars break in. We are all indebted to countless others who assist us every day in ways too numerous to mention. Not one person is entitled to everything they enjoy. We are all indebted to one another. Because of this, we must always practice humility in regards to any of our achievements or possessions. The self-righteousness exhibited by the Pharisee in Jesus' parable revels in the fact that he does not do the things he lists. But what has he left off of the list? Has he worked for justice as is demanded by Moses, by the prophets, by the Psalmists? Has he welcomed into his home the sojourner, the homeless, the widow? Has he heeded the words of Isaiah:

> The Lord says, "Is not this the fast that I choose: to loose the bonds of wickedness, to undo the thongs of the yoke, to let the oppressed go free, and to break every yoke? Is it not to share your bread with the hungry, and bring the homeless poor into your house; when you see the naked, to cover them, and not to hide yourself from your own flesh?" (Isaiah 58:6–7 NRSV).

The problem with the Pharisee's prayer is that he has set down the terms for his own righteousness, and cleverly selected those items that will show him in the best light. In contrast, the tax collector states a simple fact without qualification or whining about mitigating circumstances. He simply seeks forgiveness.

Jesus could not abide the hypocrisy and false righteousness of many of the religious leaders of his day. It is safe to say that he doesn't abide the same today. Humility in the face of the incredible generosity of love, forgiveness and mercy of God is the only true response to God. As we have received such love and forgiveness and generosity from God, so we should return it freely everywhere. We are not to sit in judgment of other people. All of that should be turned over to God, and as the Psalmist reminds us:

> The Lord works vindication
> and justice for all who are oppressed.
> He made known his ways to Moses,
> his acts to the people of Israel.
> The Lord is merciful and gracious,
> slow to anger and abounding in steadfast love.
> He will not always accuse,
> nor will he keep his anger for ever.
> He does not deal with us according to our sins,
> nor repay us according to our iniquities.
> For as the heavens are high above the earth,
> so great is his steadfast love towards those who fear him;
> as far as the east is from the west,
> so far he removes our transgressions from us.
> As a father has compassion for his children,
> so the Lord has compassion for those who fear him.
> For he knows how we were made;
> he remembers that we are dust. (Psalm 103:6–14 NRSV)

Implication: Because Jesus Forgave Us

One of the most profound and poignant prayers uttered by Jesus were among his last on earth, spoken from the agony of the cross: "Father, forgive them, for they do not know what they are doing" (Luke 23:34 NRSV). It is impossible to belabor the significance of this petition on behalf of an entire world. Yes, I mean entire world. The "them" for whom Jesus prays refers to the entire world that could not receive his words, and which still persecutes and oppresses the people he came to release and set free. None of us knows what we are doing, really. We do not know the real causes for our hurtful actions, or how our decisions may actually harm others. To the religious, military and political leaders of his time, Jesus was just a rabble-rousing nuisance that needed to be eliminated. How many people are eliminated everyday around the world because their message or belief or even their very presence is inconvenient for the status quo or threatens the tenuous hold on power those in authority wield?

The writer of the Letter to the Hebrews states that Jesus went to the cross not only as a sacrificial victim who by his death abolishes the need for any other sacrifice to be offered anywhere, but also that he took his place on the cross as the high priest offering the sacrifice. As such, the prayer Jesus prays is the prayer of a high priest, asking for forgiveness to be enacted upon the world. His prayer and his death sound a cosmic chord, like a bell sounded throughout the universe. This cosmic chord of forgiveness was struck by God not only in that moment, but throughout eternity. Either we resonate in harmony with it or clang in cacophony against it. In every act of forgiveness performed anywhere, this divine–human relationship resonates in human-human relationships. This act of forgiveness by Jesus in the midst of his crucifixion becomes the model and commandment for us to likewise practice forgiveness. When we forgive others, we are simply passing on what we have received from Jesus. Forgiveness is not ours to hoard or deny to others.

It should be clear that practicing forgiveness is not an optional activity. Forgiveness is at the core of the Way of Jesus. It is at the very center of Jesus' heart, and if we are to become men after the heart of Jesus, it must be at the center of our hearts as well.

Application

Forgiveness involves both an interpersonal dimension as well as an intrapersonal dimension. The need for forgiveness arises out of the nature of human interactions in which there is continual giving and receiving, back and forth transactions of conversations, actions, expression of emotions, words of instruction, support or words and behaviors that demean, harm and abuse. It is in the negative vectoring of these transactions that the experience of being wronged or offended against arises, with the resultant sense of indebtedness. Therefore, the need to offer and to receive forgiveness comes from this interpersonal dimension.

But there is also an intrapersonal dimension in which a person needs to address the negative feelings, emotions and judgments they may have against the other person or group. The very act of releasing a person from their moral indebtedness can affect an emotional release within a person. It may precede or come after the actual expression of forgiveness. Whenever it occurs, it can be an important aspect of forgiving another person.

The basic steps in forgiveness involve the following: confession, confrontation, releasing, accountability, and the possibility for transformation or even reconciliation. Let's look at each of these:

1. **Confession**: Confession involves recognition that an infraction, transgression, or injury has occurred. Significantly, either or both the offender and/or the offended may recognize that an offense has been committed. That offense needs to be named and acknowledged in some fashion, either by the offended saying, "This happened to me, and this is why it was injurious," or by the offender saying, "I did this to you, and it had this effect upon you." This presumes, of course, that such an interaction is possible, which involves the next process.

2. **Confrontation**: If it is possible and is safe for both parties, there must be some form of encounter or engagement with one another, in order to properly and fairly discuss what has occurred. This may occur in the context of a mediation in which the terms of encounter are carefully controlled and monitored. Sometimes, however, it is impossible to have such a face-to-face encounter, such as when the offender has moved or died, or may even be in prison or in a different country. If this is the case, then it can be helpful to stage a mock or surrogate encounter, in which the offended person can enact forgiveness in the absence of the other. This is primarily done to affect the intrapersonal experience of forgiveness because the interpersonal transaction cannot occur.

3. **Releasing**: The offended person pronounces forgiveness in order to release the other person from this infraction. It is important for the person offering forgiveness to sincerely intend or mean what they say. This is important for the offended person also to experience a sense of release within him- or herself. Because we are emotionally bonded or interconnected, this sense of inner release can restore the bonds of relationship.

4. **Accountability for new behavior**: In order for forgiveness to be genuine and to truly restore relationships, it must also be the intention of the offender not to repeat the offense, and even to make amends in some way if it is appropriate or possible. But intentions are not enough. Actual attempts to change or reform or act

differently must be evidenced. It may be necessary to establish some form of accountability, or circumstances to guarantee that the offender has truly repented and is undertaking the appropriate steps to change or make amends. This may be extremely informal, or may involve a legal settlement.

5. **Possibility for transformation and reconciliation**: Forgiveness at its most basic level is a settling of accounts to the satisfaction of both parties. But it does not address all the issues that the original offense creates. As an offense, it has created a tear in the social or interpersonal fabric. Mending the strands torn or frayed in the relationship may require more work, perhaps counseling, perhaps the passage of time, perhaps more shared occasions in which offender and offended can remain in contact and can create a new relationship. Forgiveness in the sense Jesus spoke about and modeled in his own life always holds the door open for such a transformation in relationship and the possibility of affecting reconciliation.

We all have some relationships in our lives that are in need of forgiveness. We have all had some transgression made against us, and we all have transgressed against someone else. The nature of these transgressions can differ widely, of course, but we all have work to do in this regard.

Look back over your life journey, using the life map you made in an earlier chapter of this book. Are there places in your life in which you recall hurting someone or committing some sort of offense? Did you seek forgiveness? What did you do, if anything, to make amends? Are there things for which you need to ask forgiveness and do whatever is necessary to set things right?

Are there incidents in which someone hurt you or offended you in some way, for which you still hold resentment? Is it possible to seek that person out to offer them forgiveness if they desire to set things right? What needs to be done? What internal work do you need to do so that the forgiveness you offer is genuine and sincere, and might lead to reconciliation?

Jesus instructed his followers and us: "So when you are offering your gift at the altar, if you remember that your brother or sister has something against you, leave your gift there before the altar and go; first be reconciled to your brother or sister, and then come and offer your gift." (Matthew 5:23–24 NRSV).

When the books of a certain Scottish doctor were examined after his death, it was found that a number of accounts were crossed through with a note: "Forgiven—too poor to pay." But the physician's wife later decided that these accounts must be paid in full and she proceeded to sue for money. When the case came to court, the judge asked but one question: "Is this your husband's handwriting?" When she replied that it was he responded: "There is no court in the land that can obtain a debt once the word forgiven has been written."

From the earliest days of the movement called the Way, the followers of Jesus recognized that forgiveness was at the heart of his life, and provided meaning for his death. Once they proclaimed him to be the Son of God, this meaning took on cosmic significance. "Forgiven" has been written across the accounting of all of our lives, every one of us. God has forgiven us. We are to forgive others. It is that simple.

— 20 —

Conclusion

Walking in Our Integrity

DEEP IN THE MIDDLE of the Bible, in the collection of songs and prayers known as the Psalms, is a plea to God:

> Vindicate me, O Lord,
> for I have walked in my integrity,
> and I have trusted in the Lord without wavering.
> Prove me, O Lord, and try me;
> test my heart and mind.
> For your steadfast love is before my eyes,
> and I walk in faithfulness to you.
> I do not sit with the worthless,
> nor do I consort with hypocrites;
> I hate the company of evildoers,
> and will not sit with the wicked.
> I wash my hands in innocence,
> and go around your altar, O Lord,
> singing aloud a song of thanksgiving,
> and telling all your wondrous deeds.
> O Lord, I love the house in which you dwell,
> and the place where your glory abides.
> Do not sweep me away with sinners,
> nor my life with the bloodthirsty,
> those in whose hands are evil devices,
> and whose right hands are full of bribes.
> But as for me, I walk in my integrity;
> redeem me, and be gracious to me.

Conclusion

> My foot stands on level ground;
> in the great congregation I will bless the Lord. (Psalm 26 NRSV)

This book arises out of that prayer. This prayer is that of an individual who has not only a clear sense of right and wrong, but also a deep desire to walk in the path of true righteousness and to steer clear of doing that which is wrong or harmful. In order to do that, he recognizes the vital necessity to match his deeds with his beliefs, his walk with his talk. He also recognizes the importance of associating with those who likewise walk in their integrity, and eschews associating with those whose actions are evil, injurious or immoral. What a wonderful world it would be if the Psalmist's prayer were on more lips and in the hearts of more people today. Consider the following:

- A. H. Robins went bankrupt in 1985. The company could not afford settlements for the more than three hundred thousand lawsuits filed against it as a result of its production and marketing of an unsafe intrauterine device for birth control, the Dalkon Shield.

- In 2001, Enron collapsed after Fortune magazine had named it America's most innovative company for six years in a row; it was a house of cards, built on phony books and fraudulent shell companies. Thousands of people lost their pensions and retirement plans that had invested in Enron.

- Worldcom's bankruptcy came a year later, in 2002. It had incorrectly accounted for $3.8 billion in operating expenses.

- More recently, we have seen the end of Bear Stearns, Lehman Brothers, Merrill Lynch, and numerous other financial enterprises.

- Bernard Madoff, the epitome of unethical behavior on Wall Street, now sits in a prison cell after it was discovered that his complex investment company was little more than a grand Ponzi scheme. Hundreds of people lost a cumulative total of millions of dollars, which have never been recovered.

- In 2008, Wall Street crumbled under the weight of illegal and unethical financial investment and mortgage lending schemes. This collapse threatened several of the largest banks in the world, and triggered a worldwide economic depression that put millions out of work, led to the bankruptcy and collapse of several companies, and rendered many homeless.

What was troubling about many of these incidents is the fact that many of the perpetrators of these illegal and unethical acts were regular attenders of church. Some were, ostensibly, Christian. Certainly not all fall into this category, but time and time again the newspapers report about this politician or that business leader who commits adultery, or launders campaign money, or accepts bribes, or stashes large amounts of money in foreign banks so as to avoid paying taxes, or lays off thousands of workers while receiving millions in bonuses and perks. Even sadder is how often these persons have been supported and promoted by church leaders who support them based upon their support for a narrow list of causes or positions.

The search for an integrated life is at the core of the Way of Jesus. When he confronted the hypocrisy of the religious leaders of his day, who were play-acting at their faith, puffing themselves up, strutting their righteousness for everyone to see, but who were full of meanness, abusive behaviors, and unloving attitudes and behaviors, he likened them to whitewashed tombs that were pleasing to look upon but filled with rotting corpses and decaying bones. No stronger or more vivid an image of a life without integrity can be imagined.

To truly and fully walk the Jesus Path in the twenty-first century means to live a life of integrity. But what does this life look like? Certainly, we expect a certain wholeness of life, and a trustworthiness where our word is our bond, and we don't compromise on the things that really matter just for the convenience of getting something done. It is a life that is honest, such that when we say we will do something, we do it. An integrated life is characterized by what I call the 4 C's: consistency, congruence, coherence and courage. Let's look at these in more depth, and place them in the context of what we have been talking about in this book.

Consistency

It is easy to understand what consistency is: it is where our actions match our beliefs. If we proclaim a belief in a particular way of action, or say we value a certain intangible quality like love or truth or justice, then we do those things that are loving or honest and truthful or seek to establish laws or practices that are just.

Consistency is the opposite of hypocrisy. Hypocrisy destroys belief by demonstrating that belief does not produce behavior that is dependable or in line with what is proclaimed. Consistency bolsters belief by demonstrating the necessary connection between what one believes or holds to be important, and how that can be lived out in everyday life.

Jesus came to show us the God who is love. Everything Jesus said and did was consistent with what he taught about God. He said, "If you have seen me, you have seen the Father." When he offered healing to all who sought it, he did not discriminate between rich or poor, between men or women, even between Jew or Gentile. Consistent with his preaching about love was his teaching about not wielding power over anyone else. When someone wields power, it is usually only to their own advantage. But Jesus demonstrated a way of life that looked to the advantage and welfare of others. This is consistent with an ethics and practice of love.

A Congruent Life

A number of years ago a saying went around that goes like this: "If being a Christian were outlawed and you were brought to trial for being a Christian, would there be enough evidence to convict you?" Thank about that for a while. I often wonder about myself. Would people even be suspicious that I was a Christian?

What all this is about is congruence. Congruence. Do our actions line up with what we profess to believe? Are we practicing what we preach? In the Sermon on the Mount, immediately following his list of blessings, the Beatitudes, he says this:

> You are the salt of the earth; but if salt has lost its taste, how can its saltiness be restored? It is no longer good for anything, but is thrown out and trampled under foot.
>
> You are the light of the world. A city built on a hill cannot be hidden. No one after lighting a lamp puts it under the bushel basket, but on the lampstand, and it gives light to all in the house. In the same way, let your light shine before others, so that they may see your good works and give glory to your Father in heaven (Matthew 5:13–16 NRSV).

What Jesus is talking about is congruence. What he is really saying is, "be who you say you are. Don't say you are my followers and then shame me by your actions." This is what it's about: If salt has lost its taste, it is no longer doing its job as salt. Salt by definition tastes salty. If it no longer tastes salty, then, by definition, it is no longer salt. This has to do with congruence. If a thing exhibits the characteristics that define what that thing is, then we say what the thing claims to be and actually is are congruent with each other.

The same analogy has to do with being the light of the world. The purpose of lighting a lamp is to give light to the room. If we hide the lamp, it is not acting in accord with its purpose.

There is a purpose to our lives as Christians as well. By bearing the name "Christian," we are to bear the presence of Christ to the world. Jesus came to reveal God's love to the world. It is as he said, "If you have seen me, you have seen the Father." When people see us, when they watch us and talk with us, do they see the Father? If we are the light of the world, how do we allow that light to shine through us? It is not about the content of our faith. It is how our faith causes us to live. This is the spirituality with which Jesus is concerned—a life of congruence and integrity. But it is also concerned with the nature and quality of one's relationships in family and in the world.

If people look at us, does the light of Jesus shine forth? Would anyone ever convict us of being a follower of Jesus Christ? Would anyone else want to follow Jesus because of us?

A Coherent Life

"Coherent" is from the Latin and basically means "to stick together." That's what logic is, a pattern of thinking that sticks together. Something that is *coherent* is logical and consistent; it is united as or forms a whole.

Brain researchers (neurophysiologists) tell us that there is a region in the brain that is involved with our logical thinking and decision-making processes. It specifically seeks to make logical sense of things. It is in our nature, therefore, to seek a way of life that is logically consistent, that hangs together. In other words, is coherent.

The entire Way of Jesus is all about how our life hangs together with integrity, congruence and coherence. The Way that Jesus taught is eminently logical when taken all together. Now, a coherent life needs to address at least these aspects of human life:

1. Our physical needs.
2. Our psychological and emotional well-being.
3. Our social interactions and place in society and in the natural world.

Conclusion

4. Our intimate and interpersonal relationships.
5. Our intellectual curiosity and the exercise of our minds.
6. Our aesthetic appreciation and creative impulse.

The goal of our walk with Jesus is a life that is full, that is grounded in truth and honesty, that is guided by love and compassion, and that shines forth the love of God in the world. What we have in the Sermon on the Mount is probably a collection of what Jesus taught his followers over a long period of time. The Gospels were put together by the early Christian communities as a sort of guidebook to teach new Christians about how to follow Jesus, how to be his disciple. It is in these teachings that we discover the importance of a life that is coherent, consistent and lived with integrity.

Let's look at a section of the Sermon on the Mount that gives us a glimpse of a full and coherent life, grounded in truth and honesty, that is guided by love and compassion, and that shines forth the love of God in the world.

> 'Do not store up for yourselves treasures on earth, where moth and rust consume and where thieves break in and steal; but store up for yourselves treasures in heaven, where neither moth nor rust consumes and where thieves do not break in and steal. For where your treasure is, there your heart will be also.
>
> 'The eye is the lamp of the body. So, if your eye is healthy, your whole body will be full of light; but if your eye is unhealthy, your whole body will be full of darkness. If then the light in you is darkness, how great is the darkness!
>
> 'No one can serve two masters; for a slave will either hate the one and love the other, or be devoted to the one and despise the other. You cannot serve God and wealth.
>
> 'Therefore I tell you, do not worry about your life, what you will eat or what you will drink, or about your body, what you will wear. Is not life more than food, and the body more than clothing? Look at the birds of the air; they neither sow nor reap nor gather into barns, and yet your heavenly Father feeds them. Are you not of more value than they? And can any of you by worrying add a single hour to your span of life? And why do you worry about clothing? Consider the lilies of the field, how they grow; they neither toil nor spin, yet I tell you, even Solomon in all his glory was not clothed like one of these. But if God so clothes the grass of the field, which is alive today and tomorrow is thrown into the oven, will he not much more clothe you—you

of little faith? Therefore do not worry, saying, "What will we eat?" or "What will we drink?" or "What will we wear?" For it is the Gentiles who strive for all these things; and indeed your heavenly Father knows that you need all these things. But strive first for the kingdom of God and his righteousness, and all these things will be given to you as well.

'So do not worry about tomorrow, for tomorrow will bring worries of its own. Today's trouble is enough for today (Matthew 6:19–34 NRSV).

"Do not store up for yourselves treasures on earth, where moth and rust consume and where thieves break in and steal; but store up for yourselves treasures in heaven . . ."

Storing up treasure in heaven refers to what we make as our priorities in life, and what direction our life is taking. It refers to what governs our lives, and how our decisions are ultimately made. The things to which we devote our time, energy and thoughts not only demonstrate our priorities in life, they actually shape us according to those priorities. Jesus says, "Where your treasure is, there your heart will be also." In other words, you can say your priorities are based in the Bible or are all about family or whatever you want, but I will look at how you spend your time, what you give your money to, what you do on the internet, who you vote for and support politically, what your decisions enable others to do, and so on. These will tell me what your true priorities are. These things tell the truth about our hearts. Jesus says "By their fruit you will recognize them" (Matthew 7:16 NIV).

"The eye is the lamp of the body . . ."

What we bring into our conscious awareness will affect us psychologically, emotionally and intellectually. That is what he means by the eye being the lamp of the body. This relates directly to the previous verse having to do with what we direct our attention towards in life. Some social scientists have described our society as being an entertainment-driven society. Of course, humans have always sought to be entertained. But now we have so many avenues of entertainment: TV, movies, radio, CDs, DVDs, iPods, video games, concerts, theatre, dances, rodeos, sports events, monster car rallies, animal fights, gambling, the Internet, and the list goes on. It is possible not to seek entertainment as a source of refreshment, it is also possible to become totally lost in our various forms of amusement and distraction. And that is the danger: becoming lost and distracted from the things necessary for our survival and for our fulfillment as humans. There is also the possibility that our distractions will lead us away from viewing other persons as precious beings into viewing them as commodities or objects of violence and consumption. What we continually fix our eyes upon shapes our inner world.

"Therefore I tell you, do not worry about your life, what you will eat or what you will drink, or about your body, what you will wear. Is not life more than food, and the body more than clothing?"

Worry and anxiety are common phenomena in life. So why does Jesus say not to do that which is most natural and characteristic of being a human? Once again, it has to do with priorities and direction in life. If all our attention and energy is directed at making a living, scrambling to get more stuff, battling to get ahead, then life is only about survival and competition. Jesus spars with the devil at the beginning of his ministry and renounces this sort of life: "Man does not live by bread alone but by every word that proceeds from the mouth of God." Life is more than merely material existence.

Of course, there is a corollary in this. The conditions for human life in this world should not be so severe that all of life becomes merely a daily struggle for survival. Extreme poverty, hunger, homelessness and lives devoid of loving human interaction or acts of beauty diminish and cripple human beings. If the coherent life addresses the six areas described above, then anything less is inhumane. Jesus is not telling us to ignore the material conditions in life, quite the opposite. What he is saying is that all persons should have what they need to live and thrive as full human beings, and that fullness is not ultimately measured in material terms, but in immaterial terms such as loving and joy-filled families, the production and appreciation of great works of art or music or dance, time spent in worship and spiritual devotion, meaningful human interaction and so on. Remember, Jesus said, "I have come that they might have life and have it abundantly" (John 10:10).

In this book, we have looked at how Jesus was concerned not only about curing people's physical ailments, but also addressing the social conditions and treatment of people that gave rise to their situations. He didn't elaborate a complex social theory, he simply pointed out that we all have one Father in heaven, and we are one family. He then treated everyone as family, and cared for them each equally. That simple belief and the life based upon it has spawned reforms across the world for 2000 years, has launched hospitals, centers for learning, charitable organizations and even empowered laws protecting the rights of persons and the protection of the vulnerable. We are far from creating a world entirely based upon love, but the simple influence of these teachings and the life of Jesus cannot be dismissed. In order to live a coherent life, we must address social conditions as well as the psychological condition of a person, access to medical resources as well as physical symptoms, the opportunity or ability to make moral choices as well as the choices themselves.

A coherent life will address how we function in the personal arena, the interpersonal arena and the social arena. A coherent spiritual practice will dynamically attend to all three arenas, sometimes seeking healing, sometimes challenging assumptions and beliefs that we have received, sometimes modifying our behaviors according to a better way to live and to be. Of course, it takes courage to do this.

A Courageous Life

So how do we live this courageous life that Jesus demonstrates? First, as I have said, we have to change our perspective and our very thought structure, which is the way of *metanoia*, or moving into the Next, or Bigger Mind. The perspective Jesus offers, of course, is God's perspective. It is the perspective that runs throughout the Bible, but as we are told, God's ways are not our ways, (see Isaiah 55:8) and it takes training in order to see things from God's perspective. That is why we look closely at what Jesus taught and how he lived. He said, "If you have seen me, you have seen the Father (John 14:9)."

When we do this, it becomes apparent that the world is not structured according to God's priorities. Inequity and injustice abounds. The rich oppress the poor, and then blame the poor for their poverty. On and on it goes.

So this new perspective is based upon an understanding and comprehension of God's justice. However, it is a justice that is not based upon vengeance but rather upon compassion and mercy. Justice, compassion and mercy are all components of God's love. This is the second aspect of the courageous life.

The third aspect requires us to look at ourselves through God's eyes lest we become too self-righteous and certain of our own special connection to God. This requires humility borne of an intimate relationship with God. The prophet Micah (6:8) outlined just such a program for living a courageous life:

Conclusion

- Do Justice
- Love tenderly, mercifully, kindly
- Walk humbly with your God

Do Justice—Some Practical Suggestions

There are millions of ways we can practice justice in our workplaces, or in school, or at home. Any time you come across a decision or a practice that discriminates against somebody for a reason that has nothing to do with the issue at hand, speak up. If you see somebody being bullied, speak up. Go stand with them. Any time you encounter a law that grants one set of people rights that are specifically denied to another based upon who they are, speak up! Write your legislator or congressperson. Somebody has said that the only way for evil to flourish is for good people to do nothing. As we treat one another fairly and with equity, we help society to run smoothly and calmly. But as disparities increase between people, as gaps increase between those who have and those who have not, as laws continue to be passed that grant privileges to some and deny them to many others, then the stage is set for turmoil and social upheaval. Injustice and inequity tears apart our social fabric. Justice is the act of weaving it back together.

Love Tenderly

To love tenderly means to love one another with a holy, Godlike affection, with the tenderness that God feels toward us, to love others as God loves them.

Ethics emerges out of this concern for how to treat others—such as that described by Jesus: "do unto others as you would have them do unto you." But even further, "do unto others as God would do unto them." Not taking the place of God as judge—because judgment belongs to God alone—but rather as one who loves tenderly, like a parent tenderly loving their child. "I love you so much." Doing justice is coupled with loving tenderly.

Walk Humbly

How does one do this? How does Jesus enable us to transcend ourselves in order to live in loving, justice-making relationships? That is the work of walking humbly—or of being formed spiritually by God. Walking humbly means knowing yourself, and knowing God. Be in close fellowship with God, not exalting yourself but having an intimate knowledge of who you are, a clear understanding of where you fall short of the glory of God, as Paul quotes the Psalmist. A long, clear, honest appraisal of our lives should produce humility within us.

But we don't engage in this appraisal on our own. It is done in the context of our abiding with Jesus as empowered by the Holy Spirit. The practices of prayer, Lectio Divina, contemplation and engaging in acts of compassion and justice will help you cultivate a steady reliance upon God's Holy Spirit to work within you, restoring you to God's paths, leading you in paths of righteousness, enabling you to practice justice and to love tenderly.

Walking humbly is the spiritual formation component: being formed by the Holy Spirit to be a person after the Father's Heart. It is to worship God not in form only, but in Spirit and Truth. Walking humbly with God is the inner discipline, the communing with the God who dwells within us, who is known by careful listening, by daily converse, by reading prayerfully the scriptures as if engaging in a conversation.

This is a program for a courageous life. It was also Jesus' program. He had it, he lived it, he taught it, he died for it and because of it. It is a program that will change your life, and change the world around you. It is the Realm of Heaven in the habitations of humanity.

A Comprehensive Life

Finally, I need to add an additional "C" to my description of a life of integrity, and that is "comprehensive." Jesus acknowledges the importance of the quest, of asking and seeking after a life of meaning and significance, a life that makes sense, that is coherent and congruent, in which we creatively deal with the incompleteness and shattering of our lives.

Let me tell you about my own personal spiritual quest. What I am searching for is a comprehensive life. I am searching for a way to live that fully embodies the Way of Jesus, and which searches out and dissolves everything in me that prevents me from living that Way. I am searching

Conclusion

for a way that heals and transforms all the ugliness, pain and anger within me into wisdom, compassion and mercy. I am looking for a way that harnesses that wisdom and compassion and turns it into service in the world that endeavors to transform the world into a place of justice, opportunity, kindness and beauty for all.

God honors all our earnest seeking after a more complete, integrated and truth-filled way of living that seeks to put into practice the way of life that Jesus lived and taught. Jesus encourages us to keep seeking:

> Ask, and it will be given you; search, and you will find; knock, and the door will be opened for you. For everyone who asks receives, and everyone who searches finds, and for everyone who knocks, the door will be opened. Is there anyone among you who, if your child asks for bread, will give a stone? Or if the child asks for a fish, will give a snake? If you then, who are evil, know how to give good gifts to your children, how much more will your Father in heaven give good things to those who ask him! In everything do to others as you would have them do to you; for this is the law and the prophets (Matthew 7:7–12 NRSV).

Jesus says ask, seek and knock. He's not talking about material gain. He is talking about achieving the purposes in life God has for us. It means aligning our lives and wills with God's will, to know and love God more fully and deeply, know and love our fellow creatures more fully and deeply, know and fully love ourselves more deeply. A comprehensive faith encompasses all these dimensions: God, others, ourselves.

We need to cultivate our inner lives so that compassion for ourselves and for others can arise within us. That compassion is derived from deep honesty about who we are, what we have done, and what has been done to us.

We also need to connect with the Transcendent One, who moves us from a preoccupation with ourselves alone. But we need to realize that everyone is transcendent to us. That is what transcendence is all about—moving beyond the bounds of our own individual experiences and realities to connect with the experiences and realities of others.

That becomes compassion in action, which is what Jesus, and every other God-infused, awakened, enlightened person practiced and continues to practice today. This takes us out in service.

But the vision of transcendence and the Transcendent (One) gives us a bigger picture vision of what the world could/should be like. And so we work at large-scale, world-wide, social levels as well as personal, individual, small-scale levels.

Walk in Your Integrity

This is what it means to walk in our integrity. You have a deep purpose in your life. It is to know God deeply and to manifest God's love in the world. The Way of Jesus provides a guide and a process for doing that. It will challenge your beliefs, changing some and confirming others. It will likely require a realignment of many of your priorities away from the world's priorities in order to be in line with God's. It will expand your heart as you come to see the world as God sees it, and come to love all of it as God loves it. It will make you a better spouse as you seek to serve your life partner and seek after their welfare in everything. It will make you a better father as you practice parenting not based upon wielding power, but looking to do those things that foster growth, security and trust in your children. It will make you a better citizen of the world, as you support any effort or project or law that advances the cause of justice and peace in the world. It will make you a happier and safer person to be around as you find ways to overcome violence within you and in society, and replace it with compassion, tender love and humility of spirit.

This is all that it means to walk the Path of Jesus in the twenty-first century. By taking this book seriously enough to read it and consider the applications I have suggested, you have already brought delight to Jesus' heart. Now let him bring delight to yours.

Bibliography

Akers, Keith. *The Lost Religion of Jesus: Simple Living and Nonviolence in Early Christianity*. New York: Lantern, 2000.
Ampim, Manu. "The Five Major African Initiation Rites." http://www.manuampim.com/AfricanInitiationRites.htm.
Auden, W. H. *For the Time Being: A Christmas Oratorio*. New York: Random House, 1945.
Berry, Wendell. *The Art of the Commonplace*. Washington, DC: Counterpoint, 2002.
Boyd, Stephen B. *The Men We Long to Be*. San Francisco: HarperSanFrancisco, 1995.
Buber, Martin. *I and Thou*. 2nd ed. Translated by Ronald Gregor Smith. New York: Scribner's, 1958.
———. *The Way of Man: According to the Teachings of Hasidism*. Wallingford, PA: Pendle Hill, 1960.
Christ, Carol P., and Judith Plaskow. *Womanspirit Rising: A Feminist Reader in Religion*. New York: HarperCollins, 1979.
Cohn-Sherbok, Dan. *The Jewish Heritage*. Oxford: Basil Blackwell, 1998.
Dittes, James. *Driven by Hope: Men and Meaning*. Louisville: Westminster John Knox, 1996.
Donne, John. "Meditation XVII." *Devotions Upon Emergent Occasions*. http://www.online-literature.com/donne/409/.
D'Souza, Tony, ed. *The Way of Jesus: A Contemporary Edition of a Spiritual Classic*. Grand Rapids: Eerdmans, 2004.
Ehrman, Bart D. *Lost Christianities: The Battles for Scripture and the Faiths We Never Knew*. New York: Oxford University Press, 2003.
———. *Lost Scriptures: Books that Did Not Make It into the New Testament*. New York: Oxford University Press, 2003.
Forbush, William Byron, ed. *Fox's Book of Martyrs*. Philadelphia: Winston, 1926.
Foerster, Werner. "κατεακυριευω" In *TDNT* 3:1098
———. "κατεξουσιαζω." In *TDNT* 2:575.
Foster, Richard. *Prayer*. San Francisco: HarperSanFrancisco, 1992.
Gregory, Bishop of Tours. *Glory of the Martyrs*. Translated by Raymond Van Dam. Liverpool: Liverpool University Press, 1988.
Hanson, K. C. "The Galilean Fishing Economy and the Jesus Tradition." *Biblical Theology Bulletin* 27 (1997) 99–111.
Hardy, Edward Rochie, ed. *Faithful Witnesses: Records of Early Christian Martyrs*. New York: Association Press, 1960.

Kautsky, John H. *The Politics of Aristocratic Empires*. Chapel Hill: University of North Carolina Press, 1982.
King, Martin Luther, Jr. "Facing the Challenge of a New Age." http://mlk-kpp01.stanford.edu/primarydocuments/Vol3/3-Dec-1956_FacingtheChallenge.pdf.
Lenski, Gerhard. *Power and Privilege: A Theory of Social Stratification*. 2nd ed. Chapel Hill: University of North Carolina Press, 1984.
MacGregor, Kirk R. "Nonviolence in the Ancient Church and Christian Obedience." *Themelios* 33.1 (2008) 16–28.
MacKinnon, Catherine. *Feminism Unmodified*. Cambridge: Harvard University Press, 1987.
Mason, Christopher P. *Crossing into Manhood*. Youngstown, NY: Cambria Press, 2006.
Meyer, Marvin. *The Gnostic Discoveries: The Impact of the Nag Hammadi Library*. San Francisco: HarperSanFrancisco, 2005.
———. *Secret Gospels: Essays on Thomas and the Secret Gospel of Mark*. Harrisburg, PA: Trinity Press International, 2003.
Miedzian, Myriam. *Boys Will Be Boys: Breaking the Link Between Masculinity and Violence*. New York: Anchor, 1991.
Musurillo, Herbert, ed. and trans. *The Acts of the Christian Martyrs*. Oxford: Clarendon, 1972.
Niebuhr, Reinhold. *Moral Man and Immoral Society: A Study of Ethics and Politics*. New York: Scribner's, 1932.
Pagels, Elaine. *The Gnostic Gospels*. New York: Random House, 1979.
Pagels, Elaine, and Karen L. King. *Reading Judas: The Gospel of Judas and the Shaping of Christianity*. New York: Viking, 2007.
Patterson, Stephen J. *The Lost Way: How Two Forgotten Gospels Are Rewriting the Story of Christian Origins*. San Francisco: HarperOne, 2014.
Peterson, Eugene H. "Transparent Lives." *The Christian Century*, November 29, 2003. https://www.christiancentury.org/article/2003-11/transparent-lives.
Saiving, Valerie. "The Human Situation: A Feminine View." *The Journal of Religion* 40.2 (Apr. 1960) 100–112.
Schneiders, Sandra M. "Approaches to the Study of Christian Spirituality." In *Blackwell Companion to Christian Spirituality*, 15–33. Malden, MA: Blackwell, 2005.
———. "Religion vs. Spirituality: A Contemporary Conundrum," *Spiritus: A Journal of Christian Spirituality* 3.2 (2003).
"System: definitions." *Business Dictionary*. https://web.archive.org/web/20200921005105/http://www.businessdictionary.com/definition/system.html.
Tavernise, Sabrina. "Violence Leaves Young Iraqis Doubting Clerics." *The New York Times*, March 4, 2008. http://www.nytimes.com/2008/03/04/world/middleeast/04youth.html?_r=1&th&emc=th&oref=slogin.
TDNT: Theological Dictionary of the New Testament. 10 vols. Edited by Gerhard Kittel and Gerhard Friedrich. Translated by Geoffrey Bromiley. Grand Rapids: Eerdmans, 1964–76.
Tippett, Krista. "Moral Man and Immoral Society: The Public Theology of Reinhold Niebuhr." Transcript of an audio broadcast, American Public Media. http://speakingoffaith.publicradio.org/programs/niebuhr-rediscovered/transcript.shtml.
Trull, Joe E. "Is the Head of the House at Home?" *Priscilla Papers* 14.3 (Summer 2000) 3–7. https://www.cbeinternational.org/resource/article/priscilla-papers-academic-journal/head-house-home.

Ulansey, David. "The Heavenly Veil Torn: Mark's Cosmic 'Inclusio.'" *Journal of Biblical Literature* 110.1 (Spring 1991) 123–25.
Willimon, William H. *Pulpit Resource*, 24.3, 1996.
Wink, Walter. *Engaging the Powers: Discernment and Resistance in a World of Domination*. Philadelphia: Fortress, 1992.
———. *Jesus' Third Way: The Relevance of Nonviolence in South Africa Today*. CapeTown: Methodist Publishing House, 1988.
———. *The Powers That Be: Theology for a New Millennium*. New York: Doubleday, 1999.
———. *Jesus and Nonviolence: A Third Way*. Facets Series. Minneapolis: Fortress, 2003.
———. "The Third Way: Reclaiming Jesus' Nonviolent Alternative." *Sojourners* 15 (December 1986) 28–33.
———. "Neither Passivity nor Violence: Jesus' Third Way (Matt 5:38–42//Luke 6:29-30)." *Forum* 7 (March/June 1991) 5–28.
———. "Beyond Just War and Pacifism: Jesus' Nonviolent Way." *Review and Expositor* 89 (1992) 197–214. http://www.cres.org/star/_wink.htm.

www.ingramcontent.com/pod-product-compliance
Lightning Source LLC
Chambersburg PA
CBHW050350230426
43663CB00010B/2063